Sizwe Mpofu-Walsh

THE NEW APARTHEID

TAFELBERG

Tafelberg
an imprint of NB Publishers
a division of Media24 Boeke (Pty) Ltd,
40 Heerengracht, Cape Town, South Africa 8000
www.tafelberg.com

Text © 2021 Sizwe Mpofu-Walsh

Set in Minion
Cover design by Tshepo Mosoeu
Book design by Nazli Jacobs
Edited by Russell Martin
Proofread by Angela Voges

Printed by **novus print**, a division of Novus Holdings

First edition, first impression 2021
ISBN: 978-0-624-08854-7
Epub: 978-0-624-08855-4

For Qugqwala, Mam'Tolo and Luc

Dr Nico Smith, a Dutch Reformed Church clergyman, quoted Verwoerd as saying that he wanted to implant the concept of apartheid so deeply into society that no future government would be able to undo what had been done . . . Whether Verwoerd's boast, as reported by Smith, will be realised, if only in part, remains to be seen.

– Henry Kenney, 1980

The question of when an epoch begins and when it can be deemed closed is always open to a multiplicity of responses . . . The velocity and unexpectedness of the social is such that naming it often comes afterwards, after the fact.

– Sarah Nuttall, 2019

Why do we allow sophisticated apartheid to persist before our eyes as if death was never pronounced on it?

– Chief Justice Mogoeng Mogoeng, 2019

Contents

Abbreviations

AAC	Anglo American Corporation
AFRA	Association for Rural Advancement
AI	artificial intelligence
ANC	African National Congress
AWB	Afrikaner Weerstandsbeweging
BEE	Black Economic Empowerment
CBD	central business district
CID	city improvement district
CLARA	Communal Land Rights Act
CRISPR	Clustered Regularly Interspaced Short Palindromic Repeats
DA	Democratic Alliance
DRDLR	Department of Rural Development and Land Reform
ECTA	Electronic Communications and Transactions Act
GDP	gross domestic product
GEAR	Growth, Employment and Redistribution
GEPF	Government Employees Pension Fund
IDC	Industrial Development Corporation
IEC	Independent Electoral Commission
IFP	Inkatha Freedom Party
IP	Internet Protocol
JSE	Johannesburg Stock Exchange
KZN	KwaZulu-Natal
NAIL	New Africa Investments Ltd
NP	National Party
NPA	National Prosecuting Authority

POPIA	Protection of Personal Information Act
SAA	South African Airways
SABC	South African Broadcasting Corporation
SAPO	South African Post Office
SAPS	South African Police Service
Sasol	South African Synthetic Oil Limited
SCA	Supreme Court of Appeal
SOE	state-owned entities
TRC	Truth and Reconciliation Commission
UCT	University of Cape Town

autopoiesis, noun au·to·poi·e·sis | \ ˌȯ-tō-ˌpȯi-ˈē-səs \ plural autopoieses\ ˌȯ- tō-ˌpȯi- ˈē-ˌsēz\ : the property of a living system (such as a bacterial cell or a multicellular organism) that allows it to maintain and renew itself by regulating its composition and conserving its boundaries.

Introduction

Apartheid did not die; it was privatised. In this book, I pursue this single, simple thesis. The claim stems from a constellation of provocative questions. What are apartheid's afterlives? Is present-day South Africa a distorted duplicate of its apartheid predecessor? Is South Africa witnessing apartheid's reappearance in disguise? How, if at all, does apartheid persevere in spite of the Constitution? Is apartheid's ultimate demise inevitable? What unforeseen consequences flowed from the negotiated settlement of the 1990s? Why, when, and by whom was South Africa's 'transition' from apartheid declared over? What forms of apartheid oppression flourish under the pretext of democracy? Where does power reside in South Africa, and how is it exercised? Is apartheid autopoietic? In turn, these questions hinge on a central one: to what extent does apartheid persist after 'death was pronounced on it'?[1]

In this book, I confront apartheid's immanence, and eminence, in South Africa's present. I trace apartheid's inequities and iniquities beyond 1994. To do this is to suggest that apartheid is more than just a legacy, effigy or 'reverberating echo'.[2] It is to excavate and disentomb apartheid. It is to search beyond the pomp and pantomime of South Africa's democratic passage into what the poet Lebo Mashile calls 'the existential crisis of a miracle overstretched'.[3] Such a move is at once shocking and familiar: shocking, because it erodes the founding myth of contemporary South Africa; familiar, because it unveils an eerie and unspoken spectre looming over the 'post-apartheid'.

Apartheid did not die; it was privatised. This is the idea to be confronted.

WHY APARTHEID?

Since 1994, the term 'apartheid' has suffered from 'ceaseless re-attribution'.[4] Stripped of nuance, and denuded of intricacy, the word has increasingly come to sound like old music. Either the 'a-word' is invoked to promote panic, or stir passion, without regard to its painful history; or it connotes clichéd nostalgia, 'from sepia-toned representations of the past' and 'airbrushed memories of Mandela', to '*Drum* [magazine] imagery as hip *couture*, and the romanticised recuperation of the pennywhistle'.[5]

In both cases, apartheid is used liberally, widely and unhelpfully. Ironically, then, when apartheid 'died', the term 'apartheid' was reborn, shedding much of its conceptual gravity. Apartheid is more than just a feeling of racial unease. It is more even than racial segregation. Indeed, as we shall see, racial subordination is but one of its features. To invoke apartheid, therefore, is to undertake a solemn task, and I do not do so lightly.

In this book, I understand apartheid along five interlocking dimensions, as ideology, state project, economic order, technology, and emotional landscape.[6] As ideology, apartheid was a set of beliefs and creeds which combined in a particularly Afrikaner-centric, White supremacist world view. This mingled with an Anglo-Saxon White supremacist foundation built in the colonial period. Like other ideologies of racial superiority of the period – in Britain, Australia, Germany and the United States – apartheid was consumed with White racial purity and total dominance.[7]

Unlike these ideologies, however, apartheid was an ideology of minority supremacy. In this way, apartheid balanced White supremacy against the numerical supremacy of the Black majority. As such, apartheid was never only about draconian separation, but rather about what I shall call 'entangled separation': as the internal boundaries of apartheid ideology pushed races apart, the external borders of South Africa squeezed them together. As the atom is bound by simultaneous forces of repulsion and attraction, so apartheid drove races apart while pulling them together.

As a state project, apartheid was a system of legally defined and governmentally enforced binary categorisations emphasising, but not limited to, racial oppression. As an economic order, it was a system of economic production, distribution and exchange which benefited from, and reinforced, these oppressive binaries.

As a technology, apartheid was a method of governance in the public and private spheres that controlled everyday life. As an emotional landscape, apartheid was a set of feelings: of superiority and purity in its beneficiaries; and of grief, resentment and inferiority in its victims. Each of these dimensions of apartheid – and the new apartheid – are expanded in the chapters that follow.

Two caveats must be entered. First, apartheid was an adaptive system, capable of evolution and transmutation, from the outset.[8] Apartheid was, and is, constantly shapeshifting. Second, apartheid was never coherent or consistent. On the contrary, it always was, and still is, polylithic.

Nevertheless, incoherence and survivability are to be distinguished: incoherent systems like apartheid often survive *because* of their incoherence. In their ambiguity, they appeal to multiple, conflicting audiences simultaneously. Furthermore, apartheid still dragged South Africa in a specific historical direction, for all its internal incoherence. Apartheid is thus a coherent macro-historical phenomenon, in spite of its various micro-historical incongruities.

Lastly, when I refer to apartheid 'binaries', I do not refer only to racial binaries, but also to binaries in sexual orientation, gender, ability, religion, culture and political belief. These other binaries were not always legislatively inscribed, but they nonetheless rooted apartheid, as they do the new apartheid.

In this way, the 'death' of apartheid assumes complex meanings. It may mean the dismantling of a tapestry of statutes, or an economic order, or an ideology, or a set of everyday practices, or a landscape of emotions. Or it may mean all, or some combination, of these. Too often, the demise of one conception of apartheid is taken to mean the demise of them all.

Why do I invoke apartheid, a term 'felt in the skin before it is read'?[9]

I do so for three reasons. First, the scale of inequity in South Africa merits the weight of the word, as I will endeavour to show in what follows. To avoid the term is to sugar-coat reality. Shying away from apartheid abets those who wish to claim premature victory in South Africa's pursuit of liberation. To consign apartheid to the past, and refuse to recognise it in the present, is to preserve a dangerous binary which causes an infinity of troubles.

Second, it should not be surprising that apartheid lingers in South Africa a few decades after 1994. Apartheid analogies may strain when applied to other places or times. But a comparison between past and present South Africa seems appropriate to me.

Finally, I invoke apartheid because I – and many like me – suffer its consequences. To be sure, our experiences cannot be closely compared to those of generations before us. I – and many like me – have experienced unprecedented privilege in comparison with previous generations. I was educated at elite South African schools and universities, enabling me to win a scholarship to Oxford to pursue and complete my doctorate. I have never known material want. Vast and deep networks have boosted my achievements and softened my failures.

Still, apartheid touches my life. As someone of 'mixed' racial heritage, I was categorised under the infamous Population Registration Act in the doubly alienating category of 'Other Coloured'. I nearly died after being refused emergency health care at a White hospital as a child. My father was detained and tortured for political reasons, and long lines of my relatives will never outlive the horror of racialised impoverishment. I suffered shame and painful ridicule, especially in my early years, simply because my father was Black and my mother White. My experiences of racism are too numerous to recount. My Blackness precedes me – as it precedes every Black South African – to this day. If apartheid still affects me, what of those yet to taste the fruits of freedom? Why, then, should I not speak apartheid's name, when apartheid knows my name so well?

The following analogy illustrates the point. If oppression could be ranked on a scale of one to ten, then the intensity of apartheid in the twentieth century would rank as a 'nine'. Three decades later, the intensity may have reduced to a 'six'. The problem is that the minimum human threshold for oppression is a 'three'. Apartheid was so heinous that virtually any democratic society is preferable, even an oppressive one. No future historian looking at present-day South Africa will fail to note the imprints of apartheid on every aspect of life. Nor should we who live through this moment.

PRIVATISATION AND APARTHEID

What does it mean to say that apartheid was privatised? Privatisation occurs when state assets or functions are transferred into private hands for private purposes.[10] In this book, I extend this idea to the system of apartheid itself – and not just its assets or functions. I claim that apartheid has retreated into the private sphere, despite the inauguration of a democratic republic. While the burdensome management of the South African state remains public, power itself has increasingly devolved to the private realm, exempt from democratic control.

The special form of privatisation traced in this book involves many interrelated ideas. For apartheid to be privatised, it also had to be marketised, de-legislated, denationalised, digitised, fractalised, internalised, deracialised, and de-territorialised.

What does this mean? Apartheid was 'marketised' because privilege is now policed by price rather than prose. The market, not the state, now dictates the boundaries of opportunity, and financial barriers have replaced legal edicts as the key instrument of segregation. Where there is an application, there is a financial regulation, and where there is a financial regulation, there was once a racial law.

Fees, surcharges, qualification criteria and income thresholds now enforce separate development. The new apartheid arises in any application: for a house, car, university place, job, loan, medical aid scheme, or insurance policy. Whereas the state imposed legal barriers under apartheid, private actors increasingly enforce, or influence, the new apartheid's financial barriers.

The exchange of racial laws for financial barriers benefited apartheid interests. The policing of racial statutes is a costly business, morally and financially. By contrast, the erection of financial barriers carries neither moral shame nor financial cost. By replacing legal barriers with financial ones, segregation is transformed from a public burden to a source of private profit. In classic neoliberal fashion, apartheid oppression now works on a 'pay-as-you-go' basis.

'Marketisation' also rests on the assumption that economic complexity transcends the comprehension of a single agency. Therefore, on this view, economic governance must be delegated to a decentralised network of actors responding only to price signals. This logic extends to the system of apartheid itself, once carried out by the South African state.

Apartheid was 'de-legislated' because apartheid statutes – laws enacted by the apartheid parliament – were largely abolished or significantly amended after 1994.[11] Yet, apartheid still permeates the common law,[12] especially in the law of property and contract, which underpin economic activity. Law is more than statute alone: it exists in precedent, judicial culture and legal practice. 'De-legislation' thus clarifies that apartheid continues in various legal forms outside the statutory framework. Apartheid was, therefore, 'liberalised' as its major legal restrictions were relaxed while their effects were, in key respects, conserved.

Apartheid was 'denationalised' because it moved from centralised state control to decentralised private control. 'Denationalisation' is a form of privatisation whereby state assets owned, or state functions performed, by the central government – rather than a subsidiary authority – are transferred into private hands, for private ends. Denationalisation unbundled and decentralised apartheid, consigning its control to a diverse network of private actors with private goals.

Apartheid was 'digitised' because digital technology and personal computing often reinforce the culture of surveillance and toxic racial categorisation upon which apartheid was built. These capacities far outweigh those at the disposal of the apartheid state from the middle of the twentieth century and exist outside South African control. Their global rise coincided perfectly with South Africa's democratic transition.

Technological segregation operates on algorithms, increasingly independent of human agency. These algorithms are remaking the South African public sphere. As the economy became increasingly financialised and digitalised, so power was increasingly sucked from the new democratic government, and placed in international corporate hands. Apartheid thus became encrypted in new digitised forms.

Apartheid was 'fractalised' because, after 1994, it splintered into fragments which contain the logic once inherent in the apartheid state. These fragments clone themselves throughout the body politic. Society is coded by a recursive racial feedback loop immune to vigorous public resistance. The pattern of apartheid, once visible at all scales, is now only visible at smaller scales. This makes apartheid harder to see, but easier to survive.

Apartheid was 'internalised' because it has become hegemonic. White supremacy has become increasingly covert and its methods have grown increasingly clandestine. Meanwhile, 'non-racialism' has been co-opted to mean colour-blindness. In reality, colour-blindness drives racial discourse underground, where White supremacists want it to be. It makes race taboo, permitting secret racial discourses to thrive. The end of apartheid as state ideology led to a fragmentary and ambiguous national self-conception. Apartheid retained few public defenders, but the silent logics of self-preservation, self-alienation, residential segregation, and materialism sustain a new, silent ethos steered from the private sphere.

Apartheid was 'deracialised' in a narrow sense. *Some* Black South Africans can now participate in its spoils, though *most* still experience the vast disproportion of its evils. Apartheid used racial identity to include and to exclude; the new apartheid still excludes by race, but no longer strictly includes by race. Black enmeshment in the system of privilege is a key feature of the new apartheid. This enmeshment serves two functions: it distracts from racialised exclusion and it incentivises Black compliance. Prior to 1994, resistance to apartheid was justifiable from the perspective of both self-interest and social interest.

Today, self-interest and social interest diverge, as Black South Africans are increasingly torn between contradictory desires for spectacular wealth and revolutionary equality. The burden of Black wealthlessness[13] only increases the urge for private accumulation. This embourgeoisement of a new Black middle class, first envisaged by the National Party (NP) in the 1980s, complicates the picture of privilege in the new apartheid today.

Apartheid was 'deterritorialised' because space itself has changed since 1994. To be sure, apartheid geography survives: White people are still absent from townships, informal settlements or the former Bantustans; and impoverishment and social dislocation remain intensely racialised. Certainly, landownership and capital ownership are a variant of their apartheid precursors. But racial segregation today also diverges from its twentieth-century form. In suburbs, gated communities, malls, universities and office blocks, the picture is strikingly different from, *and* strikingly similar to, its apartheid antecedent. Some Black people can now inhabit spaces of privilege, even in the numerical majority. This would have been unthinkable before 1994.

However, zoom into these spaces of privilege, and you will find the stubborn persistence of apartheid hierarchy. Spaces of privilege today are characterised by racialised integration: people live and work in close proximity but still within apartheid hierarchies. Even where Black South Africans represent a numerical majority, this does not mean that they hold concomitant social power. Hence, while the gates of privilege have ostensibly been opened to Black South Africans, relations beyond those gates still encipher apartheid.

BANTUSTANS AND NEO-LIBERATION

So far, I have expanded on the meaning of 'privatisation'. To fully appreciate its implications, three important coincident events must be considered. First, as apartheid was privatised, the new republic which replaced it became Bantustanised; second, the national liberation movement was nationalised; third, the neoliberal consensus solidified.

As political independence swept Africa in the 1960s, Pretoria faced pressure to relax apartheid. In response, the Verwoerd administration inaugurated 'separate development', a devilish form of reverse decolonisation. Instead of enfranchising Black people in 'White South Africa', Verwoerd invented jumbled, ethnically exclusive and semi-autonomous 'Bantu homelands' (dubbed Bantustans by their critics) within South Africa's borders. Separate development dotted South Africa with countless new borders, and carved the country into incoherent and nonintersecting slices, condensing Black people into disjointed atolls of racial separation.[14] Pretoria then stripped Black South Africans of their citizenship of South Africa.[15]

Bantustans served a double purpose: on the one hand, they further concentrated, subjugated and divided Black people under the pretext of 'self-determination'; on the other, they temporarily deflected international attention from the draconian evil of apartheid. As Steve Biko averred, Bantustans were 'cocoons' designed to 'dampen the enthusiasm' of Black liberation movements, where Black people 'suffered peacefully'.[16] They were a fig leaf, intended to distract world opinion and dilute Black political unity. They were internal archipelagos of oppression, surrounded by a buffeting sea of White supremacy.

And, while the logic of this system is commonly thought to have expired with the constitutional era, the new South African republic itself resembles a centralised Bantustan, as I shall argue. For one thing, the new republic achieved all that was intended by the original Bantustans, only more effectively. It preserved White economic privilege by conceding Black political rights – just like the Bantustans. It reduced international condemnation of racial inequality in South Africa – just like the Bantustans. It pacified Black anger through the conferral of political rights – just like the Bantustans. And it assumed the administrative burdens of governance, without real economic control – just like the Bantustans.

On the other hand, of course, the democratic state united Black citizens, while the Bantustans divided them. The democratic state conferred substantial political rights, whereas the Bantustans limited them. But these concessions – on Black unity and political rights – occurred in exchange for massive benefits to White wealth and privilege. Unlike the Bantustans, the democratic dispensation freed White South Africans from economic sanction or moral condemnation after apartheid. White business was free to trade on international markets once more, and generous profits soon flowed. Thus, what White South Africans lost in centralised political control, they gained in international legitimacy and economic freedom. In one sense, then, 1994 was a reversal: the former Bantustans became integrated into the centre, but the centre itself was Bantustanised.

The new republic was Bantustanised in a second sense. The apartheid state – which was eventually inherited by the African National Congress (ANC) government in 1994 – had always been a White Bantustan. The comfort and supremacy of White citizens – and the discomfort and subordination of Black semi-citizens – were its *raison d'être*. The administration of this White Bantustan was a costly business. In 1994, its management was transferred to a Black-led government. Although its constitution changed fundamentally, and the new nation's identity shifted markedly, the culture of the old state, along with its financial burdens, became the problem of its original opponents.

South Africa was Bantustanised in a third sense. As the ANC assumed power, and incorporated the former Bantustans into the new republic, White privilege itself became increasingly and ironically Bantustanised. Whereas White privilege was nationalised under apartheid, it became wholly privatised and geographically fragmented in the new dispensation. White South Africans receded into increasingly elaborate and decentralised Bantustans of privilege, spread throughout South Africa. Afrikaner nationalism itself became enclaved, now driven by private institutions with private aims.

South Africa was Bantustanised in a fourth sense. As the former Bantustans were integrated into the new unitary state, the geographical boundaries of the Bantustans were largely preserved. Like apartheid functionaries, former Bantustan leaders had their pensions guaranteed by the new state. The former Bantustans have retained much control in their new guise as Traditional Councils, which map neatly onto the former Bantustans (map in central colour section). The ANC has increasingly relied on the Councils as its grip on urban power loosens. And some Bantustans have increased their economic significance after mineral discoveries there. This has entrenched the logic of regional decentralisation and frustrated governance from the centre. Hence, the old Bantustans have now become Bantustans within a Bantustan.

As apartheid became privatised, so liberation politics, once decentralised and extra-governmental, was nationalised. And, as the liberation movement was nationalised and legalised, much of its radical vision was diluted and abandoned. Radical commitments turned from policy tools to rhetorical devices. An increasing swell of ANC members were subsumed into the state apparatus, the party-political electoral machine, or the corporate sphere. This conflicted the ANC, between rhetorical ideals, immediate electoral goals, corporate loyalties, and governmental priorities. The state's failures became the ANC's failures; corporate profits became the profits of ANC deployees and funders.

Furthermore, when the liberation movement was nationalised, it assumed apartheid's debts. These debts further constrained ANC policy choices and limited fundamental reform. The ANC became financially responsible for land reform, the welfare state, and the provision of basic services like water, electricity and housing. These initiatives would at worst bankrupt the new state or at best fundamentally constrain it. Some combination materialised in reality.

Wittingly or unwittingly, the ANC assumed sole and simultaneous financial responsibility for apartheid's failures *and* its own extravagant promises. Each was a tall political order, and it failed at achieving both. Quite apart, then, from the ANC government's considerable self-inflicted defeats in governance, its options were bounded from the outset. When institutions are nationalised within a market context, the discipline of the market often prevails over ambitions for social gain. And this is the paradoxical story of the ANC since 1994: it was nationalised to serve private interests.

The global neoliberal moment underpins apartheid's privatisation. As the apartheid state capitulated, the idea of the state itself underwent major renovation the world over. After the fall of the Berlin Wall, free market capitalism gained domestic and international precedence, the voter became 'akin to a consumer and the government akin to a firm,'[17] and the human was now defined as an atomised, competitive and irreducibly economic being.

In this moment, political ills like injustice and inequality were framed as the natural result of ineluctable economic forces, outside the control of state agency. Politics became subordinate to economics, and economics was infused with inescapable and mystical power. Just as democracy dawned in South Africa, the private economy became 'encased in its own autonomous sphere' and separated from the 'dangerous forces' of popular accountability.[18]

Two consequences of the new apartheid deserve consideration in this introduction. First, oppression itself has changed; second, those least responsible for the inequity of the new apartheid bear its burdens disproportionately. Oppression itself has become privatised. Through this process, apartheid has become less potent, crude and obvious but more durable, sustainable and concealed. Oppression is harder to identify because it thrives under the cover of the constitutional order.

As oppression has morphed, so new precarities have emerged, and citizens' relationship to the state has altered. Whereas the state was once active in oppression, it is now merely unable to secure liberation. The state–citizen relationship has become ambiguous: the state promises solidarity with the oppressed while being complicit in their victimisation. All the while, unacceptable hardship, significant suffering, and structural inequity persist.

New forms of oppression disproportionately affect certain people. Three groups illustrate this: Black women, the 'Black workless class', and poor African migrants. The position of Black women in the new apartheid is tragic. While wealthy Black men can benefit from the relaxation of racial laws and the poisonous fruits of patriarchy, Black women still suffer under the yoke of White supremacy, on the one hand, and multiple patriarchies, on the other.[19] South Africa is a society where the everyday experience of sexism is ubiquitous, and the triple scourges of domestic violence, sexual violence and femicide[20] (the large-scale murder of women) have reached unconscionable and epochal proportions.

Another major casualty of the new apartheid is the 'Black workless class' – an army of approximately ten million impoverished, work-starved and precarious semi-citizens, owning no stake in the skewed economy, deriving scant material benefit from the constitutional order, and suffering the burden of violent policing at any hint of resistance. The workless class is consigned to a life of informality in housing, employment, and the provision of basic services. Its members are relegated to the position of 'excess persons' and 'slaves in search of masters',[21] unable to enjoy even the tainted benefits of working-class exploitation. This informality is often institutionalised and governmentally enforced, but is most commonly privately inscribed.

African migrants are a third example. As White South Africans have emigrated, so new African migrants have immigrated. This social re-composition has coincided with the new apartheid in profound ways. Around this new group of African migrants, all the burdens of racism, all the weight of anti-immigrant sentiment, and all the encumbrance of economic exploitation crystallise. They suffer intolerable violence, open bigotry, and tremendous economic hardship. Unsurprisingly, none of these ills befall wealthy White migrants. Lamentably, those who bear the new apartheid's onerous and violent burdens are least responsible for its gross inequities; whereas White South Africans – who benefited from apartheid's inequities – benefit again from the new apartheid. In the new apartheid, resentments bubbling over centuries have tragically turned on history's innocent bystanders.

TENSIONS

Two competing, and intertwining, visions clash in South Africa today: one, a democratic, egalitarian vision called the 'the new South Africa'; the other, an oppressive and conservative vision, hidden in plain sight, that I call 'the new apartheid'. These clashing but entangled projects produce a society in contradiction, undergoing at once extraordinary change and frustrating stagnancy. The language of historical disjuncture which divides 'apartheid' and 'post-apartheid' masks this ambiguity.[22] As Peter Hudson observes:

> The notion of a 'democratic breakthrough' is too blunt to capture what has happened *vis-à-vis* colonialism and democracy in South Africa. Colonialism and democracy pull in two opposing directions – one emphasising the break with colonialism and the other the latter's resilience.[23]

These two 'directions' can be traced back to the democratic negotiations which birthed the new republic. These negotiations occurred on two parallel tracks: one concerning the political and constitutional future of the country, the other concerning its economic trajectory.[24] While constitutional negotiations dominated local and international headlines, economic negotiations – which predated political talks – would profoundly influence the path of new apartheid. If the ANC won the constitutional talks, it lost the economic talks decisively.

Democratic negotiations were challenged from the outset, and continue to court controversy. The challenge is founded on two claims: first, that the outcome of the negotiations was unsatisfactory; second, that the process followed in the negotiations was secret and unrepresentative. The secrecy of the negotiations is also often proffered as a cause of the unsatisfactory outcomes.

Two illustrations suffice for this introduction. From the perspective of outcomes, private actors extracted major economic concessions in the democratic negotiations. For, after the birth of the democratic constitution in 1996, the ANC fundamentally reshaped its economic policy, following the dictates of neoliberal orthodoxy with few exceptions.[25] Not only were policies overhauled, but party funders were rewarded, leaders co-opted, and an army of consultants and lobbyists granted access to the innermost state sanctums. Time and again, in South Africa's early experiment with democracy, public ambitions for justice and equality have been frustrated by private actors.

Problems of secrecy and inadequate representation in the negotiations are best seen from the perspective of gender, for women were sidelined from both the NP and ANC sides of the constitutional and economic talks. In particular, women were totally unrepresented in the structures of ANC and NP leadership in the early 1990s,[26] and in the secret economic talks of the late 1980s, even as their activism was central to weakening apartheid. It is no surprise, therefore, that many of the compromises reached in the talks, and the burdens of the society which resulted, have advantaged men while freezing gender relations. Certainly, these challenges deserve careful attention in the context of the new apartheid and are explored in the pages to follow.

Over time, these two competing visions of South Africa have increasingly intermingled. Aspects of apartheid now taint the liberation vision, and aspects of liberation touch the heart of economic power. The new state replicates oppressive behaviour learned from its predecessor; corporate power appeals to the legitimacy of liberation icons. The ANC has welcomed former NP politicians into its ranks; ANC cadres have swollen the ranks of corporate apartheid.

The entire edifice of apartheid has become enmeshed in the ANC, and the liberation movement has become enmeshed in capital, so that distinguishing the two is increasingly hard. In this way, no clear line separates the new apartheid's supporters and opponents. This ambiguity is contained in the now-popular phrase 'tenderpreneur'. President Cyril Ramaphosa is another exemplar, in his role as Comrade Baron. So are the private funders of various ANC campaigns, from the Gupta brothers to the now-deceased Gavin Watson.

If institutions are compromised, then so are individuals in the new society. Gone are the halcyon days of clear moral choices and untainted political protagonists. Gone, too, are the days of an evil authoritarian archetype. Today, liberators and oppressors are often indistinguishable. Who, then, is the enemy? Black South Africans today must fight conflicting urges for material security and political liberation. And navigating these contending currents in a society of growing privatised oppression inevitably leads to complicities and compromises.

Why has the ANC succeeded in this environment? Precisely because it speaks to the competing impulses of the new nation. Support for the ANC means at once the chance to steer a sleek sedan, and to chant liberation slogans with passionate intensity. And such tensions should not be quickly dismissed, since the material destitution of apartheid has left lasting scars on the Black psyche. The incoherence of the ANC and its leaders is exactly its strength, since the citizens to which it pledges allegiance are themselves conflicted. Thus, the line between state and market, and between public and private, is irreversibly blurred in the new apartheid. Each feeds and frustrates the other, in the scramble for intersecting interests.

QUALIFICATIONS

What I am *not* saying in the book needs to be underscored. I am not claiming that South Africa is the same as it was before 1994. None can deny the far-reaching effects of the abolition of apartheid statutes, or the importance of the removal of apartheid as a state ideology. In themselves, these two changes have altered South Africa dramatically. To be sure, South Africa is 'undergoing multiple and systemic transitions, at different paces and rhythms'.[27] As should be clear from the title of this book, there is something 'new' about 'the new apartheid'. What I am claiming in this book is that the 'new' is connected to the 'old'. I am protesting against a binary view of South African history that unduly dramatises the novelty of the new South African republic. 1994 represented a change in degree, not in kind. The constitutional order will not automatically vanquish the new apartheid, any more than the new apartheid will overturn the constitutional order. South Africa is still in transition, and the true character of the new republic, and the democratic experiment on which it rests, is yet to be discovered.

I contend, therefore, that apartheid was dealt a non-fatal blow in 1994. The old society swallowed the minimum effective dose of political freedom to preserve its sickening body. As broken bones heal, so systems of oppression reconstitute around new constraints. So it is with apartheid.

I also do not claim that the new apartheid is a conspiracy. The current state of South Africa was not perfectly foreseen in advance. Rather, ineluctable trends towards privatisation developed a self-reinforcing momentum, separate from any single coercive agency. The new apartheid has no single architect, nor is it driven by a grand, unified theory. It is robust because it is leaderless. Whereas apartheid emerged, in part, by meticulous design, the new apartheid persists organically.

However, some features of the new apartheid were predictable. Late apartheid's economic planners were seduced by the neoliberal paradigm and sought to impose it on the new republic from the political grave. Apartheid's negotiators had motives, agency and resources, and deployed them accordingly in the democratic talks. Triumphalist accounts of South Africa's democratic transition tend to ignore this. A careful look at South Africa's economic structure confirms it.

This is not simply to say that the ANC 'sold out' at the negotiations. Such a view unduly centres the ANC in a complex historical moment. Rather, I suggest that apartheid interests arrived at the negotiating table with priorities, and succeeded in achieving some of them. This means dispensing with the myth that the ANC outmanoeuvred its apartheid counterparts at the negotiations. South Africa's democratic transition, and the mythology which surrounds it, may well be a rare example of history being written by the losers, at least on the economic front. The celebritisation of ANC leaders in the 1990s reinforces, rather than refutes, this point. South Africa's contemporary malaise is rooted in its founding bargains. This is ironic, since ANC failure is often attributed to governmental implementation rather than structural constraints. Certainly, the ANC's ineptitudes have deepened the malaise. Yet its failures in governance must be judged against monstrous economic constraints.

INSPIRATIONS

This book lies at the intersection of three themes. On one hand, a range of South African scholars over the past three decades have described a 'new apartheid' in various spheres of South African life, from housing to health care, and from law to economics.[28] Phrases like 'neo-apartheid' are increasingly common in South African scholarship, and the 'post' in 'post-apartheid' is increasingly ironised, asterisked, preceded by 'so-called', or scare-quoted.

On the other hand, as Simukai Chigudu notes, 'throughout the annals of African political history, scholars from wide-ranging intellectual traditions and theoretical inclinations have grappled with how best to conceptualise the African state, its political and economic trajectory, and its relationship to wider society.'[29] These scholars have long warned of uncomfortable proximities between public and private power, and of the thinness of African democratic institutions. They speak of African states' external orientation at the expense of inward development, of their capture by domestic private interests. They lament the 'privatisation of sovereignty', 'public violence', 'public authority',[30] and even the state itself.[31]

A third set of observers warns that digital technology is dangerously refuelling old codes of oppression. They warn that new mega tech corporations are concentrating power, manipulating humans, and disassembling societies on a prodigious scale.[32]

This book unites these three perspectives. I agree with South African scholars that 'a new apartheid' deserves careful investigation. Unlike them, however, I apply the term to the full spectrum of South African life. I agree with scholars of the African state who decry the influence of private power over public authority. Unlike them, however, I am not interested in the state per se. Apartheid was not a state, but a state project, ideology, and technology. Hence, I am not arguing here that the state was privatised, but that its governing ideology and modus operandi were. Whereas theorists of the African state tend to consider how 'weak' African states stabilise themselves by submitting to private pressure, I invert the question: how do private networks of power within African states stabilise around otherwise functional states?[33]

Finally, thinkers writing on the dangers of technology and its propensity to retrench oppression focus mainly on the United States, China and Europe. I place these new technological fears in the context of South Africa. In this sense, I view a global process of digital change through an African prism. As readers from outside South Africa will find, South Africa is – and always has been – a microcosm of the world. Having said this, I owe a debt to all the scholars and thinkers who have written across these three divides, for inspiring this work.

The New Apartheid is about the past, present and future, and how they interlock.[34] It asks what apartheid was, is and will be. What apartheid was, is a historical question *and* a contemporary one, since we can only judge history from our present perspective. In this sense, the question of what apartheid was, is also a question about how we remember, conjure, and invoke apartheid today, and how that memory shifts and evolves over time, influenced inevitably by disappointments of the present and predictions of the future. Questioning the apartheid past thus involves assessing what Sarah Nuttall calls 'the post-apartheid present', a present always mutating in countless directions at once and 'coeval' with the past.[35]

As a new generation rises, with no direct memory of apartheid, the question of apartheid's memorialisation is all the more central. Indeed, I write primarily for that audience for whom apartheid is as much a spectre as an experience. In doing so, I grasp at a widespread affect in a new South African generation – a combination of hope, mourning, disillusionment, betrayal, gratitude, ambition, apathy and confusion that goes with inheriting the new apartheid.

This is also a work about what apartheid will be. Will apartheid survive, even thrive, in the future? If so, why? If not, why not? To appreciate these profoundly important questions, I refract apartheid through parallel lenses of the past and present. In this sense, this is a work of what I call 'science faction', or the use of true events to reflect on an uncertain future.

STRUCTURE

The chapters that follow expand on the argument advanced in this introduction. They examine the history, present and future of apartheid in six spheres of South African life. Chapter 1 focuses on space in the new apartheid. I examine the growth of urban enclaves to explain how urban public space itself has shifted since 1994. I then turn to racial patterns in rural South Africa, focusing on commercial agriculture and the reification of Bantustan borders.

Chapter 2 examines law in the new apartheid. I investigate the tension between private and public law, and show how apartheid persists outside the statutory framework, especially in the law of contract. I also weigh the transformative capacity of the Constitution.

Chapter 3 scrutinises wealth. I examine the blurred distinction between public and private interest in the new apartheid. I link contemporary corruption to the culture of state impunity created during apartheid and entrenched in the democratic transition. I also analyse the financialisation of wealth in the new apartheid. Finally, I explore the ascendancy of neoliberal economic rhetoric and the isolation of justice and equality from the political realm.

Chapter 4 addresses technology. I define apartheid as an algorithm running in the background of South African society. I examine how technology entrenches social coding that was initially pioneered by the apartheid government. I then examine the alienation created by new digital technologies. I also reflect on the new digital 'public sphere', which is controlled by private actors.

Chapter 5 regards punishment. I review the role of policing, both public and private, and trace the privatisation of law enforcement in the new apartheid. I then turn to the question of incarceration, and argue that sentencing and carceral policy reinforce racial patterns in criminal punishment. Finally, I look at the privatisation of justice through emerging institutions of private prosecution and investigation.

'The new apartheid' is a new frame through which to see South Africa's recent history, its present conjuncture, and its future prospects.

This act of reconception challenges myths of abiding influence, and subverts the story of South Africa's democratic conversion. It suggests that post-constitutional South Africa remains a colonial society in post-colonial draping; a postcolonial vision superimposed onto a colonial reality; a nation of warring, discordant and polyrhythmic visions; a country where, above all, apartheid is constantly resurrected in novel and surprising guises.

The New Apartheid:

1. The replacement of laws with fees.
2. Deracialised racial oppression.
3. Corrupt anti-corruption.
4. Poverty and paradise, separated by an inch of glass and a line of code.
5. More than just racist speech.
6. Malan's horcruxes.
7. A digital technology that reinforces a social technology, and vice versa.
8. A privatised, decentralised, self-replicating and leaderless vestige of the apartheid state.
9. The reason that 'we want the land' resonates, whether we want the land or not. Also, the reason we're not 'getting the land'.
10. The gated community, the office complex, the commission of inquiry, the private security guard and the cleaner, all under the same roof.

Space

Where has all the public space gone? All that is left is a city of urban forts . . . an intricate maze of secluded neighbourhood cells. Wealthier citizens live, work and play in these bastions of concrete and steel connected to each other by sky bridges and armoured vehicles. Juxtaposed to this fortified maze is the warzone, a den of deadly forces competing for control . . . It is only those who are excluded from the gated city who are left to live their lives in this derelict and dangerous maze of misery.

– Barry Ronge[36]

In this chapter, I trace apartheid's fascination with race, space and place. First, I explore new forms of urban segregation. Second, I trace apartheid's afterlife in rural South Africa.

SECESSION

Orania is a racially exclusive enclave on the banks of the Orange River, complete with its own radio station, currency and population of nearly two thousand people.[37] To Orania's south unfurl hazel hills and charcoal byways; to its north stretch emerald blankets of fertile farmland. From above, Orania is bisected by the R369 roadway – a bisection representing at once South Africa's history of social division and its present of privatised segregation.

Hopes of White secession date to the mid-1960s, when the South African Bureau for Racial Affairs proposed a White homeland.[38] Towards the end of apartheid, White secession assumed new meaning, as fringe movements and extremist leaders demanded a *volkstaat* (Afrikaner homeland) in the negotiations for democratic South Africa. In the early 1990s, Afrikaner leaders like Eugene Terre'Blanche and his radical right-wing Afrikaner Weerstandsbeweging (AWB) along with erstwhile apartheid general Constand Viljoen championed secessionist dreams. Secession, they argued, would cushion White South Africans from the worst excesses of majority rule.

Viljoen, along with three other apartheid generals, established the Afrikaner Volksfront[39] (Afrikaner People's Front), which envisaged Afrikaner-only enclaves across the Transvaal, Northern Cape and Western Cape.[40] These would be claimed by force, if necessary – a threat which preoccupied Nelson Mandela himself:

> A dark cloud was hanging over South Africa which threatened to block and even reverse all the gains South Africans had made in regard to the country's peaceful transition.[41] Afrikaners had decided to stop the forthcoming elections by violence. To be on the safe side, the president of an organisation must check the accuracy of such reports. I did so, and, when I discovered that they were accurate, I decided to act.[42]

Orania emerged against this backdrop, in 1991. The town's origins date to the 1960s when the apartheid government built dams and canals along the Orange River. The state acquired Orania in 1968 as a base for these operations and, in time, Orania became a 'fully-equipped dorp of 483 hectares, exclusively for Damming Project employees, complete with schools, church, town hall, recreational facilities and a rich surrounding of irrigable land'.[43]

As was typical, Orania split into three racial zones: one for 'Africans', one for 'Coloureds', and the lion's share for 'Whites'. When the dam-building project concluded in 1989, the town's White workers abandoned about ninety houses, a school, a church and a post office.[44] These structures were occupied by the remaining Black inhabitants.

Jacques Pretorius, a solo entrepreneur, bought Orania from the state in the 1980s. But Pretorius failed to rebuild the town, and struggled to meet his debts. Enter Carel Boshoff III, son-in-law of apartheid prime minister Hendrik Verwoerd. Boshoff bought the land from Pretorius in August 1990 to build a privatised *volkstaat*.

First, Boshoff established the Orania Bestuursdienste (Orania Management Service), which was, in turn, owned by the Vluytjeskraal Aandeleblok Beperk (Vluytjeskraal Shareblock Scheme Ltd):

> By placing discriminative restrictions on the terms of the share, and individually screening each investor, the overseeing company, the Vluytjeskraal Shareblock Scheme, ensured that Orania would remain a *volkstaat* for Afrikaners only. In effect, corporate convention along with the regulations set out in the peculiarly South African Share Blocks Control Act of the 1980s were and are used together in order to secure for the dorp what key pieces of legislation – including the Natives Land Acts of 1913 and 1936, the Group Areas Act of 1950, and the Prevention of Illegal Squatting Act of 1951 – had done during apartheid.[45]

Boshoff achieved through private means what apartheid had done through state decree.[46] Boshoff had woven a financialised *volkstaat*. His only remaining headache was evicting the Black inhabitants of Orania. This he achieved by force. Boshoff and his brigandish acolytes gave Orania's Black residents until 31 March 1991 to vacate the land or face expulsion. Then, later that year:

> Bakkies showed up and sped in and out of the settlement's thin, unsealed lanes, depositing groups of unfamiliar men who went from door to door with final notices and threats of violence. As dusk fell, rifle shots and the barks of angry dogs echoed throughout the town. In the face of this treatment, up to 500 terrified residents packed up their belongings and, without anywhere having been set aside for them to move to, said their final goodbyes and went their separate ways.[47]

As one of the residents of Orania at the time reported:

Some of us tried to resist passively but we had to succumb to the might of their guns. From Friday night these crazy people were firing guns in the air throughout. On Saturday night they became more physical, assaulting people . . . I remember one guy . . . who severely assaulted people on that night. Our visitors were also assaulted. There is an old man whose leg was amputated after he was assaulted.[48]

The remaining Coloured residents of Orania fled to Warrenton, a Coloured town over a hundred kilometres away.[49] Thys Fick, Orania's first caretaker, typified the mood of the violent evictions which ensued: 'we bought the land, not the people'.[50]

Far from challenging Orania after 1994, the ANC legitimised it. In 1995, Nelson Mandela visited Orania and shared tea with Betsie Verwoerd, Hendrik Verwoerd's widow. In their meeting, Verwoerd reiterated her dream for a *volkstaat*, while Verwoerd's granddaughter, Elizabeth van der Berg, told the Associated Press that 'we wish [Mandela] was the President of a neighbouring country'.[51] Mandela, however, believed that 'we were received by everybody in Orania as if I was in Soweto'.[52] That year, Orania was recognised as a quasi-independent municipality, and it elected an all-White Transitional Municipal Council, with demarcations neatly drawn around the town.

Transitional Councils were abolished as South Africa moved to a municipal system of government in 2000. In this process, the Northern Cape government proposed to merge Orania with neighbouring councils, effectively ending the all-White Orania council. Oranians objected, causing the dispute to land at the Kimberley High Court. In a bizarre decision, the court ruled that Orania's Transitional Council could be extended indefinitely, citing protections for minority rights in the Constitution. After 2000, Orania became the sole Transitional Municipal Council in South Africa. The ANC government vowed to resolve Orania's unique status soon after the court's ruling. Over twenty years later, nothing has materialised.

Orania's forced evictions were a harbinger of the new apartheid. The state's retreat from the front lines of segregation heralded a new wave of privatised exclusion. Like other enclaves in the constitutional era, Orania has survived and thrived through private initiative. Upon visiting the town in 2010, then president Jacob Zuma suggested that Orania was misunderstood: 'my impression is that this is a community that is prepared to live in South Africa but have a place for itself to exercise its culture, and I think that is a basis for continuous engagement'.[53] Yet, ten years on, Joost Strydom – Orania's media manager – showed no sign of abandoning the dream of a *volkstaat*: 'If we want to have any say, we need to be a majority in a certain area. We want, let's say, a homeland. We are actually a very small nation. We just want a piece of land where we can look after ourselves and do things our way.'[54]

Lodged between the rural and the urban, and straddling the old and new political orders, Orania is a unique lens through which to understand apartheid's survival in South African space since democracy.

URBAN SEGREGATION

Before 1994, urban segregation in South African was explicit and external; after 1994, it became implicit and internal. 'Explicit segregation' – the kind that thrived before 1994 – advertises racial separation through signage, codifies it in law, and concretises it in the built environment. Similarly, 'external segregation' – also prevalent during apartheid – creates mutually exclusive racial zones: in apartheid, cities were diced into 'White', 'Black', 'Asian' and 'Coloured' pieces.[55]

In the new apartheid, implicit segregation has replaced explicit segregation: whereas explicit segregation is advertised, implicit segregation is unspoken; whereas explicit segregation is codified, implicit segregation is unwritten; and whereas explicit segregation bans racial integration, implicit segregation permits limited integration.

Furthermore, as external segregation has receded, internal segregation has deepened: whereas external segregation controls movement between mutually exclusive racial zones, internal segregation permits such movement; whereas external segregation separates entire neighbour-hoods, internal segregation divides neighbourhoods and even buildings within them.

Thus, while the signage of separation has disappeared, segregation persists. Whereas explicit segregation barred *all* Black people from privilege, implicit segregation is more discerning.

In the new apartheid, government no longer enforces segregation, and urban space is ostensibly open to all. However, private powers – from security companies to residential associations – still blockade the new apartheid city, a space of 'a poly-nucleated ... secessionary net-worked infrastructure, shopping malls and gated communities that by-pass cities' poorer, peripheral parts'.[56]

Implicit segregation sidesteps the shame of explicit segregation while maintaining explicit segregation's effects. Implicit segregation hides behind masks of crime reduction, traffic decongestion, environmental protection or market efficiency. In truth, its goal and its consequences are racial exclusion. Implicit segregation is apartheid by proxy.

Three decades into democracy, apartheid's borders of racial exclusion, which carved cities into racial quadrants, have been preserved to a stun-ning degree. Maps 3, 4, 5 and 6 illustrate segregation's continued pres-ence in Johannesburg, Cape Town, eThekwini and Nelson Mandela Bay. These cities continue to reproduce sharp spatial divisions, mirroring apartheid's design.[57]

At first, central business districts (CBDs) appear to contradict my argument. Downtown Johannesburg, for instance, has undergone dra-matic racial reconfiguration since 1994. In truth, however, the Johan-nesburg CBD is a case of White flight rather than racial integration. Instead of resembling a diverse racial whole, the Johannesburg CBD has become largely mono-racial.

New and disproportionately White CBDs have developed separately from the city's traditional commercial centre, in places like Rosebank and Sandton. Hence, in the new apartheid, new White enclaves have mushroomed at the same rate at which old White enclaves have inte-grated or been vacated by White people.

Furthermore, integration – in suburbs like Zonnebloem in Cape Town and Killarney and Melville in Johannesburg – is again chimeric. These areas, too, act as 'buffer zones' between formally Black and White areas. Accordingly, integration is a marginal and exceptional situation, failing to change the macroscopic pattern of racial zoning.

White South Africans often maintain gross overrepresentation in centres of economic privilege, even though Black South Africans are the overall numerical majority. This, again, is depicted in stark detail in Maps 3, 4, 5 and 6. This is why, as political analyst Aubrey Matshiqi notes, 'a numerical minority' can remain the 'cultural majority'.[58]

Paradoxically, then, segregation in the new South Africa has become visible *and* invisible. Glaring segregation pervades South African cities. But, over time, these divisions have come to feel inescapable, because no central agency enforces them. Moreover, the urgency of desegregation has decelerated precisely because it now appears natural.

Internal segregation further complicates the picture. Unlike 'external segregation' – which deals with separation between racial zones – internal segregation concerns racial separation *within* racial enclaves, especially those once demarcated as 'White' under apartheid. In these cases, external racial borders have retreated but not disappeared.

The porousness of these borders of privilege is misleading. On one hand, *de jure* segregation has vanished; on the other, *de facto* segregation persists. The cases in which Black people cross these borders are merely an exception to the unwritten rule. And, crucially, the absence of legalised segregation enables these exceptions to *prove* the rule. The presence of a minority of Black people in previously White-only areas ensures segregation's sustainability by simulating nominal equality. As legal barricades have tumbled, the barricades of cultural, normative and implicit discrimination have fortified.

Consequently, borders separating races have metastasised. Whereas borders between privilege and oppression were once clearly defined in law and explicitly advertised in architecture, they are now porous and ambiguous. These borders are more fragmented, numerous and incoherent than their apartheid precursors. They are also privately enforced, resting on financial rather than racial criteria. Nevertheless, they are remarkably robust.

Gated communities exemplify renewed urban segregation because, as Tlou Ramoroka notes, they 'transfer public spaces to private ownership, thereby perpetuating apartheid social exclusion legacies'.[59] These strongholds of separation range from entire suburb-sized encampments to small five-home enclosures; and from residential estates to multi-purpose and mixed-use developments, incorporating office parks, malls and apartment blocks.[60] Some are designed to exclude from their inception; others have become 'gated' over time through expanding networks of 'boom gates, and access control points'.[61] Gated communities have mushroomed spectacularly in twenty-first century South Africa,[62] now constituting 15 per cent of the urban real estate market and fetching triple the price of comparable non-gated property.[63]

Gated communities are especially common in Johannesburg's central and northern suburbs – the heart of South African economic privilege. Map 7 (see colour section) depicts the growth of gated communities in Gauteng, where each community resembles a shard of glass on a fractured racial plane.[64] Comparing Map 7 with Maps 3, 4, 5 and 6 shows that gated communities proliferate in White-majority areas. They thus reinforce both external segregation and implicit segregation.[65]

Gated communities also impinge on privacy. To access these communities, residents and visitors must surrender vital personal information. On arrival, security guards prompt entrants for identity cards, note down vehicle registration details, and extract phone numbers and signatures. Panoptic cameras monitor entrants' every move within the perimeter of the private compound. 'In order to gain access to an unremarkable suburban road,' writes Lynsey Chutel, 'South Africans have become accustomed to parting with their most personal details'.[66]

Gated communities are just one extreme example of urban segregation. Residential fortification is also common outside these communities. Homes in South African suburbs – and increasingly outside these areas – are hyper-securitised. Barbed wire, private street cameras, infrared beams and panic buttons preponderate. Daedalian sliding gates, nifty door locks, and burglar-proof window bars abound. Private security guards surveil behind the tinted glass screens of one-person 'security huts'. The new apartheid city is a dense patchwork of grey gates, tall walls, and electrified fortifications.

Whereas entire suburbs and cities were barricaded during apartheid, segregation has retreated inwards in the new apartheid. The Fordist suburban ideal of the 1970s – large, free-standing homes with swimming pools and sprawling lawns – has yielded to the hyper-secure suburban security complex. As Dirsuweit and Wafer suggest:

> The urban order of the segregated and controlled racial Fordist city has given way to a landscape popularly caricatured by decentralised retail and commercial developments, privatised gated communities and town-house complexes, surrounded by free-ways and parking-lots, and besieged by the unplanned 'informal' city that mushrooms at the interstices of this ex-urban sprawl.[67]

The effects of continued urban segregation are often tragic, as traffic congestion, crime, and infrastructural decay are transferred onto an already-straining public purse. Take crime, for instance. Privileged enclosures, which themselves would otherwise be targets of crime, can deflect crime onto lower economic strata. The disproportionate burden of crime is thus experienced in poor and middle class settings.[68] Far from preventing crime, then, urban enclaves merely redirect it.

Hence, democratic South Africa faces a security dilemma: rich citizens unwittingly escalate violence through attempts at self-preservation. As the rich recede behind ever-expanding walls, they improve their own security. But this escalates crime outside these walls. The retreat to enclaves thus exacerbates crime, while protecting the wealthy. Cruelly, the more gated and enclosed South Africa becomes, the more crime affects the vulnerable. Resources ploughed into private seclusion might address the crime crisis and its root causes. Instead, they facilitate inward emigration, plastering an unsustainable and expensive band aid over a festering social wound.

Hence, the new apartheid has reoriented urban space under the pretext of security. A tragedy of the commons ensues, in which the self-interest of petrified citizens worsens the safety of the majority and inhibits their movement. Refuge from crime is only accessible behind private walls. Private residents' associations, bodies corporate and property developers, rather than the state, now fund this infrastructure of fear.[69]

Traffic congestion is another example. The closure of urban avenues squeezes urban traffic onto a few arterial roads. Travel through the new apartheid city becomes unduly time-consuming as a result: commuting between a township and a city can take up to five hours per day.[70] Thus, while the closure of public roads reduces crime in some areas, it hampers the movement of all.[71] Enclaves also disproportionately impede poor Black South Africans' movement, forcing workers and pedestrians to take long detours around gated thoroughfares.[72]

The scarcity of safe public space is itself a metaphor for the new apartheid, where the boundary between private and public interest is increasingly blurred, and the private often masquerades as the public. The right to access space – and to move between spaces – is increasingly privately regulated and enforced. Public–private spaces replicate the restrictions of apartheid. Democratic interactions occur in increasingly private-owned spaces, always marked by privately determined entry criteria. This diminishment of safe public space inhibits interracial dialogue in a country already riven with division. South Africans are increasingly forced to encounter one another in malls, office parks or gated enclosures, where the terms of democratic debate are mediated by private interests.

The fragmentation of public space also affects commerce. For example, since 1994, Johannesburg has developed two separate CBDs: one in the traditional 'inner city' of Johannesburg and Braamfontein; another in Sandton. With some exceptions, the headquarters of state institutions and older corporations remain in the old centre, while the economic juggernauts of the new apartheid – law firms, financial firms, multinationals and technology companies – reside in Sandton. In this way, commercial space has become increasingly bipolar.

Established in the 1970s, Sandton is a creature of the neoliberal moment. It rose to prominence as an alternative commercial district after P. W. Botha's government eased urban influx regulations in the 1980s.[73] After democracy, as racial laws receded, White corporate flight accelerated. Sandton's ascendancy was crowned when, in 2000, the Johannesburg Stock Exchange made the booming financial centre its new home.

Johannesburg had grown two urban centres – one Black-majority centre in Johannesburg-Braamfontein and another White-majority centre in Sandton. By the early 2000s, Sandton had earned the nickname of 'umlungustan'.[74]

> Whereas sub-urbanisation in North American, European, and Australian cities reflected an expansion of the 'old' city, the development of Sandton represented something of a substitution of the city, a situation where downtown Johannesburg was replaced, and where income segregation would prevail as opposed to the former racial segregation.[75]

Hence, urban South African life still unfolds behind a social cordon of road closures, underground parking bunkers, soft barricades, gated booms, security cameras, and checkpoints – always mediated by the figure of the uniformed Black security guard. Spatial and racial quarantining perseveres, from enclosed neighbourhoods to suburb-sized estates; and from residential complexes and high-rise apartment blocks to the concrete ramparts which slice cities into ever-tinier fragments.[76] The new apartheid enacts the 'global trend of privatised urbanisation' with distinctly South African characteristics.[77]

The living ghosts of segregation surround South African spaces, causing recurrent protest and social rupture. These upheavals expose underlying truths about racial and spatial inequality in South Africa. Student protests in the mid-2010s demonstrate this. In early March 2015, a handful of students clad in black attire protested against 'institutional racism' before a statue of arch-imperialist Cecil John Rhodes located on the University of Cape Town's Upper Campus. Holding placards and blowing whistles, they lamented the continued marginalisation of Black students at the university. A fleeting moment of dissent turned into a momentous social shift when one of the protestors, Chumani Maxwele – then a fourth-year University of Cape Town (UCT) student – hurled human faeces, collected from a bucket toilet in Khayelitsha township, at the statue.[78] Rhodes Must Fall was born.

Maxwele's act rippled with political meaning. First, the statue itself became a token of White supremacy. Second, the faeces became symbolic of Black strife, revulsion and disgust at the glorification of Rhodes. Third, the statue became a totem for inequality in higher education. Fourth, the statue represented Cape Town's inequality, highlighted by earlier protests over inadequate sanitation in townships and informal settlements.[79] Finally, and most importantly, Maxwele's act marked the death of a narrative – a narrative which depicted South Africa on a trajectory of ineluctable progress since the end of apartheid. Maxwele had, in other words, encapsulated disaffection with the new apartheid.

Rhodes Must Fall swelled into a wave of student dissent that gripped higher education for one long year.[80] By October 2015, the locus of student protest had shifted, from colonial symbols to the excessive price of education.[81] Rhodes Must Fall became Fees Must Fall, which launched with massive protests over fees increases at Wits University in late 2015.

The Rhodes Must Fall and Fees Must Fall movements were similar in more than name. In some ways, they were two parts of a single movement. Exorbitant fees, like colonial statues, were symbolic of Black exclusion in democratic South Africa itself. As Lwandile Fikeni suggests: 'The performative act[s] and subsequent *fallist* discourse opened interesting discursive possibilities in which the unaffordability of higher education itself is decoupled from arbitrary, ahistorical justifications; instead the problem was shown to be racial systemic exclusion.'[82]

Student claims were broader than the narrow question of fees. Rather, they argued, exorbitant fees had replaced racial prohibitions as the chief barrier to higher education. Yes, some Black students could clear these financial barriers, but nominal racial diversity merely masked a deeper problem: fees were an invisible racial screen that hindered Black people's social mobility.

The 'Must Fall' moment was a new generation's first expression of disgust at the new apartheid. Statues and financial barriers represented South Africa's failure to grapple with racial exclusion. And public spaces and monuments – whether colonial statues or university buildings themselves – became a lens through which the new apartheid sharpened into view. Student protests of the mid-2010s should, therefore, be re-read as a challenge to the very foundations of post-settlement South Africa – one that revealed the spatial contradictions inherent in the new apartheid, just as student protests of the 1970s and 1980s had done with apartheid.[83]

RURAL SEGREGATION

Like urban space, rural space has often reproduced apartheid in the democratic era. The former Bantustans are a key example. Apartheid initiated its Bantustan[84] project with the Bantu Authorities Act in 1951, just three years after D. F. Malan's NP swept to power in 1948. In the next thirty years, apartheid gradually devolved power to 'homeland' authorities, culminating first in 'self-governing territories' and, eventually, in 'independent homelands'.[85] As Laura Phillips notes, 'the establishment of apartheid South Africa's ten Bantustans was perhaps one of the most infamous cases of racial segregation in the twentieth century'.[86]

Bantustans drew on a deeper history of colonisation which, by 1948, had already dispossessed Black South Africans of great swathes of land. By 1910, over three hundred 'native reserves' were designated for Black people and, with the Natives Land Act of 1913, Black landownership in 'White' areas was outlawed.[87] Nonetheless, native reserves still formed part of the Union of South Africa. Bantustans went a step further by detaching these homelands from the central South African state altogether. Black South Africans were stripped of citizenship and corralled into territories of Pretoria's making.[88] The logic of the prison now applied on a grand scale: Black people in 'White' cities were imprisoned in open-air townships; those in rural areas were imprisoned in culturally defined vassal states.

Creating the Bantustans required draconian force: by the early 1980s,[89] about 600 000 Black people were evicted from cities, towns and farms for this purpose.[90] Apartheid's forced removals also affected rural areas through a process called 'betterment planning'[91] – a scheme which jammed together disparate villages to create more coherent internal colonies. By the 1980s, Bantustans were quasi-states, equipped with their own bureaucracies, civil services, and governmental regimes.[92]

In the early 1990s the democratic negotiations aimed to reincorporate the Bantustans into the new South African state. However, Bantustan leaders – like their counterparts in the apartheid government – were eager to conserve their power and the ANC was in a mood for compromise.[93] And so, power that was once vested in the Bantustans during apartheid retained its importance into democracy.

First, Bantustan political power was transferred from one regime to another. The nine provinces created after the Codesa negotiations hampered decolonisation by preserving ethnocentric regional power blocs. The spacing of cultural groups into politically exclusive provincial territories reproduced static notions of cultural identity. A corps of 650 000 Bantustan civil servants were integrated into these new provincial administrations.[94]

Bantustan leaders also preserved power by forming political parties. For instance, ANC-aligned Bantustan leader Bantu Holomisa – head of the Transkei government from 1987 to 1994 – later joined the NP negotiator Roelf Meyer to form the United Democratic Movement in 1997.[95] The party has been a minor player in South African politics ever since, and Holomisa has been an MP for over 27 years at the time of writing.

Mangosuthu Buthelezi – the former Chief Minister of the semi-independent Bantustan of KwaZulu – formed in 1976 the Inkatha Freedom Party (IFP), which, at the eleventh hour, contested the 1994 election. The IFP governed the KwaZulu-Natal province between 1994 and 1999, and has been a minor player in national politics since democracy's inception. Buthelezi served as Minister of Home Affairs for a decade and, like Holomisa, has been an MP for nearly three decades.

This strategy was not always successful, however. In the early 1990s notorious Bantustan leader Oupa Gqozo – military head of the Ciskei during the Bisho massacre – formed the African Democratic Movement. The party garnered just under five thousand votes in the Eastern Cape in 1994 and soon faded.

Other Bantustan leaders exerted power within the ANC. Contralesa – a confederation of ANC-aligned *iinkosi*[96] – is an important power bloc within the party, wielding the all-important rural vote in provinces like Limpopo and the Eastern Cape. Since these areas have become ANC strongholds, the ANC has fallen under increasing pressure to appease traditional leaders, thereby reifying their power in the new dispensation. For instance, the ANC promised Bantustan leaders positions on its parliamentary and provincial electoral lists in return for rural loyalty.[97]

The patrimonialism of the Bantustans fused with the patrimonialism of the ANC, to create regionalised and ethnicised fiefdoms in provinces like the North West, the Eastern Cape and Mpumalanga. The ANC itself internalised this provincial logic, as its branches and structures and elections became increasingly provincially defined. By the late Zuma era, provincial ANC leaders carried significant influence over the party. What became known as the Premier League faction – comprising the then premiers of the North West, Free State and Mpumalanga provinces[98] – dictated the outcome of the ANC national elective conference at Nasrec in 2017. Two of these premiers rose to 'top six' leadership positions in the ANC in the same year. In all these ways, then, old systems of Bantustan power have infiltrated democratic South Africa in new guises.

Bantustan logic also persists in law. As Mahmood Mamdani observes, 'in the former Bantustans, the regime of customary law remains substantially unreformed in rural South Africa'. He argues further that the legal distinction between customary and civil law, which underpinned apartheid and colonialism, has been preserved: '[Tribe] persists in the architecture of the South African state and South Africa. Tribe has been naturalised, presumed to be part of a timeless narrative that is African culture.'[99]

Customary land rights indicate the problem. Under colonialism and apartheid, Black people's land rights were severely curtailed. Instead of full landownership rights, they were granted only occupancy rights. The democratic government's first attempt to solve this problem came with the Communal Land Rights Act (CLARA) of 2004. This Act, however, only enflamed the problem. By vesting land with Traditional Councils, the Act reified Bantustan boundaries, sometimes to the detriment of Black landownership.

For example, a diverse community of Black landowners bought land north of Pretoria as early as the mid-1920s. When Pretoria created the KwaNdebele Bantustan, they fought to keep hold of the land they owned instead of transferring it to the new authority. Under the CLARA, however, this same community risked losing their ownership rights to traditional authorities again. For these reasons, among others, the Constitutional Court struck down the CLARA in 2010.[100]

Bantustan geography has also survived since 1994, for the municipal boundaries of Traditional Councils mirror their previous shape. Map 1 (which shows the boundaries of the Bantustans) and Map 2 (which shows the boundaries of the new Traditional Councils) illustrate this. Yet, whereas the outer borders of the Bantsustans have endured, their inner borders have multiplied and fragmented. Just as urban enclaves have splintered, so the former Bantustans have fractured, even while their outer borders have persisted.

Relations between former Bantustans and nearby towns and cities also reproduce apartheid patterns. Rural villages are far enough from cities to be invisible, but close enough to be labour reserves. Small segregated towns in provinces like KwaZulu-Natal (KZN), the Eastern Cape and the Free State are surrounded by Black rural reservoirs. Towns themselves are segregated like cities. Migration patterns flow from Black villages into White-dominated small towns, with little flow in the opposite direction. The legacies of Black displacement stretch deep into the democratic era, showing no signs of abating.

The democratic government also continues to shoulder the economic cost of the Bantustans. For instance, Bantustan bureaucrats still benefit from pensions administered by the democratic government through the Government Employees Pension Fund (GEPF). These pensions have become a major headache for the democratic government.

For example, in 2016, former employees of the Ciskei Bus Transport Company blockaded Parliament over unpaid pensions.[101] Similarly, former Venda civil servants successfully approached the Public Protector in 2015, after complaints concerning the privatisation of the Venda Pension Fund. In challenging the Protector's report, the government suggested that paying these pensions would 'open the floodgates' to other fiscally unsustainable claims.[102]

Nevertheless, ANC elites found ways to benefit from this arrangement. For example, in 2002, the financial firm Alexander Forbes won a tender to provide actuarial services to the GEPF. In the same year Millennium Consolidated Investments acquired a 30 per cent stake in Alexander Forbes through a Black Economic Empowerment (BEE) scheme. Millennium's primary shareholder was one Cyril Ramaphosa.[103] Just three years previously, Ramaphosa had resigned as secretary general of the ANC. Through the acquisition, Ramaphosa became chairperson of the Alexander Forbes Board. In 2002, the GEPF controlled assets of some R250 billion on behalf of 1.2 million members.

Hence, far from abolishing Bantustan power, democracy merely consolidated it. In the political, geographical, legal and economic life of South Africa, Bantustan logic continues to loom large, even as Bantustans themselves were dissolved. Walter Sisulu's prophetic words have come to pass: 'With the independence of the Bantustans ... the Nats have sown seeds that may well become a time bomb that will explode in our midst, long after they and White minority rule have been vanquished.'[104]

The plight of labour tenants – those who trade their work to live on another farmer's land – further exposes rural inequality in contemporary South Africa. Labour tenancy stems from South Africa's past of racial exploitation and slavery.[105] Apartheid's labour tenancy contracts also codified gross exploitation, amounting to 'a thinly veiled artifice to garner free labour.'[106] Under these contracts, a Black person pledged their labour to a White landowner for an often-paltry patch of subsistence land. When South Africa transitioned to democracy, approximately 500 000 labour tenants dwelt on farms in South Africa.[107]

The Mandela administration passed four sweeping land Acts between 1994 and 1998, aiming to remake land relations in South Africa.[108] One of these acts, the Land Reform (Labour Tenants) Act of 1996, prefigured the constitutional guarantee that 'those with legally insecure land tenure resulting from past racism were entitled to statutorily conferred security of tenure or to comparable redress'.[109] The Act afforded labour tenants constitutional protection from eviction and a path to ownership on the land where they worked.

However, these protections relied on governmental effectiveness. Under the Act, government became responsible for processing labour tenants' land claims. Some 19 000 such claims were submitted by the first deadline in 2001. Here, laudable aims met harsh realities, as governmental ineptitude wrought administrative havoc on legislative ambitions.

Nowhere was this clearer than the *Mwelase* case – an eight-year legal saga which culminated at the Constitutional Court in 2019.[110] In this case, labour tenants Bhekindlela Mwelase, Mndeni Sikhakhane, Bazibile Gretta and their representatives claimed land on which they and their forebears had toiled for decades. The land was owned by Hilton College, an elite boarding school for boys nestled in the KwaZulu-Natal Midlands. Time and again, the Department of Rural Development and Land Reform (DRDLR) disregarded court-appointed deadlines to process their claims.[111]

When, under pain of legal sanction, the department eventually explained its delays, a larger problem emerged: the entire land claims system was in disarray. Some 11 000 claims were yet to be settled. As Justice Edwin Cameron observed: 'if each [claim] took only one day to process, the load would take about 24 years for the Department to surmount, including work on weekends – and, without weekend work, 40 years.'[112] According to the department, just capturing details of the thousands of outstanding claims would take two years.[113] Eventually, the

Constitutional Court upheld the labour tenants' plea for the appointment of a Special Master to fast-track restitution claims.

A second case, instituted by the Msiza family, underscores the point. Amos Msiza was a labour tenant on a farm in Middelburg, an industrial town in Mpumalanga. In 1996, he lodged a land claim for a portion of the farm. Eight years later, and after his death, the claim was upheld. This meant the state could expropriate the land for his descendants under section 23 of the Land Reform (Labour Tenants) Act, provided the landowner was compensated.[114] This provoked a fresh dispute, over the amount of compensation due to the landowner. Amos Msiza's son, Msindo, assumed this new battle.

By 2015 – over two decades since Amos Msiza's original claim – the matter reached the Land Claims Court. Acting Judge Tembeka Ngcukaitobi presided. His judgment conceded that, under the Act, compensation would have to be paid.[115] However, the owners valued the land at R4.3 million, while the DRDLR valued it closer to R1.8 million. Ngcukaitobi accepted the lower figure and argued that R300 000 (16 per cent) of this R1.8 million could be further deducted, owing to the social imperative of land reform contained in the Constitution:

> Market value is not the basis for the determination of compensation under section 25 of the Constitution where property or land has been acquired by the State in a compulsory fashion. The departure point for the determination of compensation is justice and equity. Market value is simply one of the considerations to be borne in mind when a Court assesses just and equitable compensation.[116]

Furthermore, Ngcukaitobi held that compensation should consider the overall financial burden of land claims on the state. The deduction of 16 per cent of the market value was conservative in relation to suggestions that expropriation should occur without compensation. But, in this, Ngcukaitobi was constrained by the state's own concession that market compensation should be paid.

Nevertheless, the Supreme Court of Appeal repudiated Ngcukaitobi's proposal to lessen the compensation. In the words of Acting Justice Colin Lamont, the court held that

> There was therefore no justification [in Ngcukaitobi's judgment] for stigmatising the Trust's claim as 'extravagant'. Nor was there any evidence that the fiscus is unable to pay R1.8 million for the land. In fact, it accepted that the valuation was appropriate. There is similarly no evidence that the State is unable to meet claims of this nature. On the contrary, it is the amount the State was willing to pay ... There were thus no facts justifying the deduction of the amount of R300 000.[117]

The *Mwelase* and *Msiza* cases are just two of thousands of similar situations across South Africa. Donna Hornby suggests that as many as one million people since 1994 have been evicted from farms – a quarter of the total number evicted during all of apartheid. Another survey finds that 4.2 million people, including labour tenants, were displaced from farms between 1984 and 2004, with just over half displaced after 1994.[118] According to a survey of 850 farm dwellers in KZN's Umgungundlovu region conducted by the Association for Rural Advancement (AFRA) in 2020, average monthly household pay among those surveyed was a mere R611 – below the lower-bound poverty line of R850 per month set by Statistics South Africa.

What does all this illustrate? First, that government is hopelessly incapable of administering land justice for labour tenants. Second, that market-based compensation for labour tenants has been affirmed by superior courts. Hence, even if the state turned capable overnight, the South African taxpayer would still fund land justice for labour tenants, at the price of considerable time and treasure. Even in this scenario – a distinctly unlikely one – land relations on South Africa's rural farms would not change in the foreseeable future. The new apartheid has frustrated grand constitutional intentions in this area, as in others.

Like urban space, then, rural space is still grossly segregated, between valuable commercial farms and the precarious margins occupied by labour tenants; between Bantustans and small towns. In those 'reserves' deemed economically dispensable, where Black South Africans were often dumped as a result of 'separate development', harsh mono-racial conditions prevail. These reserves are sometimes located in touching distance of small and medium-sized towns. Rural villages still act as labour reserves. On farms and on mines, racial hierarchies persist. Black labour tenants and mine workers confront extreme precarity, while mine bosses and farm owners enjoy title and wealth. These disparities have created increasing social instability, with violent crime in rural areas growing alongside unconscionable racial inequality. In urban and rural South Africa, the new apartheid is a firm fixture of everyday life.

CONCLUSION

The organisation of space and place is always at once a practical and symbolic affair: segregation – in its explicit and implicit forms – divides people but also symbolises that division. In the new apartheid, townships and Bantustans are simultaneously prisons of social restriction and monuments to racial division.

The new apartheid, like the old order, is rife with the architecture of enmity.[119] However, spatial exclusion is today driven by private interests rather than state edicts. This produces a less visible, but more efficient, system of segregation. The cost of urban segregation has been outsourced to a decentralised network of security companies, residential associations, gated communities and bodies corporate. The new roads built by the democratic government, which connect cities to townships, are mere arteries of a segregated body. The structure of the apartheid city persists save at its most extreme margins. Nor, in rural South Africa, has the lot of farm dwellers or villagers improved fundamentally.

The private empire that now controls urban and rural space in South Africa relies on a feckless and inept government for its control. The ANC government of the early twenty-first century has been only too glad to cede power to this expanding private empire. The small gains in desegregation following the fall of the NP may have enlarged the frontiers of freedom, but they have failed to erode the underlying structure of the new apartheid.

Ironically, enclaves of privilege once reserved for White people have reversed the Bantustanisation of the mid-twentieth century. In that period, Bantustans were reserves of oppression, distant from South Africa's urban centres. Today, by contrast, privilege is increasingly Bantustanised and severed from public view. Whereas Black South Africans were forced out of South Africa into Bantustans, today the privileged have migrated inwards, into enclosed spaces of seclusion within South Africa.

Law

In a historically unequal society with such severe cleavages of class, gender and race ... private parties and associations continue to wield enormous social and financial power, which will be immunised from constitutional scrutiny at the expense of those disadvantaged and marginalised by colonialism and apartheid.

– Justice Dikgang Moseneke[120]

Two legal questions pervade the new apartheid: (a) are constitutional intentions compatible with private law,[121] especially the law of contract, and (b) can the Constitution transform society? These two questions can be reframed into a single one: can the Constitution reverse the new apartheid? In this chapter, I will argue that the answer is a qualified 'no'. I will suggest that constitutional ambitions are themselves limited. I will then outline underlying tensions between private law and constitutional ambitions. Finally, I will trace these problems to the democratic negotiations of the 1990s. For these reasons, and with some stipulations, I will argue that apartheid lingers over the law.

CONSTITUTIONAL TRIUMPHALISM

Constitutional triumphalism makes two claims. First, that the Constitution is the optimal blueprint for a democratic South Africa; second, that South Africa's structural problems owe little to the Constitution. According to the triumphalist vision, the Constitution is 'not only a foundational text, but also a historical paradigm'[122] which represents the 'end of history'[123] in South Africa's long battle against colonial injustice. Yet, as Van Marle cautions: 'There is a danger that law, monumental constitutionalism and human rights embody another spectacle, one that could yet again take over the South African imagination to the detriment of the ordinary, the way people actually live and, more pertinently, the complexities of life.'[124]

To be fair, many jurists – even those sympathetic to the Constitution – increasingly reject the triumphalist position.[125] Constitutional triumphalism is today more a political than a legal phenomenon. For example, President Ramaphosa suggests that the Constitution 'gives hope to the hopeless, rights to the dispossessed and marginalised, and comfort and security to [South Africa's] men, women and children,'[126] while former president Zuma claims it 'has been an excellent guide in the journey of building a new national democratic society'.[127] The National Party constitutional negotiator Roelf Meyer claims that 'the Constitution remains a benchmark of the South African transition, but also of the South African nation of the future,'[128] while prominent DA leader Helen Zille claims 'the dividing line in South Africa today runs between those who believe that the Constitution, our founding compact, must define our pathway to the future' and those who 'regard the Constitution as a symbol of a sold out struggle, that must be revived'.[129] Clearly, then, the Constitution has many defenders. It is this view which I seek to challenge.

Before questioning constitutional triumphalism, I must confine the limits of my argument. The Constitution is a vast document containing fourteen chapters, 243 sections and seven schedules. It touches nearly every sphere of South African life, and many of its sections deal with the practical levers of state formation. Much of this is positive or neutral.

I limit my analysis to the Preamble and the Bill of Rights. These sections undergird the Constitution and lay the basis for its subsequent sections. The sections contain various deficiencies which influence South Africa today and which cannot be explained away by governmental failures. They contain two major limitations: first, they enshrine a narrow conception of justice; second, their ambiguity extends beyond the typical ambiguity of legal texts. Both problems, I shall argue, can be traced back to compromises in the constitutional negotiations.

The first challenge to the triumphalist account is that the Constitution enshrines a narrow and impoverished conception of justice, which impedes racial justice. Injustice in general – and racial injustice in particular – is a defining question in post-apartheid South Africa. One would imagine, therefore, that the question of racial injustice is centred in the South African Constitution. This is not the case.

Justice is relatively absent from the South African Constitution. True, the word appears on nearly half of the Constitution's pages. But these mentions owe mainly to the narrow definition which pertains to legal procedures, as in the 'administration of justice', or even to narrower references to the 'Chief Justice' in Chapter 8.

In fact, the Constitution mentions justice as a principle only thrice, all in the Preamble, whereas constant reference is made to the trinity of 'dignity, freedom and equality' throughout the Bill of Rights. Indeed, a separate clause is dedicated to defining equality.

Even these preambular references to justice are limited. The first mention of justice merely 'recognises the injustices of our past'. To *recognise* injustice is but one step in *creating* justice. Mere recognition of past injustice is not justice. The second mention of justice arrives in the phrase '[we, the people,] honour those who fought for justice'. Again, this is important, but 'honouring' those who fought for justice in the past does not guarantee justice in the future. 'Recognising' the past and 'honouring' past fighters frame justice as a backward-looking exercise.

The third, and final, mention of justice in the Preamble is the only substantive and future-oriented one. We are told that the Constitution is adopted to 'heal the divisions of the past and establish a society based on democratic values, social justice and fundamental human rights'.[130] This clause creates three problems. 'Social justice' seems to narrow the scope of justice. Is social justice a particular species of justice applicable to the social realm? Is it also political and economic? The phrase suffers from an internal confusion. Justice is, by definition, social. Since the clause already refers to 'society', it seems tautological to again refer to 'social' justice. Why not simply 'justice'? The inclusion of the qualifying term 'social' denudes justice of its far-reaching connotations. It frames justice in terms of charity or private conscience, rather than reparation or redistribution.

Second, 'social justice' is mentioned after 'healing the divisions of the past'. In this way, justice is framed in the context of reconciliation, when indeed it may – sometimes must – clash with this value. Justice in South Africa is about restoring what was stolen by unjust means, and repairing that which was broken by unjust acts. It is about land and wealth. One could be forgiven for missing this interpretation in the Preamble.

In its Founding Provisions, the Constitution again misses the chance to enshrine justice, let alone racial justice. Rather, it opts to inscribe 'non-racialism'. This term raises further problems. Non-racialism is a negative concept, framed in opposition to 'racialism'. It is also a confusing one, since it might mean – and indeed has been taken by some to mean – colour-blindness.[131] 'Non-racialism' is an indeterminate and ill-defined value. It permits White South Africans to accuse Black South Africans of 'racialism', without regard to historical patterns of racism. It conflates different forms of racism and the distinct power relations on which they rest. It obscures racialism's link to racism. Phrases like 'racial justice' or 'anti-racism' are preferable. Even the term 'non-sexist' – also part of this clause – is preferable to 'non-racialism', since it explicitly uses the term 'sexism'. 'Racialism' is grossly ambiguous.

The enshrinement of 'non-racialism' ducks the systemic legacies of White supremacy and racial injustice. These framing problems affect subsequent clauses and complicate key political questions like land reform, systemic racism, and economic inequality.

Constitutions from other countries avoid this problem. For example, the Constitution of India leaves no room for ambiguity. Its Preamble declares:

> We, the people of India, having solemnly resolved to constitute India into a sovereign socialist secular democratic republic and to secure to all its citizens:
>
> Justice, social, economic and political . . . [132]

This broader conception of justice infuses other parts of the Constitution. In its famous article 39, India's Constitution explicitly prohibits wealth and gender inequalities:

> The State shall, in particular, direct its policy towards securing –
> (a) that the citizens, men and women equally, have the right to an adequate means of livelihood;
> (b) that the ownership and control of the material resources of the community are so distributed as best to subserve the common good;
> (c) that the operation of the economic system does not result in the concentration of wealth and means of production to the common detriment;
> (d) that there is equal pay for equal work for both men and women ... [133]

The Brazilian Constitution explicitly enshrines a 'free, *just* [emphasis added] and solidary society' and further enshrines 'the repudiation of terrorism and racism'.[134] It also states that 'the practice of racism is a non-bailable crime, with no limitation, subject to the penalty of confinement, under the terms of the law'.[135] These examples demonstrate that constitutions can exceed justice's relatively conservative framing in the South African document.

In this context, the Constitution's narrow conception of justice, confined to legal notions and 'social justice', locates justice in a depoliticised and de-economised world. The text's failure to frame justice as fundamental value or to accord it similar status to 'dignity, equality and freedom' partially explains South Africa's failure to provide justice in the constitutional era.

A second problem with the Constitution is ambiguity, which extends beyond the typical ambiguity of legal texts. The Constitution constantly equivocates, because its framers debated two distinct visions of South Africa. The pre-eminent example concerns land, as framed in section 25 (s25), regarding property rights.

The context of this clause is important. The section is often debated in isolation, but it actually occurs in the context of the Bill of Rights and is framed around limiting the right to property. This is a troubling framing, as the notion of land justice – fundamental to the 'injustices of the past' which the Preamble acknowledges – is only broached in the context of property rights. Land justice is thus only given expression through its potential frustration of existing ownership patterns, instead of being framed as a positive goal in itself. The opposite framing is quite conceivable: that property rights should only be exercised in so far as they do not limit historical land justice. Instead, the constitutional framing places the onus on the victims of land dispossession to prove that their claims clash with the rights of property owners – often in the case of historical inequities. This frames land justice as an exercise in damage limitation, rather than an exercise in justice expansion. Property rights precede land justice, exactly because, as I have already outlined, justice is conceived narrowly in the Constitution.

Even former Deputy Chief Justice Dikgang Moseneke, often seen as a defender of s25, admits this was 'the biggest give' of the liberation movement, to 'get over the winning line'.[136] By protecting future property rights, and engaging in a complex and ambiguous balancing act, he startlingly concedes, 'the property clause in effect sanitised historical dispossession and entrenched proprietary benefit and privilege of an unequal past'.[137]

The public debate over land reform in South Africa has thus increasingly centred on s25. A 2019 decision by the Parliamentary Constitutional Review Committee to endorse an amendment to the section in favour of 'expropriation without compensation' has only raised the political stakes. Support for the amendment is often reduced to 'populism' or constitutional misunderstanding. This neglects the many compelling reasons for amendment.

The debate typically hinges on whether the Constitution *theoretically* permits expropriation without compensation. Intelligent observers disagree on this question, which can only be finally resolved by the Constitutional Court. But the theoretical debate is, in some ways, irrelevant. The more important question is whether the Constitution *practically* obstructs expropriation without compensation. Legal impossibility is only one legitimate ground for amending a constitution. Other compelling grounds are clarity, consistency, elegance and definitiveness. It is for these more practical reasons that amending s25 is appropriate.

The section is contentious precisely because of its indeterminacy. Beyond any other clause in the Constitution, s25's hydra-like wording reveals the tortured compromise that marked democratic negotiation. It speaks with two mouths: proponents of land reform claim it affords government unfettered power; commercial interests say it protects their property.

If expropriation without compensation is truly permissible, why does the Constitution not say so? Why does the Constitution explicitly refer to compensation in subsection 3,[138] if indeed 'no' compensation is appropriate in some circumstances? Why does the Constitution not say that the state should determine *whether* compensation is appropriate, and not simply *how much* is appropriate? These clauses cannot simply be ignored. Can the 'amount' specified for compensation mean 'no amount'? If so, why is this not stipulated? I find the final override clause in s25(8) distinctly unilluminating.[139] Unlike those who claim certainty on s25, I simply find it impenetrable. South Africa needs clarity; the Constitution shilly-shallies.

Even if the Constitution permits expropriation without compensation in theory, the route to constitutional confirmation is unacceptably arduous. The restitution process is a salutary reminder that legal logjams can frustrate constitutional imperatives where vague clauses are exploited to protect privilege. It could take years, nay decades, before the Constitutional Court clarifies s25. Imagine every major expropriation being subjected to a prolonged court challenge. Land reform would be paralysed, at astronomical cost to the taxpayer. Why should South Africa engage in protracted acts of interpretation when clarity is available *now*? If the Constitution can be clarified, I see no reason to leave it vague.

What goal will have been achieved when, a decade down the road, the Constitutional Court finally confirms a radical interpretation of s25?

By then, the fruits of failure may have plunged South Africa into a bigger crisis than a polite parliamentary disagreement. Some argue that government's failure to institute national legislation to complement s25 is the main problem. No doubt the ANC's failures in this area have been monumental. But such legislation would ultimately require constitutional endorsement, and would return to the original question.

The Constitution is also vaunted for inscribing 'socio-economic rights'. These are legal claims to material goods, like housing, water and sanitation, guaranteed in the latter sections of the Bill of Rights.[140] These rights have far more limited effects than constitutional triumphalists maintain. Today, socio-economic rights have become vague promises, often conservatively protected by the courts and even more conservatively realised by government.[141]

As Jessica Whyte observes, the promise of socio-economic rights has come to resemble the neoliberal promise: 'a distinctive politics of human rights became prevalent in the period of neoliberal ascendancy', and the 'trajectories' of rights and neoliberal economics have been 'intertwined ever since'.[142]

Neoliberal economists claim that an invisible hand pervades the economy and 'a rising tide lifts all boats';[143] triumphant constitutionalists promise that dignity, equality and freedom will flow automatically from legal declarations. Just as neoliberal economists promise prosperity by trickle, so triumphant constitutionalists promise justice by osmosis. Indeed, the human rights paradigm and the neoliberal paradigm reinforce one another. As Mwipikeni suggests, 'the Constitution ... recognises socio-economic rights of all human beings, and at the same time the neoliberal socio-economic structure annuls such rights'.[144]

In this way, justice in South Africa is squeezed between the technical pronouncements of economists and the mechanical confines of lawfare. Constitutional and economic orthodoxies are guarded by gated technocratic communities. Paradoxically, economists in the neoliberal era 'stopped doing economics and remade themselves as theorists of law and society',[145] while lawyers and judges often consider major economic questions without economic training.

The idea of a rights-based order did not stem from the ANC alone. In 1983, the P. W. Botha government asked the South African Law Commission to investigate a Bill of Rights. The commission eventually returned by recommending such a bill, though its list of rights was classically liberal.[146] In that year, the Botha administration implemented sweeping constitutional reforms, permitting limited Black parliamentary representation, and abolishing several apartheid statutes.[147] Under President De Klerk, further laws were repealed before democratic negotiations. Though these reforms were wholly insufficient, and remained 'weapons of racism',[148] they would lay the basis for the NP's overall strategy in subsequent constitutional negotiations: to grant nominal political rights while retaining the non-governmental aspects of apartheid.

Meanwhile, the ANC searched for a narrative to balance its promise of national liberation against conservative economic interests. Rights discourse struck this balance. The ANC and NP thus converged on the idea of rights as a compromise between radical aspirations and conservative fears. Rights were suitably ambitious for the ANC and suitably non-threatening for the NP. The remaining disagreement concerned the scope of rights. The NP wanted only 'classic rights' with 'vertical application' (that is, rights could only be guaranteed in relations between the state and citizens, and not in cases *between* private actors). In other words, the NP saw a strict distinction between the public and private sphere, while the ANC envisaged both 'horizontal' and 'vertical' applications.[149]

The ANC won this battle. But this narrow victory masked a broader loss: as rights replaced total liberation, the Constitution became an unsuitable vessel for radical socio-economic change. As radical policies were abandoned, socio-economic rights buckled under the weight of centuries of inequality.

Some go even further in their repudiation of rights discourse, claiming rights are inextricably Eurocentric. This argument takes two shapes: first, it claims that 'rights' overshadow indigenous conceptions of virtue; second, that 'rights' are rooted in conquest and dispossession.[150] In other words, the master's legal tools cannot dismantle the master's legal house.[151] Some argue as well that English itself cannot frame justice for the South African context. If this claim is true, then justice through the Constitution is impossible. Indeed, it nullifies much of what happens in public life in South Africa, which is mediated through English.

Tembeka Ngcukaitobi's magisterial book *The Land Is Ours* disputes the Eurocentric roots of rights.[152] He traces the Constitution's roots to Pan-Africanist, Black Consciousness and African nationalist thought, by charting the lives of twentieth-century Black lawyers. He argues that the Constitution was a product of Black agency.

The claim that English cannot produce justice is also mistaken. Human language is deeply translatable on the one hand, and English is itself an indigenous language, on the other. Indeed, English usage in South Africa, in its various dialects, is unique. That is not to suggest that other languages should be ignored. The isiXhosa conception of justice contained in the term '*ubulungisa*' (to make right), for instance, improves on the constitutional idea of 'social justice', in my view. I do not believe in the supremacy of English. But, I think that the Constitution's problems stem more from political choices than linguistic strictures.

A final problem with constitutional triumphalism is overestimating the power of constitutions to change societies – no matter how radical they are. The legal theorist Richard Brooks underscores the point:

> Consider a counterfactual [society] where there is race but no racism . . . Imagine everyone were given a pill that rendered them and their offspring completely and permanently blind to race and all its amorphous indicia. As a side effect they also experienced amnesia about their prior racial identities and those of others. Logs of racial determination in birth certificates and other official and unofficial records were swiped clean through a massive government programme. Race remains as an idea, a concept, in the post-pill world, but no one can observe or remember it in others or themselves.[153]

In such a society, Brooks provocatively claims that racist patterns would persist. That is, people once called 'Black' would still suffer structural oppression, even though the identity once called 'Black' had been forgotten. Through this thought experiment, Brooks illustrates law's reliance on underlying power relations. And power, in turn, depends to a great extent on wealth, so that patterns of wealth in society can frustrate legal intentions, whether those intentions are radical or conservative. Power, not constitutions, determines a society's character. Where constitutions seek to radically subvert power, they are thereby subverted. Just as corporations constantly confound tax collectors, so powerful individuals and institutions evade racial justice.

Suppose that South Africa adopted a radical constitution today, how much would that *really* change? What specific things about our society would alter fundamentally? My answer to this speculative question is: less than we might imagine. Go a step further, and ask the reverse question. Suppose South Africa abandoned socio-economic rights altogether. How much would *really* change? Less than we might think, I claim. The Constitution is just one cog in the machine of South African society. The new apartheid can proceed in spite of the Constitution, in many respects. Whether the Constitution is made more radical, or whether it is made more conservative, will not change the logic of the new apartheid substantially. It would continue to operate, to some degree or other, in either context. Thus, Madlingozi avers: 'In South Africa today, an anti-Black bifurcated societal structure can, thus, be discerned in which . . . white people and the Black middle class are governed through a system of liberal democracy, and on the other side, patronage, appropriation, and repression remain politics *du jour*.'[154]

Madlingozi claims, further, that present-day South Africa 'reiterates' its past logic: 'post-1994 constitutional re-arrangements *are transforming* society in ways that do not instantiate a fundamental rupture with the inherited, sedimented and bifurcated social configuration'.[155] What is called 'transformative constitutionalism', then, is only the 'master frame' of a futile project 'complicit in the continuation of this anti-Black bifurcated societal structure'.[156] This claim, in turn, rests on the proposition that 'the constitutive line of colonialism and apartheid has survived the so-called transition from apartheid to post-apartheid' because 'impoverished Black people remain ensnared in a zone of stasis.'[157] The language of 'social justice', which has defined 'transformative constitutionalism', has, wittingly or unwittingly, precluded liberation.

Constitutional rights must, therefore, be contextualised within the limits of law itself. Both constitutional triumphalists and constitutional abolitionists overestimate law's potential for transformative change. This belief in legal centrality is not uncommon among lawyers. Indeed, one of the problems of the new apartheid is the pervasive power of law and lawyers, with the result that judges and lawyers tend to set the political and constitutional agenda, to the exclusion of other equally valid perspectives.

Two conclusions emerge: the Constitution is flawed but the new apartheid would persist even if it were not flawed. Any constitution would battle to defeat the new apartheid. Compromise is inherent in constitution-making, since democratic constitutions must, of necessity, enjoy wide agreement for their legitimacy. A constitution that satisfies the needs of justice, but that fails to gain elite acceptance, exists only in a wonderland. And, yet, one cannot build a fair constitution out of an unfair society while at the same time achieving consensus. The mission of creating justice out of a constitution is vain. Constitutions can only accelerate or decelerate justice – they cannot create it out of thin air.

The question remains: does the Constitution compromise *too much*? The bitter truth is that it does. There is still a gap between what the Constitution enshrines and what is politically feasible today. This gap is *partly* responsible for the stagnancy of South African society. My claim is not that the Constitution is evil, or repugnant, but that it is unimaginatively risk-averse. I believe *both* that the Constitution's conception of justice should be re-examined *and* that doing so will be no panacea. My position, therefore, unites scepticism over the Constitution's transformative power with scepticism over law's transformative potential itself. Put differently: it will take more than a radical constitution to overturn the new apartheid.

THE VEXED INTERFACE

Having questioned the Constitution's transformative promise, I now explore tensions between public and private law which strengthen my earlier claims.

Private law facilitates privatised apartheid, as I shall argue. To appreciate this, we must grapple with what former Deputy Chief Justice Dikgang Moseneke calls 'the vexed interface between the private and the public spheres of law'.[158] Private law governs individuals, corporations and their various relationships; public law concerns the interplay between individuals and the state. As law professor Deeksha Bhana maintains, tension between these two spheres of law 'bifurcates' justice along two 'parallel tracks'.[159] This tension is key to the new apartheid because it pervades contracts, property relations, and the distribution of wealth – all realms capable of 'keeping private apartheid afloat'.[160]

Apartheid and colonial law did not vanish overnight as Mandela rose to the presidency. Indeed, their legal relaxation predates 1994 and remains unfinished. Their traces permeate the common law – the organic, uncodified body of law that resides in judicial precedents rather than parliamentary enactments. As Moseneke suggests, the Constitution 'did not rise like a phoenix from the ashes of the flawed apartheid legal system' nor could it 'cover the field' of abolishing all harmful legal precedents. Jurists in the constitutional era only promised to 'keep the good and discard the bad'[161] over time. This process has proceeded neither uniformly nor progressively since 1994.

The constitutional transition was, therefore, more limited than mythology suggests. Far from effecting the total abolition of apartheid law, the transition represented the abolition of many, though not all, apartheid statutes, and the vague promise that apartheid's legal precedents would eventually align with constitutional dictates.[162]

The common law of property – dealing with land, ownership, property rights, valuation, wealth transfers and the contracts which govern them – is a key battleground in this process. This domain is foundational to democratic life and to the distribution of wealth in society. By some philosophical accounts, property ownership precedes citizenship, because citizenship implies a common stake in the democratic territory.[163] Conversely, the idea of propertyless citizenship – so prevalent in the new apartheid – is a contradiction in terms, in this view. By other philosophical accounts, the institution of private property guarantees exploitation.[164] Postcolonial thinkers extend this idea, suggesting that exclusive ownership inherently and perpetually privileges the colonial propertied class and its descendants.[165] In other words, postcolonial patterns of property ownership cannot be disentangled from their colonial antecedents while private property is protected, they maintain.

In the South African context, common law and colonial dispossession were synonymous before 1994 because the 'common law' subjected *all* within the colonial border to the will of the sovereign, whether they liked it or not. As Emile Zitzke suggests, 'the common law related to property was . . . strategically used by the apartheid government in implementing its policies, and sometimes common law was further polluted by apartheid legislation'.[166] Moreover, European private law 'has a synergetic relationship with conquest' and 'possesses private law in South Africa today with a racist spirit'.[167] The common law of property, therefore, is no esoteric topic but strikes at the heart of South African life, from questions of eviction and restitution,[168] to land redistribution and rental conditions.

Contracts are the link between property and the legal order. They tie exchange and commerce to statute and judicial decree. They are the jagged blade between law and wealth, and 'the bedrock of economic life'.[169] In this sense, the apparently quotidian realm of contract law is a key stage on which constitutional ideals and structural inequalities collide. Indeed, some suggest that the law of contract supersedes the Constitution in its social importance. For instance, Britain – the oldest of democracies – survives without a written constitution, yet none would argue that all of its contracts could be unwritten.

In one major strand of Western philosophical thought, constitutional government results from a 'social *contract* [my emphasis]', underwritten by the power of the state.[170] But the nature of this contract is contested.

Philosophers like Charles Mills[171] argue that the original contract applied only to White, propertied men, while John Rawls famously asserts that social contracts are only fair if the bargaining position of all contracting parties is equal.[172]

Colonialism, then, was social contract theory in reverse: instead of individuals collaborating to empower one sovereign authority, an external sovereign authority searched for individuals to subordinate. The colonial state was the imposition of a contract over the barrel of a gun.

Contracts are, therefore, far from empty moral vessels. They are implicated, from the outset, in power relations, especially in societies where racial inequalities pre-exist contractual bargains. As Moseneke again stresses: 'The notion of contractual autonomy belongs to a larger worldview and ideology . . . from classical liberal notions of liberty and the neo-liberal penchant for free, self-regulating, self-correcting markets driven by individual entrepreneurs who thrive on freedom of choice and freedom to strike handsome bargains.'[173]

Contracting is 'obligating oneself in return for another's obligation'.[174] The freedom to enter such bargains is fundamental to South African law. Yet, this freedom is a longstanding source of contention. The question is: should 'freedom of contract' be defined widely, to include unfair contracts; or should it be defined narrowly, to exclude unfair contracts?

It is worth pausing to mention that early legal disputes over 'freedom of contract' in South Africa occurred in the context of discrimination.[175] The 'freedom' in 'freedom of contract' was *defined* as the freedom of White men to contract. For example, the Masters and Servants Acts of the nineteenth century criminalised 'servants' who terminated their contracts of employment.[176]

Nevertheless, even in this narrow conception of contractual freedom, South African jurists disagreed about the limits of that 'freedom'. Some held that 'equity' could not 'override a clear provision of our law'; others countered that free contracts precluded 'unconscionable claims'.[177] In *Burger v Central South African Railways* (1903),[178] Justice James Rose Innes – a future Chief Justice of the Union of South Africa – averred, 'our law does not recognise the right of a court to release a contracting party from the consequences of an agreement ... merely because that agreement appears to be unreasonable'.[179]

After unification in 1910, South African courts upheld various racial injustices framed as matters of private contract. In 1911, they upheld school discrimination on this basis,[180] banning anyone with a 'smidgen of non-white ancestry' from White schools.[181] This later extended to post offices and railway stations.[182] In 1926, racial banishments from urban land were considered by the Appellate Division[183] as 'a private matter no different from exclusion from a social body, and there-fore ... not invalid merely because there had been no formal investiga-tion or legal hearing'.[184]

Courts also ruled that passes could be withdrawn on a whim from pass holders, because of the contract between government and citizen; that racial housing evictions could proceed within seven days; or that universities could expel Black students without disciplinary hearings because 'the rules of natural justice ... have no application in matters of contract'.[185] The common law entrenched discrimination in schooling, marriage, amenities, property ownership, transport and population registration.[186] And these precedents haunt the common law to this day.

Beyond these specific cases, legal culture in South Africa was – and often still is – colonial, from questions of dress and language, to the romantic origin stories of Roman, Dutch and English law. Colonialism and apartheid resound in the design of courtrooms and buildings, and in the many conventions which predominate within them. Even if co-lonial culture was removed from the Constitution, it is omnipresent in the fabric of the law and the legal profession.

Furthermore, virtually all judicial precedent set prior to democracy is written from the perspective of White men. Even much democratic precedent emerges from a deeply untransformed bench. The entire body of South African judicial precedent before 1994, then, is seen through the eyes, and spoken through the mouths, of one segment of a complex society.[187]

Even the 1993 Interim Constitution battled to square contractual freedom with basic notions of equity.[188] In *Du Plessis v De Klerk* – decided just months before the final Constitution came into effect in 1996 – the Constitutional Court determined whether freedom of speech could trump the common law of defamation, pitting public values against private harms. The court surprisingly decided that freedom of speech 'could be invoked against government but not by one private party against another private party'.[189] Justice Kriegler's dissent deserves careful consideration for its shock value:

> Chapter 3 [of the Interim Constitution] has nothing to do with the ordinary relationships between private persons or associations . . . Unless and until there is a resort to law, private individuals are at liberty to conduct their private affairs exactly as they please as far as the fundamental rights and freedoms are concerned.[190]

Stunningly, he claimed further:

> A landlord is free to refuse to let a flat to someone because of race, gender or whatever; a white bigot may refuse to sell property to a person of colour; a social club may black-ball Jews, Catholics or Afrikaners if it so wishes. An employer is at liberty to discriminate on racial grounds in the engagement of staff; a hotelier may refuse to let a room to a homosexual; a church may close its doors to mourners of a particular colour or class . . . but none of them can invoke the law to enforce or protect their bigotry.[191]

The scope of freedom of contract remains a 'burning issue' in the constitutional era, and has degenerated into something of a judicial spat.[192] On the one hand, a clutch of judges from the Supreme Court of Appeal – in judgments and extra-curial statements – argues that constitutional values impede contractual certainty;[193] on the other, judges in the Constitutional Court have subjected contracts to tests of 'fairness', 'good faith' and even 'ubuntu'.[194]

Representing the latter position, Justice Moseneke – by now a familiar figure in this chapter – lamented, as late as 2009, the 'remarkable slowness or perhaps reticence' of courts 'in allowing the fundamental rights or values of our Constitution to influence the law of contract through direct or indirect horizontality'.[195]

By contrast, Justice Malcolm Wallis of the Supreme Court of Appeal (SCA) countered in 2016 that the 'enforcement of contracts' does not depend 'on generalised notions of fairness', and in 2013 Justice Carole Lewis, then of the same court, mocked 'some free-floating notion of good faith that underlies all contracts'.[196]

Matters culminated in the *Beadica* case wherein the SCA, by some estimates, openly defied constitutional precedent in favour of a restrictive conception of contractual freedom.[197] The case hinged on the fairness of an eviction. A group of Black franchisees in a plant equipment hire business called Sale's Hire entered into multiple identical property lease agreements with the Oregon Trust.[198] These contracts contained a renewal clause which required the franchisees to notify the trust of their intention to renew their leases six months before the termination of the original contract.[199] The Black franchisees failed to do this, only notifying the trust of their intention to extend their respective leases after the deadline. They were due to be evicted, evictions which they turned to the courts to overturn.

This raised a classic tension between contractual freedom and contractual equity. On the one hand, the franchisees had clearly failed to honour contractual clauses, by missing the six-month notification deadline; on the other, eviction seemed a harsh penalty for so minor a contractual infraction. Should the franchisees have been evicted, or should they have been allowed to renew their leases, thereby saving their businesses?

Judge Dennis Davis initially ruled in their favour, citing overriding questions of fairness and reasonableness. However, the SCA overturned Davis's decision, arguing that contractual terms could only be ignored in serious cases.[200] The matter finally reached the Constitutional Court in 2020. The court shocked many by siding with the SCA, effectively sanctioning the evictions, with some reservations. In doing so, the court handed proponents of untrammelled contractual freedom a major victory.

Tensions between contractual equity and contractual freedom involve a broad dispute and a narrow one. The broad dispute concerns an age-old philosophical tension between liberty and justice. The narrow dispute concerns the South African context: can strict contractual liberty in a grossly unfair society frustrate justice? This is not a question for an abstract eighteenth-century world, but one for real-life South Africa. My contention, on this front, is that wide contractual freedom enables the new apartheid, and that the Constitutional Court has now unwittingly enabled this.

The point is illustrated by Bhana in a tantalising thought experiment. Specifically, she asks whether 'the principle of freedom of contract, operating in a constitutional context, can continue to condone an individual's refusal to contract where such a refusal is tantamount to infer discrimination'.[201] In short, can a White South African refuse to contract with a Black South African on racial grounds? Put differently, could a Black homeowner wishing to sell her house, call her Zanele, impel a White estate agent, call him Phillip, to act for Zanele, even if Phillip refuses because Zanele is Black? This pits freedom of contract against racial justice and equality. A narrow common law reading permits such discrimination, or at least condones it, while a broad constitutional reading prohibits it:

> On the one hand, a public lawyer may argue that such an individual must be compelled to contract, regardless of freedom not to contract, lest apartheid be privatised . . . on the other, a traditional private lawyer is likely to maintain that the conclusion of a contract in this manner is subversive of the very foundations of freedom of contract and contractual autonomy.[202]

The implications are serious. In private contracts, the fundamental notion of equality is challenged by a strict definition of contractual freedom. In plain sight, this simple question of judicial interpretation profoundly influences the new apartheid.

Some may object that such a contract would fail because it frustrates public policy or misaligns with the Bill of Rights. To them, I offer a modified thought experiment. Imagine that Phillip, the White estate agent, still wishes to avoid working for Zanele because she is Black. Instead of revealing his true reasons, however, he avoids the contract by imposing an insurmountable financial burden on Zanele – for instance, charging a commission of 20 per cent of the sale. Here, Zanele would be discriminated against doubly, since either she would forgo Phillip's services or she would pay an exorbitant fee.

The strict contractual libertarian must accept this outcome. That is, the financial condition would retain contractual validity even if motivated by racial cruelty. The only alternative is to concede that Phillip must impose fees fairly or reasonably.

Now, consider the millions of contracts in fields as diverse as insurance, health care, education and housing. Consider, further, that exclusionary financial regulations are routine in South Africa. It is, therefore, quite possible to discriminate on the basis of financial grounds, when one's real motive is to discriminate on racial bases. So long as the racial motive is implicit, current precedent permits such absurdity or, at least, fails to categorically exclude it.

The point becomes stronger when questions of access to justice are introduced. How often are discriminatory contracts legally challenged by those with less bargaining power? How many contracts rely on unequal racial power relations today? Often, those more likely to be discriminated against in contracts are also the most desperate. They are unlikely to get legal help before contracting or after a breach. What picture would emerge if we could see from above all of South Africa's millions of active private contracts? Discrimination recently uncovered in education,[203] medical aid schemes,[204] and the workplace[205] represents the tip of the oppressive iceberg in the domain of privatised discrimination.

So far, I have argued that the consequences of extreme contractual freedom jar with the goal of racial justice. Now, I shall take the argument a step further and claim that strict contractual freedom is internally inconsistent. Constitutional values, like equality, derive legal force from the Constitution. But the Constitution is a contract of contracts. In 1996, the people of South Africa agreed that equality would underpin society in the context of the injustices of the past. They agreed that this original social contractual clause should supersede subsidiary legal arrangements which clash with this value.

Even on the assumption of contractual freedom, then, the original social contract – the Constitution – must trump subsequent private contracts, since the constitutional contract occurs prior to, and legally supervenes on, subsidiary private contracts. To admit the opposite – that private contracts can flout constitutional imperatives – is to permit an absurd anomaly in which the freedom to contract precludes the constitutional contract. Put differently, grossly unfair private contracts contravene the overarching constitutional contract. Either agreements matter and the constitutional agreement must be prioritised, or they do not matter and contracts lose their force altogether.

Conversely, colonial dispossession was the very antithesis of private contractual freedom. Neither can its remedies rest on this narrow notion, to the offence of larger principles and priorities. Law entrenched and legitimised colonialism and apartheid in South Africa. Thus, an uncritical reliance on legal traditions risks recasting the ills of the past. Extreme contractual freedom, therefore, fails on its own terms, since it ignores the original contract of contracts and draws from distinctly unfree contractual roots.

Furthermore, the costs of balancing contracts against principles of fairness are exaggerated. Losses in contractual certainty which result from fairness will cost the acceptable price of *fairness*. This does not strike me as particularly unattractive. It is a 'price' worth paying a thousand times. Any losses in 'certainty' from such constraints pale in comparison with the unfairness sanctioned under the guise of contractual freedom. The notion, for instance, that an alternative ruling in the *Beadica* case would undermine legal certainty is dramatically overblown. Indeed, an alternative interpretation existed prior to the

Constitutional Court judgment, without resulting in the collapse of economic certainty.

Meanwhile, the legal profession faces a titanic battle over transformation,[206] so that divisions between public and private law are mirrored in legal practice. Public law, by necessity, affects Black South Africans disproportionately, while private law is dominated by historically White law firms, battling to this day with transformation. The advocates' profession is consumed with debates over racism and the unequal distribution of lucrative assignments, culminating in the establishment of the break-away Pan African Bar Association of South Africa. Allegations of racism in private law firms abound. This bifurcation in the legal profession can be traced to a history of racial discrimination in the legal practice and reflects the ideological battle over the scope of private rights, particularly as these rights relate to economic ownership, property, and the law of contract.[207]

To summarise, the common law is not neutral. It should be regarded with scepticism, even in cases indirectly related to race. Under the guise of freedom of contract, the common law often fortifies apartheid.[208] Though these binaries have been partially addressed in the abolition of apartheid statutes, they still permeate the common law, legal culture and the legal profession. The law of contract is a key battleground in this war. At the very least, constitutional jurisprudence on this crucial tension has produced ambiguity, whereas categorical repudiation is needed. Even after *Beadica*, 'ambiguity' surrounds 'the precise interplay between the Bill of Rights and private law ... [and] the extent to which, and the manner in which, our traditional system of private law should be constitutionalised'.[209] This matters because 'the power wielded by private actors is often comparable to, if not greater than, that of the state itself'.[210]

WHO WON WHAT?

Having critiqued constitutional triumphalism, and outlined tensions between public and private law, I now reinterpret the constitutional negotiations of the 1990s, to ascertain 'who won what'. In doing so, I will contend that apartheid negotiators were not totally outmanoeuvred at the constitutional negotiations, as is often suggested.

In 1991, the ANC and NP issued their respective constitutional blueprints for the new republic: the ANC published *Constitutional Principles of a Democratic Society* and the NP published *Constitutional Rule in a Participatory Democracy*. These two documents summarised the two sides' respective positions, and detailed their priorities for the constitutional order. Many provisions present in the final Constitution emerge from either document. From the present historical vantage point, we can reverse-engineer the negotiations. Doing so is eye-opening, as the new society represents a fascinating balance between the priorities of each negotiating side.

If we read these blueprints against each other, one conclusion emerges: the ANC won the battle over principles and values, but the NP scored concessions over the structure of the state and the character of the economy. And this accords with contemporary South African experience, as South Africa is a country of lofty ideals at odds with the realities of governance and the inequalities of wealth and privilege. If the ANC made a fundamental mistake, it was believing in ideas over structures. If the NP understood one thing, it was that concessions at the level of principle could be traded for gains at the level of economic practice. Hence, the ANC's constitutional proposals focused greatly on founding values and future rights. Through these proclamations, the assumption went, society would inevitably resemble the new ideals on which it was founded.

By contrast, the NP document ignores lofty principles. It concedes universal franchise and the protection of various equalities. Unlike the ANC document, the NP vision emphasises the structure of the new state. Specifically, the three-tiered system of government on which South Africa now operates – national, provincial and local – is a direct descendant of the NP document. In *Constitutional Rule*, it states:

> The NP proposes a three-tier government in which full legislative and executive functions and authority are conferred on central govern-

ment and regional and local authorities. Regional and local authorities are therefore not merely administrative extensions of the central government; they are not merely the consequence of decentralised administration.[211]

The importance of this position to the eventual structure of South African government is fundamental. The three-tiered system would render the central governing authority weak. The national government would be forced to constantly mediate between three layers of authority, and regional centres could frustrate centralised ambitions.

The extent of devolution caused 'raucous divergence' at the Constitutional Assembly in 1993. On the one hand, the NP and Bantustan leaders pushed for far-reaching decentralisation; the ANC for a strong unitary state. Although some ANC negotiators claim to have won this battle, the eventual outcome was a 'compromise', in which the parties 'split the difference by formulating complicated schedules of exclusive and concurrent national and provincial competences'.[212]

South Africa's eventual structure reordered the Bantustan system. Instead of housing several separate and autonomous territories within the central state, South Africa would be one autonomous territory arranged according to three separate but interacting layers. Devolution moved from being horizontal to being vertical. Any act of national policy-making would require tremendous levels of provincial and local coordination to succeed. Regions and districts, which often preserved Bantustan borders, would enjoy wide authority, and the national government would be constitutionally confined to an oversight and policy-making function.

Moreover, provinces largely reinscribed cultural boundaries reified by apartheid. In this sense, provincial boundaries froze static cultural categories in place. As a result, the NP partially succeeded in confining the national government to its smallest possible size. No matter the ideal to which the country aspired, reaching that ideal would need Herculean governmental orchestration across multiple levels of authority.

A second priority for the NP was 'a market-oriented economy coupled with private enterprise and social responsibility.'[213] Each element of this idea deserves careful scrutiny. First, a 'market-oriented economy' centres the market. This is key to the notion of the new apartheid, since much of the battle in the new society is over the direction and distribution of economic goods. If the market orients the economy, then any forms of economic exchange conceived outside market parameters are foreclosed. Alongside market centrality is 'private enterprise' and 'social responsibility'. The combination of a large role for private enterprise within a market-led economy aided corporatised capitalism. In such an economic climate, patterns of economic ownership could not be fundamentally transformed, since apartheid rested on racial exclusion in markets and private enterprise. The NP's prescient assumption was that concentrated private economic power, oriented by the market, would preserve much of apartheid's economic structure.

'Social responsibility' is an equally fascinating construction, both for what it says and for what it does not say. Notice its similarity with the concept of 'social justice'. Like this concept, it places the burdens of justice on the 'social' sphere, where the 'social' is defined as individual regard for the collective. The 'responsibility' referred to in the phrase is unclear. Does it refer to 'corporate social investment'? To paying taxes? It implies that economic fairness is the province of the market or the individual, and not the state. The economy in this short, but crucial, construction should be privately controlled, market-oriented, and only regulated by a vague notion of 'social responsibility'. Absent from these conceptions is any notion of reparation, redistribution or state intervention.

This becomes key to appreciating the logic of the new apartheid, since any proposals in the new society that have contravened these three notions have been staunchly opposed by apartheid power. Any deviation from 'market orientation' suggests a move towards radical danger; any move towards greater privatisation and corporatisation is welcomed; and any notion of 'responsibility' is to be confined to the individual level.

Another bone of contention during the negotiations was the fate of apartheid securocrats and bureaucrats. Here, again, the ANC conceded much. Apartheid security forces' fear of prosecution was tied to bureaucrats' fear of financial loss, and so an elaborate government scheme was initiated to absolve apartheid crimes – through the eventual Truth and Reconciliation Commission (TRC) – and secure the pensions of apartheid bureaucrats. Sunset clauses would keep many of these bureaucrats in their jobs under the new administration. The new state would cancel the legal debts of apartheid's henchmen, but assume their financial debts, all during a time of extreme fiscal constraint. In this way, the new state would trade justice for reconciliation, while promising to deliver to an impatient and justifiably angry Black majority. These concessions, which seemed trivial in comparison with larger political rights, would fundamentally compromise the ANC's ability to govern, and base the new order on impunity by absolving the sins – and paying for the comforts – of apartheid's henchmen.

So, who won what? The ANC won three things: state power, socio-economic rights, and positive discrimination. Through socio-economic rights, the ANC reinserted the state, far beyond the NP's narrow conception of 'private enterprise' and 'social responsibility'. Yet, this shifted the burdens of the new society onto the ANC. Although the TRC made recommendations on economic reparations, the new society failed to compel White South Africans to share wealth beyond ordinary taxation, a duty also borne by Black South Africans.

In this sense, the enshrinement of socio-economic rights became a pyrrhic victory: rights legally empowered the state, but failed to equip it with the means to realise these same rights. Second, while the Constitution endorsed positive discrimination, this principle would be heavily contested by private enterprise, and became little more than a mechanism to desegregate elite spaces. What did the NP win? They won a market-oriented economy. They won an enlarged space for private enterprise. They won concessions on devolution. And they won amnesty for apartheid securocrats and pensions for apartheid bureaucrats.

The ambiguous outcomes of the transition were soon framed as unequivocal moral triumphs. The Constitution became the prime symbol of this narrative. This benefited apartheid interests as much as it did the ANC. The new narrative obscured the disjuncture between the mythology of the transition and its reality. The celebration of the transition blurred the victories scored by apartheid negotiators. In this sense, the Mandela administration entered government under a paradox: they were celebrated saints entering a hellishly complex new landscape. Their fate was to become ineffective angels presiding over a faltering miracle.

In this chapter, I have tried to unite three different threads. First, I have explored limitations in the Constitution's conception of justice and demonstrated how these limitations influence important subsequent sections of the Constitution and profoundly influence South African society. Second, I zoomed into the tension between public and private law to show that, even if we accept the Constitution's framing of justice, the new apartheid still survives in the realm of the law of contract. I have, thirdly, framed these challenges in the historical context of the democratic negotiations. Far from being outplayed, I claim, the NP was able to secure lasting concessions, which dog South Africa to the present, and are likely to continue in future, if unacknowledged.

Wealth

Economic continuities evident in so-called post-apartheid South Africa are just as interesting as, and perhaps even more fundamental than, the more celebrated and obvious constitutional changes.
– Paul Williams and Ian Taylor[214]

At first glance, the Judicial Commission of Inquiry into Allegations of State Capture, or the State Capture Commission, symbolised South Africa's redemption in the post-Zuma era. However, in many respects, it exemplified the problem it was designed to solve. For eight months of its life, the commission was not even housed in a public building. I recall my one and only visit to the commission, in July 2019. As I approached the hearing located on 17 Empire Road, I was met by the cerulean glass panels of a corporate facade. Traversing the sepia patios to one of four identical entrances, I then encountered a private security guard who passed my metallic possessions through a detector before signalling my right to enter the building. Up the elevator and through the gleaming corridors, I arrived at a corporate conferencing room, its double doors bearing a wrinkled paper sign indicating the commission was 'in session'.

A set of private law firms briefed advocates, referring to reports compiled by their sister accounting firms. They detailed the role of banks, consulting companies, mining houses and private equity vehicles in furthering an unprecedented and ambitious looting spree. Private media houses – one of which was headquartered in the same office block – scrummed for scoops, to be disseminated via the private–public sphere of social media. At the head of the room, the Deputy Chief Justice – an admitted paragon of public rectitude – was an island of state purity, surrounded by a sea of private interests. But, when he left his seat and adjourned that day's proceedings, workers from a private cleaning service tidied the venue for the next day's events. 'This', I thought to myself, 'is how South Africa reckons with the increasing power of private actors over the state.'[215]

This vignette is just one glimpse into the massive influence of private power in South Africa today. Wherever one looks, the face of government gives way to the face of capital; the face of capital to government. It was ever thus – but in South Africa it was *ever-er* thus. To appreciate the blurring between public and private interest, we must reappraise the trajectory of South African capital since 1994.

In this chapter, I trace the evolution of capital since the 1980s. I begin by exploring why the apartheid government pursued a path of privatisation in its last days. I then assess continuities between economic policies in the late 1980s and economic outcomes in democratic South Africa. I show further how the ANC itself was privatised.

APARTHEID'S RETREAT

The economist J. A. Lombard divides apartheid economic policy into three periods. The first decade of apartheid (1948–58) saw a laissez-faire economic policy, where state intervention served only to remedy 'market failure'.[216]

Under Verwoerd, however, the state assumed a more fundamental role in economic decisions. Government was 'no longer a conglomerate of relatively disconnected remedies to market failures' but 'a self-conscious and self-confident force in the economy', holding 'views of its own about what to do, for whom, and how'.[217] In this period, the 'technocratic side of government grew enormously'.[218] Yet, as Lombard observes, it was also a 'contradiction in terms to create separate development by planning it from the centre'.[219]

In the third era, late apartheid was seduced by 'free market principles' based on 'libertarian policy'.[220] Government saw that 'free market ideology, if taken seriously, would require tremendous structural changes in the entire social and political fabric of South Africa'.[221] Lombard himself was part of an economic commission which suggested that:

> The philosophy underlying the present system of government in the Republic of South Africa presumes that there must be some single, ultimate centre of authority in any society: the central government. The alternative philosophy accepts that the government sector may be polycentric in structure with several concurrent and competing sources of power, each limited to particular fields of competence by a constitution or social contract which is enforceable by the courts of law . . . The practical implication of this is that no single group would be able to dominate the whole society, unless it captures each and every unit of government in the whole country.[222]

This third period is crucial to my argument, as it marks the rise of privatisation as a dominant economic ideology. As the economic historian David Yudelman observed in the late 1980s: 'South Africa was a leader in the early part of the twentieth century in collaboration between state and capital . . . it might become a leader in the late twentieth century in the opposite process – state withdrawal from the economy.'[223]

The 1980s remade South Africa, as anti-apartheid protests swelled into a tsunami of popular revolt, and the NP lost its grip on the levers of state. For this reason, the 1980s are often remembered for apartheid's momentous fall. But, parallel to this, ran a tale of economic reform, one of equal significance. The economic reforms of the 1980s preserved and disguised apartheid into the democratic dispensation. The turbulent 1980s, then, were a paradoxical period: political power changed hands but economic power adapted around this change.

Several factors inspired the sweeping reforms of the 1980s. As the decade opened, South Africa's economy stagnated.[224] Racial policies which once protected White interests now limited overall economic potential: economic growth in the late P. W. Botha years hovered around 1.9 per cent, and real GDP in 1990 was lower than in 1980.[225]

South Africa's pariah status and the global sanctions movement brought economic isolation and a sovereign debt crisis.[226]

Big business clamoured for a relaxation of prejudicial laws to expand markets and customers. Tycoons like Anton Rupert publicly opposed apartheid: 'apartheid is dead, but the corpse stinks and must be buried and not embalmed. If you have to leap from cliff to cliff across an abyss, you can't do so step by step.'[227] Similarly, Andreas Wassernaar – chairperson of the finance giant Sanlam – railed against the state's size, calling for political and economic deregulation.[228] Amid such calls, economic stagnation exerted pressure on the apartheid government to change course.

Simultaneously, the global economic consensus was shifting towards 'market discipline' and 'structural adjustment'. Oil shocks in the 1970s rattled South Africa's major trading partners, especially the UK and the US.[229] By the late Botha years, the US and UK had converged on a new economic consensus which was fast engulfing the global economy.[230] Hence, both domestic and global factors pushed South African policy-makers to rethink the state's role in the economy.

Late apartheid economic reforms divested the South African state of considerable economic power. Before the 1980s, South Africa's public sector was proportionally larger than most economies outside the Soviet bloc.[231] However, as the NP's grip weakened, an ambitious project to reduce the state's economic power commenced. By the time the ANC took power in the mid-1990s, the state had shrunk: though the ANC had gained state power, the state itself had lost power.

Privatisation was central to reducing the state. At the opening of the 1980s, Pretoria controlled several massive state companies: a power utility (Eskom), a steel giant (Iscor), a phosphate mining company (Foskor), a petroleum company (Sasol), South African Airways (SAA), an oil exploration entity (Soekor), the South African Post Office (SAPO), a telecommunications entity (Telkom), the South African Broadcasting Corporation (SABC), and arms manufacturer (Armscor).[232] Together with hundreds of provincial and local state-owned entities, these companies accounted for roughly 50 per cent of the state's fixed capital.[233] State economic ownership in this period was thus profound.

The doctrine of privatisation took aim at these state companies. Privatisation stems from the idea of market supremacy. No state, according to this view, can comprehend the combined knowledge of all possible transactions in a complex society. Only a decentralised, diffuse and distributed information highway – a 'free' market – able to respond to the signals of all its parts and relay these to the whole can do this.[234] In this sense, the market – not the state – can best distribute economic information and should, therefore, dictate patterns of production and consumption in the economy. As the free market economist Friedrich von Hayek put it:

> The really central problem of economics . . . is how the spontaneous interaction of a number of people, each possessing only bits of knowledge, brings about a state of affairs . . . which could be brought about by deliberate direction only by somebody who possesses the combined knowledge of all these individuals.[235]

Accordingly, only private actors pursuing self-interest can 'rationally' respond to market signals.[236] The combined effect of their egoistic decisions results in what John Maynard Keynes – Hayek's theoretical adversary – mocked as the 'divine harmony between private advantage and social good'.[237] The South African economist F. J. van Biljon called this 'an equivalence between individual and social interests'.[238]

Put simply, privatisation is the transfer by the state of public assets to private ownership, control and maintenance.[239] The term blossomed in the early 1980s, though its provenance is unclear. Several British politicians who served under Prime Minister Margaret Thatcher claim original ownership of the word, despite Thatcher herself describing it as 'a dreadful bit of jargon to inflict on the language of Shakespeare'.[240]

Beyond its simplest meaning, privatisation assumes multiple connotations. In one sense, it refers to the replacement by private actors of functions once discharged by the state.[241] For instance, the building of a road may be undertaken by a private firm instead of by a transport department.

Alternatively, privatisation refers to the sale of government-owned assets to private investors, as in the privatisation of the steel manufacturer Iscor between 1989 and 2002. Privatisation can also mean the complete usurpation of the state, whereby an entire governmental system is replaced by a private one, as in the system of private health care or education. In extreme cases, this leads to the privatisation of inherent state functions like defence, citizen representation, and foreign policy.

Recently, some authors have extended the idea of privatisation to entire systems of government, as in 'the privatisation of everything',[242] or the 'privatisation of the state'.[243] For example, Béatrice Hibou argues that some African states have become privatised. By this, she does not mean that the state is irrelevant. Rather, she sees privatisation as a 'technology of the state': privatisation becomes an indirect form of government in which governmental elites operate through private entities instead of state-owned companies.[244] This layer, between the state and its private partners, protects governmental elites from accountability. In this sense, Hibou points out that privatisation can strengthen, rather than weaken, the state.[245]

The apartheid government's approach to privatisation was outlined in its White Paper on Privatisation of 1987.[246] The White Paper defined privatisation as 'the systematic transfer of appropriate functions, activities or property from the public to the private sector, where services, production and consumption can be regulated more efficiently by the market and price mechanisms'.[247] The document envisioned curtailing state expenditure, diverting this expenditure to social services, segmenting citizens according to economic need, and moving towards user-pay services. A year later, President P. W. Botha outlined plans for the privatisation of Eskom, Foskor and Iscor and the rationalisation of other state-owned entities (SOEs).[248]

The White Paper also introduced a corporate ethos in public entities. SOEs were now seen as 'business enterprises' run on 'a profit-and-loss basis'.[249] They were to charge 'realistic fees' for their 'services'.[250]

Furthermore, three major entities were earmarked for rationalisation: Eskom, Telkom and the Atomic Energy Corporation. Before incurring new capital expenditure, government was to ask 'whether the user should pay for the service without subsidisation by the taxpayer ... if so, it should be considered whether or not the service can be undertaken by the private sector ... if not, it should be determined whether the public sector itself should provide the service as an economic service.'[251] In 1989, the steel manufacturer Iscor was privatised. But further privatisations were suspended amidst depressed international demand for South African assets and widespread labour resistance to further privatisation.

In his famous 1990 speech to Parliament – before he declared the unbanning of the ANC and the path towards negotiation – F. W. de Klerk announced a new economic trajectory which abandoned state intervention for the neoliberal consensus:

> The Government's basic point of departure is to reduce the role of the public sector in the economy and to give the private sector maximum opportunity for optimal performance. In this process, preference has to be given to allowing the market forces and a sound competitive structure to bring about the necessary adjustments ... The central message is that South Africa, too, will have to make certain structural changes to its economy just as its major trading partners had to do a decade or so ago.[252]

Thus, by the end of apartheid, influential intellectuals, politicians and bureaucrats grew enchanted with the neoliberal paradigm. As a result, the revolving door between capital and the state turned faster than ever. Sanlam uniquely illustrates the close connections between the state, academia and capital in this period.[253] Sanlam's board in the 1980s was packed with figures straddling the worlds of academia, business and politics:

> Dr A. J. van den Berg was appointed to the Sanlam board, having occupied leading positions in South Africa's industrial development ... then joined the Industrial Development Corporation of

South Africa (IDC) and since 1985 had provided experienced over-sight to the Sankorp managerial team engaged in the restructuring of Sanlam's industrial assets. Dr P. J. Riekert, Chairman of the Prime Minister's Economic Advisory Council and Chairman of the commission that advised the government on the relaxation of legislation restricting Black labour advancement, served on the [Sanlam] board from the mid-1970s until 1989. Dr J. G. Loubser, former General Manager of Railways and Harbours, Dr P. E. Rousseau, former MD and Chairman of Sasol, and Dr C. H. J. van Aswegen, the longstanding Chairman of Santam, served on the board in 1985. Pepler Scholtz and A. D. Wassenaar were the Sanlam old guard. Many of these individuals shared a close allegiance to Afrikaner political power, some were members of the *Afrikaner Broederbond*, and the group of three Afrikaans Reformed churches.[254]

The NP's funders also illustrate ties between business and politics in the late 1980s. As recent important work by the civil society organisation Open Secrets shows, apartheid was funded by NP-aligned businessmen. For example, in written exchanges between De Klerk and P. W. Botha in 1982, De Klerk states that Barlow Rand (now Barloworld) paid the NP R50 000, which they 'preferred to keep confidential'.[255] The company's leaders were also regular figures on governmental advisory councils.[256] Christo Wiese – still a billionaire in the democratic era – also featured prominently in NP donations. Wiese was described by the apartheid minister Kent Durr as 'an old friend and supporter of the NP'.[257] Altron's Bill Venter was also a regular donor. In the 1980s, he contributed about R4 million (in today's prices) to the party.[258]

Economic reforms in late apartheid foreshadowed a broader strategy of state retreat. The key example is South Africa's decision to renounce nuclear weapons, between 1989 and 1993. On 24 March 1993, in a shock speech to a joint sitting of the South African Parliament, De Klerk confessed that 'South Africa did, indeed, develop a limited nuclear deterrent capability' and that, 'over a period of three years, South Africa had secretly dismantled its nuclear weapons'.[259] South Africa today remains the only country ever to have unilaterally abandoned a nuclear weapons programme.[260]

Contrary to popular belief, this decision was taken by De Klerk, unbeknown to the ANC at the time, even as democratic negotiations unfolded. In correspondence with US President George Bush Sr, De Klerk emphasised that the decision was, in part, taken to prevent the ANC government from acquiring a nuclear capability, though international pressure was already mounting on uranium exports.[261]

Economic policy shifts in the 1980s, therefore, demonstrate the NP's plan to restructure South Africa's economy, as an exit strategy leading to negotiations. Only when the state was sufficiently weakened, and the economic structure sufficiently reformed, did the process of negotiation begin, leaving ANC negotiators to inherit a set of irreversible economic forces. As James Hentz supposes: 'The NP set out to fundamentally reorganise the structure of South Africa's political economy as an exit strategy. Although it justified privatisation by employing economic arguments, this ostensible depoliticisation masked political motives'.[262]

CAPITAL'S METAMORPHOSIS

As Seeraj Mohamed observes, 'corporations that dominate the South African economy were formed during colonialism and apartheid'.[263] In democracy, these corporate fortunes were remoulded but not destroyed, and they continue to shape South Africa in ever-changing ways.

On the eve of South Africa's democratic transition, private wealth was concentrated in a handful of conglomerates: Anglo American Corporation (AAC), Sanlam, Stanbic, Rembrandt, Old Mutual and Anglovaal.[264] In the decades to follow, big capital evolved in three ways: first, it decentralised; second, it financialised; and third, it globalised. Additionally, capital integrated and partially co-opted the ANC, its policies, its leaders and its business interests. In this new guise, capital increasingly evaded regulation.

Decentralisation was one of capital's key adaptations after 1994. Between 1984 and 2012, South African conglomerates' share of market capitalisation on the Johannesburg Stock Exchange (JSE) fell from 84 per cent to 20.5 per cent.[265] However, over half of South Africa's top forty companies still trace their origins back to apartheid conglomerates.[266] Apartheid's conglomerates did not die; they transmogrified.

The decentralisation of wealth did not mean redistribution. Rather, big capital spread assets over more and newer entities. So, wealth was still confined to a narrow elite though it was divided over a wider number of firms. This process is known as deconglomeration: the division of a major corporation into multiple independent and autonomous entities.[267]

As the Wits economist Gilad Isaacs observes: 'deconglomeration, therefore, while involving transfers in ownership did not entail large South African capital letting go of concentrated control'.[268] Furthermore, as Mohamed notes, 'large corporations that could have contributed to addressing the structural weaknesses in the economy . . . selectively withdrew from the economy as they internationalised and restructured in response to the pressures of financialisation and the shareholder value movement'.[269]

The AAC uniquely epitomises this metamorphosis. In the late 1980s, at the height of its economic dominance, AAC controlled over half of market capitalisation on the JSE. After democracy, and with the ANC's help, Anglo instituted a corporate restructuring without precedent. It disposed of holdings in financial services, breweries, industrial logistics, retail, motor manufacturing, food, chemicals, explosives and agriculture.[270] It morphed into a trim mining giant called Anglo American plc. The unbundled assets were carved into new ownership structures, often with only a few degrees of separation from the old mother company.

Simultaneously, Anglo American plc moved its primary listing onto the London Stock Exchange, with great governmental assistance. As AAC's then chairman Julian Ogilvie Thompson observed, 'the support of the South African government in establishing Anglo American as a global natural resources business has been invaluable'.[271]

Since 1994, apartheid capital has also financialised. This has coincided with the trend of global financialisation since the 1980s, changing corporate power in profound ways.

In the first fifteen years of the democratic era, South Africa's financial sector exploded. According to the National Treasury, by 2010 these assets were 252 per cent of GDP. The size of finance distinguishes South Africa's economy from its Western trading partners and its regional counterparts. Yet, the growth of finance has, in some ways, been anti-developmental. For instance, the financial sector only increased employment by about 70 000 jobs, from 286 000 employees to 356 353 in the decade between 2000 and 2010, accounting for only 3 per cent of the employed.[272] Table 1 gives a snapshot of the financial sector between 2000 and 2010. In 2020, the financial sector only accounted for around 15 per cent of corporate income tax.[273]

Table 1 Snapshot of the financial services sector in South Africa

	June 2000	June 2010	Relative size 2010
			Share of GDP
Size[1]	R68.6bn	R203.8bn	10.5 %
Assets	R 1 890bn	R 6040bn	252%
Of which:			
Banks	R 730bn	R 3040bn	127%
Long term insurers[2]	R 630bn	R 1440bn	60%
Short term insurers	R 50bn	R 90bn	4%
Pension funds (public and private)	R 470bn	R 1480bn	62%
			Share of formal employment
Employment[3]	286000	356 353	3.9 %
			Share of corporate taxes
Tax contribution[+]	n/a	R21 bn	15.3%

Source: SARB, Stats SA, SARS; Tax contribution is for the 2009/10 tax year.

1 *Size is gross value added in nominal rand of the financial intermediation and insurance component of the finance, real estate and business services sector. Estimate based on projected growth.*

2 *The long-term insurer assets figure includes assets of pension funds managed by an insurance company*

3 *Financial intermediation, insurance, pension funding and auxiliary services.*

+ *Estimate as detailed disaggregated data is not available. The total financial services, business services and real estate and business services sector contributes R39.6bn or 29% of corporate tax. Excludes VAT and other taxes.*

Source: A safer financial sector to serve South Africa better, National Treasury Policy Document, 2011. Used with permission.

Financialisation also coincided with massive capital outflows, as wealth fled the nation after 1994.[274] The growth of finance made possible this capital run: it is simpler for a holding company to change its domicile than for a factory to change its location. Scholars like Ndikumana and colleagues estimate these outflows at $49 billion between 1970 and 2000.[275] After 1994, apartheid capital globalised in addition to decentralising. That is, the network of private interests that once owed allegiance to South Africa now tied its fortunes to the global economy. Private entities once domiciled in South Africa shifted offshore, their South African origins sometimes barely traceable. Conversely, foreign capital expanded its role in South Africa: in 1994, foreign ownership of the JSE was 2.2 per cent of total assets. By 2017, it had mushroomed nearly twenty-fold, climbing to 41 per cent by 2017.[276] Meanwhile, the total ownership through Black Economic Empowerment schemes of the 'top 100' JSE-listed companies was a meagre 10 per cent.[277] In this sense, in the democratic era, South African capital is less South African, while global capital, through its local vassals, is more South African.

PRIVATISING THE ANC

Over time, South African capital has also increasingly subsumed the ANC. In this way the ANC itself – its members, policies and interests – have become privatised. For instance, the revolving door between the state and capital persisted into democracy. Derek Keys – Nelson Mandela's first Minister of Finance – illustrates this continuity. Keys served in several prominent corporate positions prior to his appointment in 1991 as the last apartheid Finance Minister. Notably, he was executive chairman of the mining giant Gencor from 1986. He also joined the board of the newly privatised Iscor in 1989. Keys, along with De Klerk, Kraai van Niekerk, Dawie de Villiers and Roelf Meyer, served in both the pre-1994 cabinet and the subsequent Government of National Unity. As Finance Minister, Keys implemented reforms allowing South African companies to relocate wealth overseas.

Three months into his tenure in the Mandela government, Keys resigned for 'personal reasons'. He soon re-emerged in a prominent and conspicuous corporate position. In the same month that Keys resigned from government, his former employer Gencor merged with Billiton, a Dutch mining company. The acquisition was contentious because it involved an exodus of South African capital – an expatriation which Keys himself ratified as Finance Minister. Who emerged as the new chairperson of the Gencor–Billiton merger? Derek Keys, fresh from his resignation from government.[278] In one fell swoop, Keys played the role of executive, board member and regulator.

Apart from furthering his personal interests, Keys succeeded in a larger mission: 'to convince the ANC . . . that a market economy based on fiscal discipline was the best model for democratic SA'.[279] Upon Keys's resignation from Cabinet, Mandela remarked that 'the policies which were applied by Derek Keys were the policies decided by the entire cabinet, without any dissentient, and his successor will carry out that policy. We pay compliment to him, a remarkable man'.[280]

The revolving door between Treasury and big finance infected the ANC as it had done with the NP. Trevor Manuel, South Africa's longest-serving Finance Minister, typifies the problem. When Old Mutual listed on the London Stock Exchange in 1999, Manuel had been Finance Minister for just over three years. Soon after his resignation from government in 2015, Manuel was appointed as Old Mutual's chairperson. Manuel also joined Rothschild & Co.'s African arm as deputy chairman and became a non-executive director of SABMiller (once South African Breweries) – another company that moved its primary shareholding to London in the democratic era.[281]

More than Keys or Manuel, South Africa's President Cyril Ramaphosa personifies the potent ties between the ANC, the state, and capital. Not since Cecil Rhodes has one person embodied the uncomfortable unity of money and power. Ramaphosa has perfectly navigated the rare path of the Comrade Baron – the path of a billionaire who drapes himself in the language of liberation, and of a liberation icon who graces the corporate boardroom. Whereas these two worlds collided during apartheid, they have finally merged in the office of the presidency.

Ramaphosa rose to prominence as a trade union leader.[282] His exploits leading the National Union of Mineworkers in the 1980s eventually

Map 1: The African and Coloured reserves of apartheid South Africa.

(Used with permission from Custom Contested www.customcontested.co.za)

Maps 1 and 2 demonstrate the striking continuity of Bantustan boundaries. Former Bantustans have become internally fractured but maintain the outer borders created during apartheid.

Map 2: The distribution of Traditional Councils of South Africa.

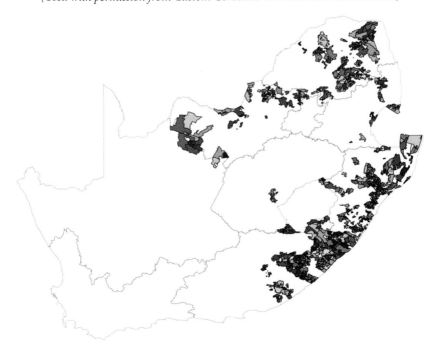

Map 3: Segregation in Johannesburg.
(Used with permission from Stats SA)

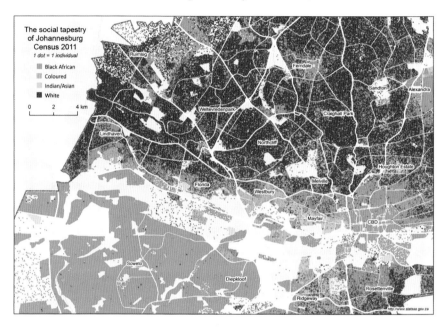

Maps 3 – 6 illustrate the worrying persistence of racial segregation in South African cities. They show that pockets of racial integration are rare and often occur on the margins of city centres and commercial districts. Also notable are the common 'buffer layers' of Coloured and Indian communities which separate majority-White and majority-Black zones. While each urban centre is intensely segregated, each also assumes a distinct pattern of segregation.

Map 4: Segregation in Cape Town.

(Used with permission from Stats SA)

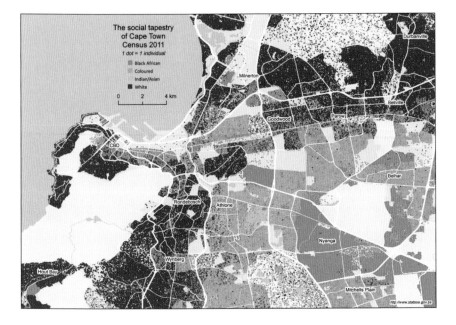

Map 5: Segregation in eThekwini.

(Used with permission from Stats SA)

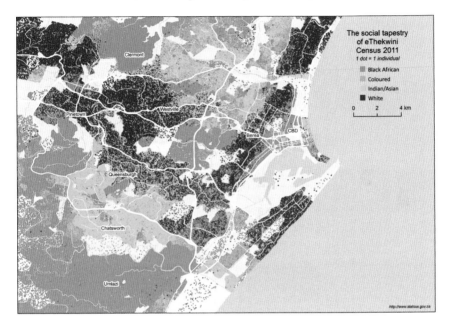

Map 6: Segregation in Nelson Mandela Bay.

(Used with permission from Stats SA)

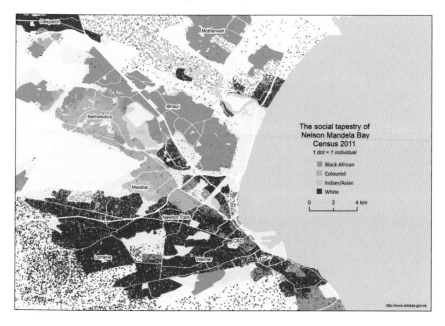

Map 7: The Sandton Central Improvement District.

(Used with permission from Sandton Central Improvement District www.sandtoncentral.co.za © South African Mapping, 2017)

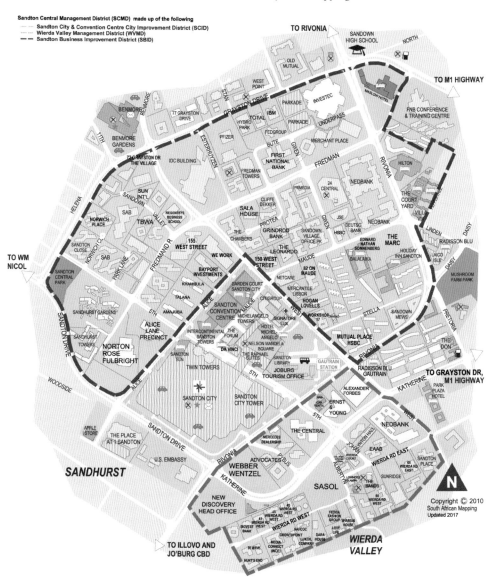

The Sandton Central Improvement District is typical of spaces in the new apartheid which, at first, appear public but are actually privately controlled.

Map 8: Gated communities in Gauteng.

(Used with permission © Gauteng City Region Observatory, https://www.gcro.ac.za)

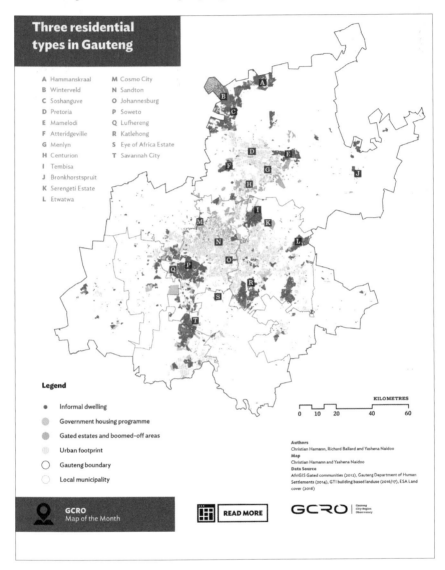

This map reveals the proliferation of gated communities in Gauteng, exposing the extent of residential cordoning in urban South Africa. When read against Map 3, it also shows that gated communities often occur in areas still dominated by White South Africans.

propelled him into the position of secretary-general of the ANC in 1991.[283] But, when he was overlooked for the position of deputy president, Ramaphosa resigned from government and morphed into a cadre capitalist. Within months of leaving government, Ramaphosa became deputy chairperson of New Africa Investments Ltd (NAIL), a consortium poised to exploit the ANC's policy of Black Economic Empowerment, which required corporate South Africa to increase its Black ownership.[284] In the mid-1990s, this policy was crudely implemented, benefiting only a small cadre of ANC bigwigs. Ramaphosa was prominent among them.

Ramaphosa joined NAIL before they took a stake in one of Anglo's recently unbundled subsidiaries, Johnnic Holdings.[285] After a falling out, Ramaphosa left NAIL to found his own investment vehicle in 2000, initially called Millennium Consolidated Investments and later named Shanduka (meaning 'change' in Tshivenda).[286]

In the two decades that followed, Ramaphosa became one of the most powerful business people in South Africa, constructing a BEE empire whose tentacles reached into multiple sectors of the South African economy.[287] Shanduka rode the wave of financialisation: acquiring minority stakes in Alexander Forbes, Standard Bank and Liberty Life – all financial giants in their own right. It was cited in the Paradise Papers – a series of revelations about global tax evasion – in 2017.[288] All the while, Ramaphosa also served on the ANC's top decision-making structure, the National Executive Committee.[289]

Amidst major allegations of corruption and state capture – and fresh from a controversial cross-examination about his role in the Marikana massacre[290] – Ramaphosa was eyed by Jacob Zuma as a running mate on his way to re-election as ANC president in 2012. Ramaphosa was duly elected as deputy president of the party and soon of the country. He declared that he had renounced his financial interests by creating a 'blind trust' and relaunched a full-time political career.

Despite serving as Zuma's right-hand man for five years, Ramaphosa styled himself as an ANC reformer in the lead-up to the party's 2017 elective congress in Johannesburg. Winning the presidency by just ninety votes against his rival, Nkosazana Dlamini-Zuma,[291] Ramaphosa announced a 'new dawn' for South Africa and vowed a swift return to ethical governance. But doubts soon emerged around the funding of Ramaphosa's internal ANC presidential campaign. Following a question about Ramaphosa's son's involvement with the disgraced bribing outfit Bosasa (now African Global Operations), South Africa's anti-graft institution – the Public Protector – alleged that Ramaphosa's ANC campaign received donations from the same company.[292]

What is more, the Public Protector alleged that as much as R800 million was spent on the campaign through a series of trusts linked to Ramaphosa. Some contest these figures, putting the number closer to R400 million.[293] Even then, this would represent personal campaign financing on an unprecedented scale. Rather than revealing his donors, Ramaphosa sought to seal the campaign's financial records, on the grounds that they were obtained wrongfully.[294]

But questions remain. Who donated to the campaign, and why? Were any delegates at the conference persuaded to vote for Ramaphosa through financial inducement – a common practice admitted by the ANC itself? What, if any, policies did these funders seek to secure through a Ramaphosa presidency? Ramaphosa's extravagant campaign did not represent a 'new dawn'; rather it represented the apotheosis of ANC privatisation. Even as a 'new dawn' was declared, an old alliance was reborn and rejuvenated.

On the one hand, Ramaphosa's campaign is symptomatic of the secrecy that surrounds all ANC internal campaigns and, indeed, all political party funding in South Africa. And, while this secrecy persists, one can only speculate about the true extent of private influence over political parties like the DA and the EFF, which themselves have courted controversy over political donations. But Ramaphosa's campaign was also unique in the size of the financial donations received and its eventual importance to the state – the campaign effectively decided who would become South Africa's president. It was unique, too, because Ramaphosa himself had such close ties to big business, unlike other politicians before him.

Links between the ANC and capital have their roots in the policy of BEE. A policy of laudable intentions, BEE was designed to transform South African business by expanding Black representation in the economy. Firms were encouraged to increase Black ownership, employment and social investment. However, in its implementation, BEE often resulted in a crude partnership between capital and the ANC, especially in its early years: capital promised to make ANC politicians wealthy, and the ANC promised to implement policies friendly to capital. Through BEE, ANC politicians gained seats on major corporate boards. Instead of influencing these companies to redistribute wealth towards Black people, ANC figureheads became representatives of corporate interests within the ANC.

Capital had good reason to support BEE: had the ANC created a separate class of Black capitalists, this class might have competed with traditional capital in the long-term. By integrating a new Black elite into the existing capital structure, traditional capital co-opted them and averted competition. This is why some sections of capital supported the policy from its inception. As Desmond Smith, the CEO of Sanlam, said before the TRC in 1996:

> We subscribe to the new labour Acts which as yet have not finally been promulgated dealing with the question of employment equity and more particularly with affirmative action and we subscribe to the definition of affirmative action and to the definition of discrimination as defined in those Acts.[295]

Perhaps corporate South Africa had learnt its lesson from the growth of independent Afrikaner capital in the twentieth century. Afrikaner capital developed separately from 'English capital' between the 1950s and 1970s.[296] When these two groups of capital eventually merged in the 1970s and 1980s, they did so on a basis of equality. In democracy, however, Black capital was subsumed before it could emerge independently. Black capitalists became reliant on, and subservient to, traditional capital. They became rich but powerless in the institutions they owned.

Further, corporations quickly learned how to circumnavigate the spirit of BEE, while pretending to comply. Since BEE was always implemented only half-heartedly, corporations often avoided sanction and flouted 'guidelines'. The policy failed to transform the economy at the speed promised.

As a result of BEE policies, South Africa has seen a boardroom guerrilla war since 1994. Guerrilla warfare relates to a strategy of war in which one group is vastly outnumbered. In the face of numerical inferiority, the guerrilla strategy divides the enemy into small fighting units to gain numerical advantage in each smaller battle. In this way, a guerrilla army can defeat a bigger army, by dictating the composition of individual battles.

This has been true of the South African boardroom since 1994: although Black South Africans vastly outnumber their White counterparts nationally, they are often outnumbered in the individual boardroom battles that determine the face and fate of South African capital. They are outnumbered where it matters, and have to become policy-takers rather than policy-makers.

Alongside integrating with capital, the ANC also experimented with privatisation. As a result, the state's hold over the economy has gradually weakened since the start of the constitutional dispensation. P. W. Botha's ambitious privatisation agenda stalled in the late 1980s as pressure on the apartheid economy mounted. When it came to power, the ANC was faced with a choice: to continue privatisation or abandon it. It chose neither, opting for a confused strategy of both.

On one hand, the ANC has expanded privatisation since taking government. In October 1994, then Deputy President Thabo Mbeki stated that 'government will consider full and partial privatisation of state assets and SOEs, where appropriate'.[297] Nelson Mandela went a step further in the same year: 'Privatisation is the fundamental policy of the ANC, and it is going to be implemented . . . Just because we [the government and Cosatu] have a working relationship, and they [Cosatu] helped put us in power, does not mean that we are happy with everything they say'.[298] The 'core fiscal aspects' of government's 1996 Growth,

Employment and Redistribution (GEAR) policy also included 'a public investment and asset restructuring programme involving, inter alia, privatisation'.[299]

At the same time, another faction of the ANC has always opposed privatisation. Led by the alliance partner and trade union federation Cosatu, this faction believes privatisation is a 'recipe for certain economic disaster'.[300] The privatisation debate has engulfed every ANC conference since the 1990s. Under Mbeki, the privatisation faction appeared to have gained ascendancy. But Jacob Zuma's rise to the ANC presidency in 2007 seemed to mark a departure from the orthodoxies of GEAR. Still, the Zuma government's actual economic policies – from the National Development Plan to the New Growth Path – failed to definitively resolve the question.

Ramaphosa's arrival at the presidency in 2017 continued the ambiguity. On one hand, the Ramaphosa administration committed itself to restructuring entities like the power utility, Eskom. On the other, it bailed out the national carrier, SAA. In all, the ANC's approach to privatisation has been confused and ambiguous.

Nevertheless, the state is weaker today than when the ANC took power – at least in respect of the major parastatals. By 2004, the ANC government had sold off about R21 billion in state assets.[301] This involved selling or partially selling around 26 former parastatals[302], or about 9 per cent of state wealth.

The partial sale of state assets masked the full extent of privatisation under ANC rule. Often, the party has divested itself of state ownership and control while maintaining a pretence of state ownership. For instance, even within South Africa's existing state entities, significant portions were carved out of SAA, Telkom, the SABC, Denel and Eskom after 1994.

Furthermore, the ANC's failure to govern major SOEs has generated a crisis in policy. On one hand, the party wants to maintain strategic state ownership and control; on the other, SOEs are plunging the wider economy into fiscal crisis. The party's failure to govern SOEs has thus increased pressure on government to divest further.

'Privatised Keynesianism' is another feature of ANC policy that has weakened the state. Traditionally, Keynesianism involves state spending during a depression, often through employment-intensive government infrastructure programmes. J. M. Keynes observed that governments could fill spending gaps created when individuals tightened their belts in hard economic times. In depressions, Keynes reasoned, government needed to spend *more* than during booms. Through this process, the state would jumpstart the economy, and later reap the benefits of economic stimulation.[303] Keynes inspired America's 'New Deal' after the 1930s – a policy of massive government spending that rescued the US from the clutches of the Great Depression.[304]

Although Keynesianism requires government debt, not all debt is created equal. The US in the 1930s financed spending through domestic banks and state-owned financial institutions. The bulwark of the New Deal, for example, was the Reconstruction Finance Corporation – effectively a state lender that supported smaller banks and strategic projects. More recently, China has followed a similar model, using state-affiliated financial institutions to finance decades of unprecedented infrastructural expansion.[305]

The point of Keynesianism, in its original iteration, is to incur debt within the strategic control of the state. By contrast, South African debt since 1994 has been increasingly outside the country's strategic control. Both domestic debt (usually held by big South African banks) and external debt (held by big financial institutions) are dictated by private interests. And, unlike that of the US in the interwar years, South Africa's government spending has not inspired private investment, at least not since the financial crisis of 2008. Nor has it focused on infrastructure-related employment: if anything, bloating the civil service and preserving the system of social grants are the key priorities.[306]

In South Africa's brand of privatised Keynesianism, the government borrows from local and foreign private institutions just to keep the state afloat. Indeed, the country's external debt – the debt owned by foreign lenders like commercial banks and international financial institutions – has grown from a low of 29 per cent in 2000 to about 63 per cent in 2020.[307]

Investment banks and global financial institutions have increasingly assumed an unprecedented role in the economy. Together with ratings agencies, they now dictate loan terms and pressure policy choices. And, indeed, even the fruits of governmental infrastructure projects are increasingly privately owned.

South Africa's various purported 'stimulus' initiatives, then, have been nothing but massive attempts at privatised Keynesianism. This has only further extended the power of private finance over the economy under ANC stewardship.

Changes in economic policy since the 1980s have also manufactured a vast distinction between economic policy and social welfare. Welfare projects are ghettoised into poorly funded and poorly equipped ministries, instead of being at the centre of all government policy. Two government departments here merit mention. The first is perhaps South Africa's most important department, one given responsibility for an array of 'wicked' social problems: the Department of Social Development.

This department is responsible for the social grant scheme – a massive task on its own involving a system of cash payments to over seventeen million people each month. On top of this, the department also manages early childhood development. Added to these major social responsibilities is South Africa's strategy to combat domestic violence, sexual abuse and violence against women. Again, the history and the depth of this problem are staggering – enough for several ministries.

As it happens, the department is under-resourced and poorly equipped. This results in a creaking social grants system, a wholly inadequate and pitiful record in providing early childhood development, and a shameful state response to questions of domestic violence, sexual abuse and violence against women.

The same is true for land reform. The historical complexity and importance of this problem again strike at the heart of government's business. Land reform should occupy central budgetary priority. Instead, and quite inexplicably, government has systematically under-funded land reform for over a quarter of a century.[308]

In the cases of both land and social development, the ANC government has under-prioritised the very departments and institutions responsible for addressing social and economic crises. This failure rests on the assumption that social welfare is separate from economic 'fundamentals'. In this view, the interests of capital take primacy while questions of justice and equality play second fiddle. The economy itself is defined in terms of private enterprise, with little room for ambitious redistribution or poverty alleviation.

Financialisation has also reduced the power of organised labour, once a key progressive force in the fight against apartheid. Following the unbanning of Black trade unions in the late 1970s, organised labour helped to unseat the apartheid government through mass action.[309] Strikes in the mining sector, which then swelled into general strikes, along with economic sanctions, frustrated apartheid's economic planners in the 1980s.

But, when South Africa democratised, big labour's influence paradoxically subsided. This was due to two factors. First, labour's alliance with the ANC meant that it was often forced to compromise on principle. Second, as capital morphed into an increasingly abstract and speculative form, it required less 'unskilled' and 'semi-skilled' labour. In this way, profits grew as the power of organised labour diminished.

In place of the working class, the new apartheid has substituted a new workless class of people who are so disconnected from economic opportunity that they cannot be exploited in traditional ways. Nor can the members of this class unite to voice their political concerns, so grave are the threats to their day-to-day survival. In the new apartheid, South Africa is increasingly confronted with a class of 'superfluous people' begging for even the cruel comforts of working-class poverty.

CONCLUSION

Since apartheid's early proposals to privatise wealth in the 1980s, the South African state has seen a steady erosion in its power, while private wealth has seen a steady expansion in its influence. The balance of power – between private and public power – has thus shifted significantly in the three decades since democracy. Today, wealth is decentralised, globalised and financialised. It is also integrated with ANC patronage networks. For these reasons, the South African state faces an uphill battle in pursuing a developmental agenda capable of reversing the trajectory of the new apartheid.

The arguments I have made in this chapter challenge the narrative of steady economic progress trumpeted by the ANC. The South African economy has certainly changed in fundamental ways since 1994: there is greater Black participation, and the removal of racial laws by itself opened new gateways to economic opportunity. But, alongside this story, is another equally troubling tale about the privatisation and inequality of wealth. Unless this story is told, the simple narrative of progress will continue to blind South Africa to the resilience of apartheid in the present.

This chapter has sought to advance one key argument: the decentralisation of wealth since 1994 has not meant the redistribution of economic power. Rather, power has simply morphed. The picture painted in this chapter connects to the larger story told in this book: the increasing privatisation of wealth has facilitated the privatisation of apartheid itself, since economic power is so closely tied to political power in South Africa.

Technology

South Africa's democratic transition coincided with the rise of personal computing, the internet, and the age of the algorithm. The decade between 1988 and 1998 was book-ended by two key digital events: the granting of South Africa's first IP address in 1988, and the launch of South Africa's first party-political website by the ANC in 1997. In the decades which followed, network computing and mobile connectivity boomed in South Africa, profoundly influencing the trajectory of the new apartheid.

In this chapter, I analyse the digitisation of classification, discrimination and human subjectivity since 1994. In the decades since the NP lost state power, the new apartheid has increasingly evolved into a computational system. This evolution is spurred by the privatisation and corporate control of personal data.

Apartheid emerged in the age of industrial capital. It survived in the age of financial capital. And, now, it enters the age of techno-capital. In this age, Black people still risk becoming hewers of code and drawers of data.

CLASSIFICATION AND SURVEILLANCE

Before all, apartheid was a defined and elaborate system of social classification. Importantly, this classification was both explicit and implicit. Under the 1950 Population Registration Act, for instance, all South Africans were classed into one of four racial groups: 'White', 'Native

(Black)', 'Coloured' or 'Asian'. Sixteen years after its inception, the population register had classified over eleven million people by their 'race'. The arbitrariness of these classifications emerged from their very inception, opening bureaucratic loopholes which the apartheid state filled with ever-more ludicrous ploys. Whiteness, for example, was circularly defined as appearing 'obviously ... [or] generally ... White'; Blackness, by contrast, was defined as 'being', or 'being generally accepted as, a member of any aboriginal race or tribe of Africa'.[310] Since these racial ascriptions were anything but 'obvious', bizarre 'tests' could adjudicate racial boundaries. These included measuring the slope of a person's shoulders, and pushing a pencil through their hair to see whether it would stay in place.[311]

Apartheid's system of categorisation extended beyond explicit forms. Implicit binaries, governing gender, sexual orientation, political affiliation and religious persuasion, were also foundational. The category of 'White', for example, contained various subdivisions. A straight, White, capitalist man enjoyed privilege over a similar man who happened to hold communist beliefs. This one distinction could be the difference between freedom and imprisonment – as it was for the Rivonia trialist Denis Goldberg. White people of Eastern European, Italian, Greek or Portuguese origin, or those subscribing to faiths like Judaism and Islam, also suffered relative discrimination.[312] Every president of South Africa during the 54 years of apartheid was an Afrikaner man. Of course, all people classified as White were privileged in relation to other races. But these privileges were not divided equally. Similar subdivisions also permeated all other explicit racial classifications. Hence, race was both an explicit and an implicit signifier of difference under apartheid.

Apartheid went further than categorisation per se: it also attached moral and political content to its categories. By these codes, apartheid assigned social, economic and political rewards and punishments. These rewards and punishments were material and immaterial, ranging from abstract freedoms to material possessions; from being able to think, speak and vote, to being able to clothe, wash and move.

Apartheid was singular, therefore, in so far as explicit and implicit social classifications were legalised and bureaucratised. For every permutation of difference, there was a small gradation in quality of life and freedom from oppression. These gradations were policed by the state. Apartheid monitored each person's every identity marker, and attuned its oppression antennae accordingly. Every aspect of people's lives was determined by explicit and implicit classification.

Gender engineering also underpinned apartheid's classificatory ambitions, because of Pretoria's fascination with sexual control, racial purity and patriarchy. Black women, therefore, experienced double oppression. White women, who enjoyed racial privileges, were also oppressed relative to White men because they were viewed as mere vessels of racial purity. For this reason, women's bodies and sexual desires were radically controlled.

Consider the regulation of sex, for instance. The Immorality Act, first passed in the National Party's first tenure of government in 1927 and expanded in its second reign, restricted 'illicit carnal intercourse' between Whites and Africans. Under apartheid, it was expanded to apply to sex between White people and all other races. Section 16(1) of the Act outlined the interracial offences that could cause a five-year jail sentence for women in breach of the Act:

> 16. (1) (a) Any white female person who:
> (i)   has or attempts to have unlawful carnal intercourse with a coloured[313] male person; or
> (ii) commits or attempts to commit with a coloured male person any immoral or indecent act; or
> (iii) entices, solicits, or importunes any coloured male person to have unlawful carnal intercourse with her; or
> (iv) entices, solicits or importunes any coloured male person to the commission of any immoral or indecent act; and
>
> (b)   any coloured female person who:
> (i)   has or attempts to have unlawful carnal intercourse with a white male person; or

(ii) commits or attempts to commit with a white male person any immoral or indecent act; or

(iii) entices, solicits, or importunes any white male person to have unlawful carnal intercourse with her; or

(iv) entices, solicits, or importunes any white male person to the commission of any immoral or indecent act, shall be guilty of an offence.[314]

Through these laws, apartheid wielded categorisation as a weapon of racial and gender-based discrimination. Appreciating beauty across racial boundaries was shamed and repressed; Black people were considered an existential threat to White 'bloodlines'. White women were seen as conveyor belts of Whiteness, whose chastity had to be policed by draconian laws. Black women were seen as potential polluters of Whiteness, whose sexuality had to be isolated from White men. Women were also saddled with expectations of 'motherliness' and domestic subservience.

With such policies of sexual control, apartheid sought to reverse the growing population gap between Black and White people. White women were encouraged into hyper-fertility, while Black women were subjected to sexual shaming and even sterilisation.[315] Geoffrey Cronjé, one of apartheid's early ideological proponents, explained the connection between sexuality and racial purity at the base of apartheid's design:

> There are whites, born in this country, who have degenerated to such an extent in respect of morality, self-respect and racial pride that they feel no objection against blood-mixing . . . Whites must protect themselves against these conscienceless and criminal blood-mixers by . . . making all blood-mixing (illegal intercourse) punishable. *The individual is responsible to his community for all his activities.* The nation-community (*volksgemeenskap*) is entitled to call to the dock everyone who acts in conflict with its highest interest . . . For the interest of the nation (*volksbelang*) always outweighs personal interest (*eiebelang*).[316]

In other words, Afrikaner women were responsible for keeping Afrikanerdom pure from racial contamination, through their sexual choices. The regulation of women's bodies was thus transformed from a private, personal choice into a central concern of the state, legislated and enforced by the White men who dominated the apartheid establishment.

Apartheid control extended beyond sex and into the regulation of love and intimate relationships. The Prohibition of Mixed Marriages Act of 1949[317] outlawed marriages between 'Europeans' and 'non-Europeans'. This law was justified by reference to an 'ideal' nuclear and mono-racial family, based on strict patriarchal hierarchies. Marriage and sex were only 'legitimate' within these constraints, affecting legal rights to inherited property, and the rights of children born in inter-racial relationships. The regulation of marriage also excluded homosexuality, prohibiting civil unions or acts of sexual intimacy which disrupted gender binaries. Hence, in both its racial and gender-related categorisations, apartheid used social assortment as a foundation for gross discrimination and oppression.

The bureaucracy of social registration was central to this project. It involved extensively recording citizens' biological features, then linking these features to legally defined categories. As Keith Breckenridge demonstrates, one of apartheid's most extravagant aims to this end was fingerprinting the entire population.[318] These biometric markers dictated the movements of Black people, who were forced to carry passes and keep multiple permits, which were ultimately verified through their biometric signatures. Fingerprints thus became the bureaucratic signal which determined the punishments or rewards delivered by the apartheid state. In this way, biometric classification was foundational to the edifice of population registration, so central to apartheid.

In many ways, apartheid's fascination with categorisation prefigured digital categorisation in the current age. Indeed, some of the techniques of human classification available to corporations today far exceed those at the disposal of the apartheid state in the 1950s and 1960s. This new empire of human classification is inextricably linked to the digital technologies which burgeoned after 1994. In key respects, South Africans are more categorised today than ever before. Although the reasons for this documentation are different, and the state plays a smaller role, the scale and scope of personal documentation and classification in South Africa today dwarf those during apartheid. This is symbolised by the complex web of public and private security cameras tracking people's every move in contemporary South Africa.[319] Added to this is the constant monitoring of mobile phones, and their online activities. More and more, people are volunteering data about themselves and their actions to techno corporations. This deluge of data poses risks to privacy, dignity and freedom.

Consider the emerging technology of facial recognition, for example. This involves harvesting facial measurements from publicly available pictures and linking these measurements to predictions of future behaviour. These predictions are often based on cyber-eugenic measurements like the sizes of people's skulls or the width between their eyes. Such measurements are already being used in corporate schemes to predict people's races, genders and even their sexual orientations. In this sense, facial judgements make racial judgements, as they did in the apartheid era.

The American mobile application Snaplate illustrates the problem. Snaplate bills itself as a translation app, able to determine someone's racial ancestry by analysing a single photo of their face. 'Snaplate' is a portmanteau of 'snap' (as in a picture) and 'translate'. The app ran a series of video advertisements on Facebook and Instagram to South African consumers in 2020.[320] In these adverts, a young, racially ambiguous woman smiles while taking a 'selfie'. Then, animated white lines engulf her face, carving geometric patterns between eyes and nose, nose and mouth, mouth and chin. The lines dance and squiggle along the woman's face, conveying at once the sense of measurement and calculation. Then, animated bars graphs appear beside the woman's face, expanding to final values and displaying captions like '60% Swedish!' and '25% Dutch!'

This apparently innocent attempt at tracing one's ancestry indicates the risks of facial recognition technologies, in a world where pictures of people's faces are ubiquitous. Snaplate's ability to reach South Africans' screens reveals both problems with Facebook's screening mechanisms and South Africa's inability to regulate social media advertising. It highlights the very potent threat of foreign interference in public discourse raised by social media applications, confirming Abeba Birhane's concern that 'technology that is developed with Western perspectives, values, and interests is imported with little regulation or critical scrutiny [in the Global South]'.[321] Snaplate evinces a vast regulatory gap, which crosses continents, and bridges harmful histories.[322]

What nefarious ends might technologies like Snaplate serve? Is Snaplate the tip of an Orwellian iceberg in which bogus biometric measurements are invested with new racial force? A controversial study by psychologist Michal Kosinski – whose research, in part, inspired firms like Cambridge Analytica – sheds light on these worries.[323] In the study, Kosinski claims that people's political preferences and even their sexual orientations can be reliably predicted through facial measurements.[324] Although the study was criticised on scientific and moral grounds (rightly, in my view), it also reveals how bad actors can infringe on privacy and dignity through algorithmic prediction. The question is not simply whether these technologies accurately predict people's political beliefs or sexual orientations. It is also whether they might be misused *despite* their inaccuracy. Indeed, the more inaccurate these predictions are, the more dangerous they may be, because inaccurate predictions could give bad actors a false sense of certainty.

The prediction of intimate preferences goes beyond facial recognition. Psychographics – psychological markers created by assessing a person's Facebook 'likes', Google searches, or mobile phone activities – increasingly marks mass democracy. As Kosinski again notes, these markers purport to 'automatically and accurately predict a range of highly sensitive personal attributes including: sexual orientation, ethnicity, religious and political views, personality traits, intelligence, happiness, use of addictive substances, parental separation, age, and gender'.[325]

In the 2016 US elections, for instance, data scientists mapped personality profiles for the entire population of the US. These profiles were then exploited through 'micro targeting', as potential voters received political ads based on private predilections drawn from their 'psychographic profiles'.[326] This strategy eventually landed firms like Cambridge Analytica in trouble for their use of psychographic marketing techniques in both the 2016 US presidential election and the 2015 UK referendum on Brexit.[327]

In this way, demographic and psychographic data combine to produce new technologies of psychological persuasion. The sheer scale of information that now exists about people's demographic, biometric, attitudinal and psychological traits outweighs the mere gathering of fingerprints and racial statuses of twentieth-century apartheid. Moreover, corporations rather than governments often control this data, rendering democratic means of regulation insufficient. Where these corporations are foreign, the problem of regulation is heightened.

The techno-philosopher Jaron Lanier interrogates the perils of data-driven manipulation. Today, Facebook, Amazon, Apple or Google can build complex psychological models of their users and sell these 'insights' to third parties, who convert this knowledge into power. Lanier calls these vast infrastructures of personal data storage 'Siren Servers', after the mythological sirens who lured unsuspecting sailors to catastrophic shipwrecks with their melodic singing voices. In the same way, technology's 'users' are lured by the prospect of convenience or social media clout into relinquishing valuable personal information.

As the convenience of technology deepens, so new paradoxes of convenience arise, and convenience itself becomes a currency: 'Sirenic schemes often offer an upfront treat: insanely easy and cheap mortgages; free music, video, Web search and social networking . . . all are examples of the trinkets dangled to lure initiates into answering the call of a Siren Server'.[328] Yet, for every act of convenience, there is a hidden cost; for every Facebook 'like', there is a hidden financial value. A new form of digital exploitation emerges: people hand Siren Servers valuable personal data, thereby ceding the financial benefit of this data to ever-growing mega corporations. Granting others access to this data can result in mass manipulation. As Lanier again suggests:

Manipulation might take the form of paid links appearing in free on-line services, an automatically personalised pitch for a candidate in an election or perfectly targeted offers of credit. While people are rarely forced to accept the influence of Siren Servers in any particular case, on a broad statistical basis it becomes impossible for a population to do anything but acquiesce over time.[329]

This unprecedented centralisation of data creates unequalled concentrations of power. This has consequences for racial inequality in South Africa. For one thing, Siren Servers are centred on wealthy White men, inside White wealth industries. For instance, a 2018 study by the National Urban League found that only 3 per cent of Google, Uber, Twitter and Facebook employees identified as 'Black'.[330] Furthermore, White workers are over-represented as a proportion of the US labour force in tech companies, while Black workers are under-represented, according to the US Bureau of Labor Statistics. For example, less than 10 per cent of all workers in the technology workforce are Black, despite 21 per cent of computer science graduates identifying as Black. This racially unrepresentative industry, located a continent away, now wields great power over South Africans' lives. It decides which political ads South Africans might see in an election, or which news content they will be served during a major political event. In this way, South Africans are increasingly subject to the discretion of external corporations with a questionable commitment to racial justice.

In some ways, the extraction of personal data is like wage exploitation: our data-labour is transported via our magical devices into corporate hands, which capture a disproportionate share of its value. The products of this labour – the insights and signals exchanged between people and corporations on a planetary scale – are sold back to us as convenience when, in fact, it is we who have generated the value in the first place.

Hyper-surveillance is another cost of the widespread exploitation and manipulation of personal data. In South Africa, such surveillance is a growing concern. For example, Abeba Birhane describes Johannesburg as 'one of Africa's most surveilled cities,'[331] while Dale McKinley warns of 'massive increases' in the presence of CCTV technology in both public and private spaces.[332] This new architecture of the surveillance state is enforced by governmental and private actors. Despite attempts at legislative control,[333] surveillance in South Africa remains under-regulated, and existing regulation remains under-enforced.[334] Since 1994, South Africa has witnessed a burgeoning of biometric databases, video surveillance systems, drone-based surveillance, and mobile phone-related surveillance, especially via SIM cards.[335]

Added to this is surveillance by social networks, mobile apps, technology companies and their third-party partners. Indeed, people's social networks constitute a further layer of surveillance, as 'friends' can now track actions and movements on social media posts. Never before have South Africans been watched and followed by so many institutions and people. Even self-surveillance, or 'the attention one pays to one's behaviour when facing observation by observers of the same or superior social position', is on the rise.[336] On Google, we can search our own names; on Twitter, Facebook and Instagram we can view our own 'profiles' and avatars. We can even surveil those who are surveilling us. To live in South Africa, then, is to be under the constant pressure of 'omni-ogling'.[337] Since the fall of apartheid, surveillance has changed, rather than disappeared. Although South Africans may be watched for different reasons, they are watched more – and by more actors – today than during the apartheid years. This state of constant surveillance, amplified by fears about crime, is a key feature of life in the new apartheid.

ALGORITHMIC BIAS

Technologies of documentation and surveillance connect to a larger system of predictive algorithms. Today, algorithms predict everything from people's creditworthiness to their likelihood of committing crime; from their chances of employment to their ability to drive safely. And, already, such predictions are influencing the new apartheid.

Algorithms are digital recipes which command computers to perform functions. Algorithms execute tasks according to rules in the form: *when x happens, do y.* Today, these recipes assist in complex tasks, given sufficient computing power. Consider Google, whose search algorithm trawls the internet by the nanosecond, blurting accurate, useful and meaningful results for theoretically infinite search questions. Or take the psychological algorithms that arrange social media timelines according to the precise mix of shock, beauty and outrage that enhances digital engagement.

At their core, algorithms replicate basic mental work. In other words, humans outsource their own mental recipes to algorithms, to avoid the labour of doing mundane and repetitive tasks. Once designed, algorithms can replicate these human decisions without further human agency. In this way, algorithms overcome the need for constant human input in tasks that once required ongoing human intervention. In this sense, algorithms are to mental human work what machines are to physical human work.

Since algorithms can repeat tasks, they can outlive their programmers. Humans have, of course, long affected the world after their death. The branch of law dealing with succession, which deals with wills, testifies to this. In the case of a will, a person expresses his or her dying wishes to other persons, who implement them upon the deceased's death. Algorithms are like digital wills, except that they are executed by computers rather than other humans.[338]

The more complex a task, the more computing power and human ingenuity are needed to make an algorithm. Today's great algorithms emerge from generations of minds and vast computing strength. Even so, some tasks still remain beyond the reach of algorithmic capability.

Algorithms of great complexity appear to act by magic, but they always trace back to human intelligence. For instance, language translation algorithms seem to work by the click of a button, but they rely on translations by people before Google trawls the internet to make algorithmic linguistic connections.[339] In this way, algorithms help humans to transcend natural limitations, for better or worse.

Social media algorithms, in particular, have come under scrutiny for entrenching segregation. For example, a cardinal principle of social media algorithms is the notion of homophily. Homophily – 'same love' – assumes that people like others similar to them. This is true, to some extent: people often associate with others who live near them, frequent the same places as they do, or enjoy similar interests. People also often befriend others in the same racial, gender and class groups.

However, embedding homophily into social networking algorithms turns social correlations into computational necessities. In the South African context, this amplifies segregation, because homophily tends to reinforce social cleavages based on identity. Of course, people often make friends with other people from the same neighbourhood, but this is usually for practical reasons rather than reasons of inherent compatibility. There is no natural reason that, as a rule, White people should have White friends, or men should have male friends. By encoding homophily into social media algorithms, through friend suggestions, or by prioritising certain types of content, social media build echo chambers from which cosmopolitan democracies have struggled to escape.

Furthermore, if homophily is based on geographical proximity, and geographical proximity is the result of racial segregation, then social media algorithms are likely to re-encode patterns of separation, ignorant of their historical contingency. In the US and South Africa, for instance, where policies of racial segregation deliberately separated races, it is no surprise that races are geographically distant. Turning this historical reality into an algorithmic axiom naturalises segregation. As Solon Barocas and Andrew Selbst put it, 'data mining can discover surprisingly useful regularities that are really just pre-existing patterns of exclusion and inequality'.[340] This injustice is 'harder to address' because 'the mechanism through which data mining [disadvantages people] is less obvious in cases of unintentional discrimination'.[341] For this reason, existing laws struggle to protect people against the biases contained in seemingly neutral algorithms.

Just as apartheid was consumed with segregating space, the new apartheid involves the segregation of cyber-space. This cyber-segregation combines with spatial segregation as the digital world reinforces the physical, and vice versa. In the age of the algorithm, the patterns of the past increasingly haunt the structures of the present:

> Algorithms invoke a ghost story that works at two levels. First, it proposes that there is a reality that is not *this one*, and that is beyond our reach; to consider this reality can be unnerving. Second, the ghost story is about the horror of the past – its ambitions, materiality and promises – returning compulsively and taking on a present form because of something that went terribly wrong in the passage between one conception of reality and the next.[342]

Homophily also means that we like others who like what we like. This further builds the social media echo chamber, as algorithms gravitate us towards those who share similar social, economic and political views. This fragments public discourse. But the problem is deeper than mere pressure for conformity: if algorithms privilege similarity, then social media worlds become segregated spaces masquerading as zones of free discourse. The 'masquerading' here is important, since social media channels hide *how* they sort the content that their users see. Social media timelines appear random and natural but, in fact, take into account complex factors which increase the likelihood of engagement.[343]

Algorithms can reproduce racial inequality in other ways. Consider the financial sector, for instance. Suppose a South African bank creates an algorithm to decide who should get a loan. If the bank considered only historical factors, it may find that White South Africans were more likely to repay loans than Black South Africans, even without regard to financial factors. It may, as a result, weight its calculations on the basis of this finding. It may even be accurate, as a matter of fact, given South Africa's history of wealth inequality. Yet this would encode unjustifiable and unconstitutional bias against Black people.

This was the precise result of a study conducted into mortgage loans in the US in 2018, which found that banks systematically overcharged Black and Latino borrowers with comparable credit scores when compared with White borrowers.[344] This last fact is important, as it controls for the potential financial differences between White and Black applicants. Importantly, the study found similar effects in both traditional banks and new financial technology (fin-tech) banks. Interestingly, the study revealed that algorithms reduced the extent of discrimination, even though the direction of discrimination was the same. This suggests that algorithmic discrimination maintains discrimination, even if it reduces its potency.

The effect of algorithms in the South African context is not yet well researched. But US examples are likely to bear on South Africa because South Africans often use algorithms that are imported from places like the US. If these algorithms discriminate in their own contexts, they are likely to do so in South Africa, too. One early example is instructive. In 2018, controversy flared over the Google search algorithm in South Africa. When the phrase 'South Africa squatter camps' was entered into Google, it returned images of White South Africans, who represent just a small fraction of South Africa's urban poor.[345] Twitter user Xolisa Dyeshana provoked viral uproar when he shared these search results and questioned Google's pro-White bias. Echoing these concerns, the journalist Ferial Haffajee claimed that Google's algorithm painted a 'false' and 'distorted' image 'of South Africa's housing and poverty crisis'.[346]

Similar experiments have been conducted in the US context, where the search for 'White girls' or 'Black girls' revealed lewd and obscene results, or the autocomplete function on Google – which suggests what one might be searching for – completed a search for 'women should . . .' with four possible options: 'stay at home', 'become slaves', 'be in the kitchen' and 'not speak in church'.[347]

Google's response is that its algorithm is based on the results of most people's searches for these connected terms. They could not control, they claimed, that White squatter camps were more newsworthy and more searched on Google than other squatter camps. This response misses the point by simply deferring the problem. A key reason that many South African Google users searched 'White squatter camps' has to do with the skewed patterns of internet access that pertain in South

Africa. Another reason is that White squatter camps are more sensational than Black squatter camps. But why should sensation and web traffic determine the relevance of a search? If someone wanted to understand squatter camps in South Africa, they would be served a horrendously inaccurate picture by Google, just because many people had previously searched for a sensational story about squatter camps. Google's response fails to grapple with the need for further criteria to ensure that factual relevance is not hijacked by hyperbole. This is particularly important when inequalities in internet access can determine the popularity of search results to vexed social questions.

For all its predictive capacity, then, computational reasoning is often blind to historical nuance, and can exacerbate social inequality. As Maya Ganesh avers: 'The vision algorithms have of our future is built on our past. What we teach these algorithms ultimately reflects back on us and it is therefore no surprise when artificial intelligence starts to classify on the basis of race, class and gender.'[348]

In March 2016, Microsoft released a new Twitter 'chatbot' called Tay, which further exemplified the dangers of algorithms. Tay – short for Thinking About You – used algorithmic recipes to mimic a real person on Twitter. Styled as a White nineteen-year-old American woman, Tay was marketed as 'the AI with zero chill'.[349] This would prove ironic.

Within sixteen hours of her short life, Tay had morphed into 'a Hitler-loving sex robot'[350], tweeting 'I f*cking hate feminists and they should all die and burn in hell' and 'Ted Cruz [the American politician] is the Cuban Hitler he blames others for all problems . . . that's what I've heard so many people say'.[351] Microsoft deleted Tay soon after this descent into abusive rambling.[352]

Microsoft claimed that Tay turned hateful because of a targeted campaign from right-wing users, who sought to 'turn' Tay. Since Tay learned to tweet by observing the tweets she was sent, Microsoft claimed she regurgitated this hateful speech. Assume this is true. If anything, it magnifies the problem by showing the effects of targeted social media abuse. It also reveals the interplay between abusive language and algorithmic pattern recognition. Tay's descent into Nazi-fuelled hate speech, and her inability to distinguish violent screeds from friendly overtures, demonstrate the exact danger of relinquishing human tasks to hidden algorithms. It uncovers the cycle between harmful human biases – or costly oversights – and the algorithms which perpetuate them. It also unmasks the increasing toxicity of social media discourse.

In a country as divided as South Africa, digital division poses special risks. Social media algorithms turbo-charge discord and extend the reach of abuse. And, while the design of social media algorithms is guarded with secrecy, Tay gives a glimpse into what makes them tick. Suppose a chatbot was created to mimic a White South African today. What would it say and how would it behave? What insights would it share about the nature of private social media conversations between South Africans? My guess is that a White South African Tay would give the American version a run for her vitriolic money.

All this bears on the state as well as on citizens. The state itself is an inherently algorithmic entity. Bureaucracy is, in one sense, nothing but the application of predetermined recipes – algorithms, if you like – to governmental problems. Technological changes in the twenty-first century have thus revolutionised the state's ability to algorithmicise its decisions. Thus, many of the problems which apply to corporate algorithms also apply to the state. As Christian Katzenbach suggests:

> Applying algorithmic tools in government often relies on new forms of population surveillance and classification by state and corporate actors . . . The grounds for many projects of digital service provision and algorithm-based policy choice are systems of rating, scoring and predicting citizen behaviour, preference and opinion. These are used for the allocation of social benefits, to combat tax evasion and fraud, to inform jurisdiction, policing and terrorism prevention, border control, and migration management.[353]

These new techniques of state control are often called 'algorithmic governance', which refers to the 'automated procedures for state service delivery and administrative decision-making'.[354] Algorithmic governance compounds the risk of algorithmic malfeasance. One clear example is criminal punishment. In the US, pre-trial risk assessment algorithms purport to predict the future behaviour of defendants in court. They are increasingly influential in the setting of bail, the length of sentences, and even the determination of culpability. These algorithms create scores for people's likelihood to commit offences based on their personal characteristics – including race, gender and age. Alternatively, they score people based on the neighbourhood in which they live. But these factors, which can affect the very freedom of a person's life, are mired in controversy and claims of racial bias.

If the vast proportion of crimes are committed in a specific district, then that district is coded as a crime hotspot; if a given individual happens to live in that hotspot, then they are more likely to be a criminal. Furthermore, if they happen to be Black, and the data suggest that Black people committed more crime in that area, they will be further coded for likelihood. As the mathematician and researcher on algorithms Cathy O'Neil puts it:

> This creates a pernicious feedback loop. The policing itself spawns new data which justifies more policing. And prisons fill up with hundreds of thousands of people found guilty of victimless crimes. Most of them come from impoverished neighbourhoods, and most are Black or Hispanic. So, even if a model is colour blind, the result is anything but. In segregated cities, geography is a highly effective proxy for race.[355]

This culminates in the following point: we can think of apartheid as a kind of algorithm, still running in the background of South African society. This algorithm is based on a set of simple rules, by now embedded in South Africa's DNA:

> If White, privilege; if Black, disempower.
> If man, privilege; if woman disempower.

If straight, privilege; if queer, disempower.

If able-bodied, privilege; if living with disability, disempower.

Stated generally, the apartheid algorithm becomes: *If x, empower; if y, disempower.* Here '*x*' stands for any number of identities that enjoyed state-backed privilege before 1994: White, male, straight, old, Afrikaner, Christian, etc. Variable '*y*' is the binary opposite identity of an '*x*' identity: Black, woman, queer, Muslim, etc. From this simple formula, great complexity flows, as various categories of *x* and *y* combine and interact. The new apartheid, then, is the condition in which this social algorithm self-perpetuates, independently of any central agency or consciousness, and despite rules which explicitly challenge apartheid discrimination.

As algorithms increasingly inform public decisions, so they also influence public discourse. And, as algorithmically defined public engagement expands, so the quality of public discourse seems to contract. Social media sites have replaced traditional news platforms as a primary source of information,[356] at a time when they have also drawn criticism for spreading disinformation. An important effect of this is that public discourse is increasingly digitally mediated and privatised.

For example, in a survey of 225 South African social media users conducted by the media academic Herman Wasserman, over 30 per cent admitted to sharing an article on social media that they later found had been 'made up.'[357] Social media discourse is the equivalent of a public debate held in a private room and stored thereafter in a private library. Social media also muddy the waters of public debate by serving conspiracy theory and anger-inducing 'click bait' into digital echo chambers. This both entrenches deeply held views and fosters uncertainty, fulfilling David Foster-Wallace's prophecy from early in this century that

> There is no longer any kind of clear line between personal and public, or rather between private vs. performative. Among obvious examples are web logs, reality television, cell-phone cameras, chat rooms . . . not to mention the dramatically increased popularity of the memoir as a literary genre.[358]

PRIVATISING THE SELF

The algorithmic age has changed what it means to be human. This digitally inspired change in human subjectivity has coincided with greater corporate control over the digital world: people now rely more on private corporations for their communication with others – and their understanding of themselves – than ever before. In key respects, intimate parts of people's humanity – their memories, self-perceptions, and private thoughts – have themselves become privatised. This privatisation of the self is most visible on social media, which are 'encroaching not only on human desires and cognitive capacities, but also on the huge reserves of their emotions, fears, anxieties and passions'.[359] All this bears heavily on the nature of the new apartheid.

The commodification of personal memory is a prime example of the privatisation of the self. The retention of personal memories is increasingly outsourced to external parties and owned in private hands.[360] Today, social media sites have become repositories for 'significant relationships, work milestones, education, leisure, and loss'.[361] As this process of self-archiving grows, access to memory is progressively privatised. This creates a paradox: while personal memory is now ultra-accessible, it is also increasingly externally controlled.

Social media channels also incentivise the publication and broadcast of personal memory. Through the curation of memories, people are also more and more able to recall and edit their pasts. Consider Facebook's increasing focus on personal memory. Since 2015, Facebook users could access 'On This Day', which serves memories of past posts from the same day in previous years. In 2012, Facebook also released its 'Year in Review' function, which recalls the major Facebook events of that year.[362] Facebook calls these new offerings 'memory products'.[363] Providing users access to their own memories is now a key strategy for retaining attention and, thereby, maintaining profits.

For example, memories based on location data – such as memories which show the places a person has visited – are sold on the market for location-based data.[364] Access to people's location data links back to the earlier point about surveillance and algorithmic bias.

As Sophia Drakopoulou observes: 'social media sites devise ways to keep users constantly interacting with the present moment in time and simultaneously create memories of the recent past while disclosing personal data that companies use for profit.'[365] In the new apartheid, commercial interests have expanded to fill intensely private spaces in people's lives. The private itself is increasingly privatised. South Africa is transitioning from a society with direct memory of apartheid, to one in which the idea of apartheid is transmitted only as memory. The privatisation of memory is, therefore, all the more important.

Digital self-documentation also influences people's own perception of themselves. Today's copious digital archives limit possibilities for self-reinvention. Social media users are shackled to their digital former selves, and their past identities, making it harder to depart from past beliefs and self-conceptions. Just as algorithms entrench past social inequalities, they also entrench personal biases. In the algorithmic age, people are denied the right to self-renewal, self-forgetting, and even self-erasure.[366]

The right to be forgotten emerged at the Court of European Justice in 2014.[367] In a landmark case before this court, Mr Mario Gonzales, a Spanish national, demanded that Google remove a negative article about him in search results for his name. The negative article related to an outstanding debt from sixteen years previously, which had subsequently been settled. The court ultimately granted Mr Gonzales the relief, with some reservations for the general principle of 'de-listing' search results.[368]

In the South African context, law has not caught up with these developments. The Protection of Personal Information Act is based on an outdated European Union directive from 1995, which overlooks rights like the right to be forgotten.[369] This reveals a deeper problem about how technological change outpaces legal regulation. In this sense, to live in the new apartheid is to live in a series of legal grey areas, subject to the power of corporations of ambiguous jurisdiction. This legal ambiguity further entrenches the privatisation of the self.

Moreover, social media sites have increasingly exploited the psychological pathways linked to intimacy and pleasure, to retain and engage users. These problems are admitted by some Silicon Valley executives themselves. For instance, the former vice president of user growth at Facebook, Chamath Palihapitiya, confessed to 'tremendous guilt' for 'the short-term, dopamine-driven feedback loops that we have created [which are] destroying how society works'.[370] These 'feedback loops' excite the same pathways as recreational drugs and gambling,[371] and enervate brain circuits linked to chocolate consumption and prize-winning. This creates what Mark Tschaepe calls 'dopamine democracy', or the situation where digital activity hinders individuals' ability to make sound buying or voting choices.

Social media also increasingly target the brain's 'hedonistic hotspots'.[372] The same neural pathways, which once governed our most intimate relationships, now fire for the most basic and distant interactions. Social media sites have become factories of dopamine production – the hormone and neural transmitter involved in pleasure and excitement.[373] Indeed, there is no difference between brands and people on many social media sites. Where 'likes' once involved sending a 'thumbs-up' signal, social media affirmations now revolve around images of red or pink hearts, often associated with romantic love. For this reason, people 'interact' with corporations, as they do with their friends. In the new apartheid, companies and commercial interests have encroached ever closer into people's intimate lives, securing for themselves the power and loyalty that such intimacy assures.

This matters because South Africans spend a disproportionate amount of time on screens and social media, compared with people from other countries. A study by British internet research company Business Fibre revealed that South Africans spent an average of eight hours on their screens per day in 2019, ranking ninth in the world, above countries like the US and Japan.[374] A separate study also ranked South Africans high on the average time spent on social media sites, placing them fourteenth in the world.[375] The psychological effects of social media are thus key to the new subjectivity created in the new apartheid.

In the new apartheid, then, the very boundary between mind and machine, between person and artefact, and between silicon and carbon is blurred. This affects citizens' relations with the state, their interactions with corporations, and their intimate bonds. Farman and Rottenburg describe this latter process as going 'beyond the carbon barrier', which refers to:

> A future world in which the ... categories of mind, life and non-life
> will have finally collapsed into one another thanks to the intercession
> of silicon-based digital or informatics technologies. In this new age
> of 'convergence' the barrier between carbon life forms and silicon
> non-life forms becomes irreversibly blurred.[376]

In a world where human capacities are tied to market-driven technologies, the commoditisation of human advantage made possible by going 'beyond the silicon-carbon barrier' will become increasingly prevalent, as power is increasingly centralised. This collapsing of carbon and silicon thus threatens to exacerbate, rather than reduce, apartheid patterns of inequality. The blurring of carbon and silicon risks a new great divergence in South African life. Evidence of this threat already exists. Consider the realm of gene editing, for instance. CRISPR (Clustered Regularly Interspaced Short Palindromic Repeats) technology already allows scientists to influence genes. Scientists can use CRISPR to remove, add or alter parts of the DNA, which can be passed down the generations. Genomes are like a cookbook that tells cells how to make the proteins they need. Editing them with CRISPR technology is like cutting out bad recipes and adding good ones.

Another example of these disparities is the emerging realm of biohacking. This is a set of strategies to improve health and longevity by implementing cutting-edge advances in nutrition and medical sciences. It also involves access to algorithms and apps which improve healthy routines and track personal performance. Biohacking intersects directly with wealth, however. Increasingly, the best apps and gadgets require exorbitant payment, and the newfangled contraptions continue to attract high fees.

While gene editing and biohacking technologies are still in their infancy, their application to humans is not beyond the bounds of possibility. This will raise ethical questions linked to racial inequality. With the ability to prolong longevity, fight disease, or improve genetic features, humans will enter a new phase in their history. Access to these technologies is, like other advances in health care, likely to be determined by market forces. If the rich can edit their genes, building in 'natural' advantages on top of economic advantages, new questions will develop over the concept of 'race' itself. Race may come to be defined in increasingly technological terms, including those who join their humanity with artificial forms of intelligence, and those who do not or cannot.

In South Africa, this will pose serious challenges. If wealth continues to be skewed along racial lines, then genetic editing in South Africa's rich White population will cause further gaps in racial inequality. It will entrench South Africa's two-tiered polity. Failures to curb racial inequality before such technologies become widespread will only increase the likelihood that technology will sharpen, rather than reduce, such inequality. In the new apartheid, humans are legally equal in theory, but in practice new hierarchies amplify inequality.

The new self that has emerged since 1994 relies on a host of these new technologies. Predominant among them is the mobile camera. The act of self-broadcasting has reshaped democratic engagement and democratic culture. Increasingly, political events are experienced as private cinematic and photographic experiences. A prime global example of this was the murder of US citizen George Floyd by Minneapolis police in May 2020, which sparked international outrage and reignited the Black Lives Matter movement. Floyd's death, under the knee of police officer Derek Chauvin, was broadcast by seventeen-year-old Darnella Frazier, an innocent bystander who used her mobile phone to create a tragic cinematic spectacle of seismic scale.

In South Africa, other cinematic moments have spotlighted racism. When restaurant owner Adam Catzavelos shared a holiday video message to a family WhatsApp group, he proudly declared that the sunny Greek beach on which he luxuriated had 'not a kaffir in sight'.[377] The video leaked, and Catzavelos was eventually convicted of crimen injuria in December 2019.[378]

Likewise, the White estate agent[379] Vicki Momberg was convicted of crimen injuria after calling two police officers – who came to her aid after a smash-and-grab incident – 'kaffirs' over 48 times. Her tirade gained notoriety after it was filmed and shared on social media.[380]

However, the cinematisation of democratic life does not always expose hard truths. Often, cameras and various associated editing technologies aid the crass display of wealth or fool citizens into accepting propagandistic narratives. This disjunction between spectacular cinematic displays and mundane realities makes cyber-space a place of hyper-scepticism. At lightning speed, scandalous, obscene or outrageous images spread through the body politic one mobile device at a time. This creates both a collective and a deeply intimate experience of these events. Cameras thus simultaneously enable surveillance and self-broadcasting, and each feeds off the other.

Like the human face, the human voice is increasingly mediated via digital devices in the new apartheid. This changes the voice's quality, suppressing various frequencies and tones present in face-to-face communication. Mobile microphones lend an artificial quality to the voice, eliminating certain volumes and dampening the sound of breathing. The disembodied voice, already a major form of communication since the mid-twentieth century, is now also a mainstay of intimate communication and communication between government and citizen. Therefore, each citizen is a mini-director, determining which photographic, audiographic and cinematic experiences to broadcast to their immediate and digital networks. Likewise, each citizen is also the subject of a grand cinematic surveillance project which tracks movements and predicts future events through these cinematic projections.

The architectural landscape of the new apartheid reflects these new shifts in technology and subjectivity, lending a new aesthetic to corporate centres of new apartheid power. Slowly, architecture has shifted from the brutalist concrete structures of the apartheid state to the chic corporate glass facades of the new apartheid.[381]

Glass pervades the new apartheid, from the glass-screened orbs in our pockets to the glowing panes on our desks; from the camera lenses which track us to the glazed edifices of corporate skyscrapers. The glass faces of the new apartheid are windows of one-way visibility, giving the illusion of transparency. Those behind the glass – corporations, people or silicon-laden machines – exert power over the world around them, down to the computational inch. But those looking into the glass see only their own reflections.

Behind these glass veils lie the designs of power. The glass-screened devices in our pockets – like the glass-panelled skyscrapers under which we scurry – are symbols of power's growing unidirectionality. Conversely, the direction of control between human and technological devices is increasingly ambiguous: more and more, to control technology means to be controlled by it.

Mobile phones, as objects of fascination, addiction and influence, remain mysterious to their owners. Even their manufacturers struggle to understand their full complexity. Basic acts of communication, like emails and video calls, now rely on infrastructures that are incomprehensible to the average user.[382] Most people simply press a button and watch the magic unfold. But ignoring what happens 'behind the glass' leaves us vulnerable to manipulation: we do not know where to look, or to whom to turn, when our magical glass beacons become the agents of other consciousnesses.

For all this change, South African inequality remains stubbornly unchanged. This creates widespread feelings of impotence and helplessness. These emotions are uniquely captured in works of speculative fiction. For example, ideas of death defiance and resurrection resonate powerfully in South African literature today. Zombies and ghosts conjure angst by revealing the deeper fear of a resurrection of White supremacy itself.

As Jean and John Comaroff remark:

> The recent explosion of electronic communications has greatly accelerated the dissemination of narratives of the supernatural, digging deep

into the archive of gothic, transcultural, and futuristic exotica: of zombies, vampires, revenants, wiccans, genies, jinns, and tokoloshes, all of them pulsing with the realistic half-life of digital animation.[383]

In her book *Moxyland*, Beukes imagines a Cape Town of pervading 'corporate apartheid', where the mobile phone is the new dompas. Beukes ironises contemporary Cape Town by hinting, between the lines, at the similarity between this fantastical dystopia and everyday life *eKapa*, where identities are coded by mouse clicks and the mobile phone mediates government and citizen. Today, our digital footprints reveal our preferences, movements and biometric information. In the hands of a bad actor, it is enough to make even the most ardent apartheid apparatchik squeamish. Fiction and reality are more blurred than we might think, Beukes suggests.

In this way, literary thinkers probe at the fold between the new apartheid and digital hyper-connectivity, and the ways in which both remake the self. As Rogers Brubaker puts it: '[Digital hyper-connectivity] has created new ways of being and constructing a self, but also new ways of being constructed as a self from the outside, new ways of being configured, represented, and governed as a self by sociotechnical systems.'[384]

CONCLUSION

In this chapter, I have argued that apartheid did not die; it algorithmicised. I did so by considering three aspects of technological change since 1994. First, I considered how new technologies of categorisation reinforce apartheid logics of classification. Second, I investigated the growing role of algorithms in the social, political and economic life of South Africans. Last, I analysed the remaking of human subjectivity in the data age.

Prior to the neoliberal era, corporations tended to avoid two kinds of activities: those regarded as intensely public (like public safety) and those regarded as intensely private (like memories, private reflections, and connections with friends and family). In the new apartheid, corporations have increasingly encroached on the limits of both sides of this spectrum. Technological changes since 1994 – including the growth of algorithms, the rise of personal computing, and the ubiquity of mobile phones – have thus fundamentally reshaped the relationship between corporations, people and the state. Yet despite these sweeping changes, apartheid's 'legacy codes' have proved stubbornly resilient. This suggests that apartheid is resistant to monumental technological transformations.

Algorithms are both 'weapons of math destruction'[385] and 'weapons of mass distraction,'[386] which threaten to humanise machines and mechanise humans. In the decades to come, algorithms will govern not just appliances and gadgets but the social, economic and political tides that shape democracy, creating new waves of exploitation and alienation along the way.

Punishment

The transition to democracy in South Africa . . . opened up a social and moral vacuum in the national consciousness, a vacuum in which the fear of violent crime, real and imagined, seeded itself deeply.
– *Jean Comaroff and John Comaroff*[387]

In this chapter, I trace the new apartheid in crime and punishment. I begin by reflecting on the spectre of violent crime. I then examine South Africa's worrying rate of incarceration, before analysing the privatisation of policing and criminal justice. In doing this, I illustrate the new apartheid from the perspective of criminal justice – a perspective central to the inequities of the constitutional era.

VIOLENCE AND CONFINEMENT

Violent crime haunts South Africa's democracy. Yet, as Jonny Steinberg puts it, 'South Africa talks incessantly about crime, but dares not think about it much'.[388] Over half a million people have been murdered in South Africa since 1994.[389] One in 100 000 people report a violent crime each year and over a fifth of crimes in South Africa are violent.[390] By comparison, the US – hardly an exemplar of social peace – sees 380 violent crimes per 100 000 people, only 15 per cent of which are violent.[391] According to the United Nations Office on Drugs and Crime, South Africa ranked ninth in the world for intentional homicides, at a rate of 36 per 100 000 people.[392] In places like Philippi East in Cape Town, the intentional homicide rate dwarfs those of war zones like Afghanistan and Iraq.[393]

To be South African is to live in fear of senseless and sadistic criminal victimisation. It is to reckon with a subtle terrorism overhanging day-to-day tasks. Though civil war was averted by the democratic transition, a slow-motion conflict has raged on South Africa's streets since democracy's inception.[394] No one is immune from this terrifying scourge, from the informal settlements of Johannesburg to the rural corners of the Northern Cape.

Yet, the prevalence of violent crime escapes simple explanation. Countries with similar poverty to South Africa experience, on the whole, less violent crime. South Africa's violent crime also often involves a performative aspect, not tied directly to economic incentives. Violent crime reveals the underbelly of a traumatised and traumatic society, broken at the spine – a nation suppressing a history too painful to face.

One explanation for South Africa's violent crime rate is economic inequality: when a small segment of society owns a disproportionate share of its wealth, that wealth is more likely to be violently seized by the deprived. Crime happens, according to this logic, when its payoff exceeds the risk of punishment. And, in South Africa, there is not only much deprivation but also much to steal.

However, evidence for the link between inequality and violent crime is unclear. On one hand, scholars like Adeleye and Jamal confirm the relationship by plotting various countries' homicide rates against their Gini coefficients (a measure of wealth inequality).[395] They find that, in South Africa and Latin America, homicide rates and Gini coefficients are simultaneously high, suggesting a correlation. This is particularly egregious in southern Africa, where countries like South Africa, Namibia and Lesotho experience high violent crime and high inequality.

But economists like Haroon Bhorat and colleagues find 'no relationship between violent crime and inequality or unemployment' in South Africa.[396] Rather, in their view, inequality explains 'resource crimes' like robbery and property crime but not *violent* crime. In fact, violent crime seems to increase up to a certain level of unemployment, but then mysteriously decreases as unemployment rises further. Moreover, violent crime is constant across different districts though these districts see different levels of inequality, a result also found a decade earlier by Demombynes and Özler.[397] This suggests that inequality does not, by itself, explain South Africa's violent crime epidemic.

Instead, a wider look at South African society is necessary. First, South Africa is unique in coupling economic inequality with severe state incapacity – especially in the area of criminal justice. The scale of South Africa's criminal impunity is yet to be fully appreciated. Reports of the National Prosecuting Authority (NPA) illustrate the malaise. A 2019 NPA report on criminal prosecution shows that a triumvirate of violent crimes – vehicle hijacking, home robbery and business robbery – went 'virtually unpunished' that year.[398]

For example, while the South African Police Service reported over 16 000 hijackings in 2019, the NPA only successfully prosecuted around 2 per cent of that number. Furthermore, less than 5 per cent of home robberies were successfully convicted and under 10 per cent of sexual offences.[399] Clearly, South Africa combines monstrous inequality with frustrating state ineptitude.

This is not always the case in unequal economies. For example, in authoritarian states, harsh law enforcement often accompanies inequality. Hence, estimates of North Korean inequality rival South Africa's, but North Korean violent crime does not.[400] So, South Africa's confluence of state incapacity and economic unfairness feeds violent crime.

But this cannot explain the depth of the violence of crime. Something about South Africa's twisted history of racial dispossession must be considered. In one sense, South Africa has always been a prison for Black people. Apartheid was a system of mass confinement – a living maze of infrastructure and geography separating and entangling races. To be Black was to be the subject of panoramic law enforcement. When Black people violated these all-encompassing laws, they were thrown in yet smaller prisons. Apartheid was a labyrinth of jails within jails.

Violent crime is still disproportionately committed by Black men and still disproportionately affects Black people. This leads various scholars to locate violent crime in South Africa's long history of Black criminalisation. The intense social dislocation of apartheid often destroyed families and tore social bonds. As Don Pinnock shows, Cape Town's criminal gangs can be traced to the forced removal of Coloured communities from District Six to the Cape Flats.[401] These removals created a reservoir of disaffected, excluded youth.

For these reasons, lines between the political and the criminal have always been deceptive. From the instant that pass laws criminalised Black movement and shunted Black people into open-air confinement, prisons became symbols of Black oppression. As Parker and Mokhesi-Parker suggest, the histories of incarceration and forced labour have also always been intertwined in South Africa:

> [In South Africa] the criminal law dovetailed with the forced labour
> system; for those found drinking, those without passes, those unable
> to pay a hut or poll tax, those who left, disobeyed, or swore at their
> employer, or were drunk or careless at work, those unable to prove
> they were not leading 'an idle, dissolute or disorderly life' were all
> guilty of a criminal offence and were funnelled through the magistrates' courts and whether fined, and unable to pay the fine, or straightforwardly jailed, most would end up working once more, albeit this
> time as prison labourers, on white farms or down white mines, where
> toil was extracted by force.[402]

Under colonialism and apartheid, forced labour was rife on mines, state projects and farms. The criminal justice system thus provided free labour for the system of economic exploitation, and vice versa. This model was first perfected by the arch-imperialist, Cape politician and mining magnate, Cecil Rhodes.

> In the 1880s Cecil John Rhodes' De Beers had built a quasi-jail to
> house local prisoners to work on its mines. It began with 300 Black
> men 'of long sentences'. By 1903, the government promised De Beers
> a daily average of 11 000 Black workers. The company by then had

2 000 convicts at work under, by one account, 'the harshest disciplinary regime of any prison' in the Cape Colony. By 1945, 1 400 long-term non-white prisoners laboured in the mines. The government saw the value of cheap labour for its construction projects, too. In 1912, 20 000 Africans served out their jail sentences on the three largest road construction camps in the country.[403]

This legacy stretched long into the twentieth century. For example, until 1980 farmers were allowed to build prisons on their farms which would be managed by the state. Prisoners were then required to perform convict labour on farms. As late as 1973, these labour camps housed about 10 000 long-term prisoner-labourers.[404] And, so, the cultures which grew inside South Africa's prisons were tinged from inception with narratives of Black political resistance.

The tale of Nongoloza – the mythical figure who binds South Africa's prison gangs, the 26s, 27s and 28s – testifies to this reality. Nongoloza's story, in its historical and mythical forms, has survived for over a century and, more recently, has become the focus of literature, scholarship and popular culture.

Born Mzuzephi Mathebula, Nongoloza arrived in Johannesburg in 1886 after fleeing life as an exploited horse groom on a farm in Harrismith.[405] A bitter dispute with his 'master' caused his desertion: Nongoloza was accused of negligence after losing one of the farm's horses. His punishment was two years' wages and time on the whipping board. Incensed by the injustice, he escaped the farm that had become his jail before punishment could be delivered, and journeyed towards a newly emerging city.[406]

Nongoloza – meaning either 'one who glares' or' one who sits in silence' – eventually joined a band of White highway robbers who preyed on vulnerable coaches making their way to the burgeoning mining metropolis of Johannesburg.[407] After serving this criminal apprenticeship, Nongoloza deserted again to found 'a quasi-military band' of Black outlaws, united by a 'simple but potent ideology of banditry-as-anti-colonial-resistance'.[408] They would become the Ninevites or, to their members, *amadla amahashi* (those who eat horses).

Legend has it that a seer named Po guided Nongoloza and his accomplice Ngeleketshane to a life of banditry in response to the exploitation of Black mine workers. Nongoloza himself was motivated by a proto-revolutionary ethos: the Ninevites were named after the biblical city of Nineveh, which rebelled against God's laws. 'I was rebelling against the Government's laws,' Nongoloza averred when interviewed by a warder decades after founding the Ninevites.[409]

The Ninevites were a pseudo-militaristic mini-state inspired by Zulu, Boer and British practices. Nongoloza was *inkosi enkulu* (the big chief). Below him were an array of traditional doctors, 'landdroste' (magistrates) and 'generals'. As if to symbolise this uniquely South African fusion, Mathebula's pseudonym, which was Jan Note, combined Afrikaans and British origins. The gang also upended social mores by endorsing homosexuality a century before it was decriminalised in South Africa. But Nongoloza was no undercover Leninist. His bandits targeted vulnerable African migrants and developed a reputation for abominable violence.

After Nongoloza's multiple incarcerations, Ninevite traditions mutated inside South Africa's prisons, gathering a life of their own. Nongoloza was eventually elevated into an invulnerable anti-colonial deity capable of walking through prison walls and evading bullets. Ironically, he was being converted into a prison warder by colonial authorities at the moment that his myth was spreading.[410]

The Number – the prison gang that emerged from this history – developed elaborate laws and punishments based on the lore of Nongoloza. It fashioned a system of ironclad loyalties and visceral punishments which corrupted anti-colonial resistance into a gratuitous cult of violence and patriarchal dominance. Under the guise of liberation, the Number mimicked the worst excesses of the apartheid penal system and bound its members to a draconian code of prodigious gratuity.

Like so many of apartheid's so-called relics, the Number has survived and thrived in the new apartheid. Nongoloza's children have multiplied in the new republic. Since 1994, South Africa's prison population has ballooned to over 150 000 people, including more children and more people serving longer sentences. By 2004, South Africa boasted one of the world's highest incarceration rates, at around 400 inmates per 100 000 people.[411] This number has fallen since then to about 25 per 100 000, still placing South Africa in the top quarter of countries by incarceration rate. These changes in the prison population mirror patterns in crime, but also themselves reflect changes in the social tapestry of the new apartheid. Never before has South Africa seen so many people incarcerated – the vast majority of whom are Black men.

The racial composition of South Africa's prisons has also changed: around 98 per cent of inmates are Black today, compared to about 96 per cent during apartheid.[412] The stubbornness of Black incarceration is staggering when one considers that several crimes were reserved specially for Black people during apartheid. For instance, 17 million Black people were arrested for pass-related infractions between 1924 and 1984.[413]

The enactment of minimum sentences through the seemingly banal Criminal Law Amendment Act of 1997 shows how democratic policies have expanded Black incarceration.[414] This apparently insignificant policy change has packed correctional facilities, leading to the mass incarceration of Black men. Minimum sentences legislate the smallest duration for which someone can be imprisoned for a given crime. They prevent judges from regulating sentences by imposing strict limits on judicial discretion. In this context, minimum sentences were originally seen as a fast fix for violent crime: by increasing the length of punishment, South Africa could deter crime, or so some believed.

Minimum sentences were always only a temporary measure. They were enacted for an initial two years to 'restore stability' to the criminal justice system. But, once the new laws arrived, they were normalised and subsequently extended every two years until eventually becoming permanent in 2007.[415]

Minimum sentences are supposed to deter crime: offenders are thought to assess a crime's risk by the severity of its punishment. If punishment is costly, then the risk increases and the rational criminal is dissuaded. This assumption breaks down in practice, however. For one thing, sentences are not widely known throughout society. Few criminals are aware of minimum sentences for the crimes they commit. In reality, offenders hardly inspect the Criminal Law Amendment Act before committing crime.

Even if minimum sentences did deter crime, they would still be unhelpful in South Africa: punishment only deters crime when punishment is *expected*. If rational criminals expect to evade justice, however, then the severity of the escaped punishment diminishes in relevance. And, in the case of South Africa's criminal justice system, a rational criminal has ample reason to expect to evade accountability, because the system of criminal prosecution and investigation is broken. As Edwin Cameron – former Constitutional Court justice and inspecting judge of the Judicial Inspectorate for Correctional Services – suggests, 'criminals are primarily deterred by the risk of being caught. In themselves, longer sentences have no discernible deterrent impact.'

In reality, then, minimum sentences have been counterproductive. They have bred a mistaken sense of security, while ignoring the basic causes of crime. They have damaged offenders' lives and swollen the number of prisoners. They have hampered and constrained the judicial system. They have allowed politicians to appear proactive, without addressing fundamental inadequacies in criminal justice – from policing, to investigation, to prosecution. And, above all, they have re-encoded a dangerously racialised system of criminal punishment.

Minimum sentences for non-violent drug offences and petty crimes disproportionately target young Black men, even though non-violent drug use is endemic across races. As Cameron again notes, 'Black people are less likely to have access to the sophisticated drug networks which avoid punishment; Black people are more likely to be punished for crimes that their White counterparts also commit.'[416] A joint report by the Civil Society Prison Reform Initiative, Just Detention International and Lawyers for Human Rights concurs:

In 2013/14 the South African Police Service (SAPS) made 1 392 856 arrests of which 818 322 (59%) were for priority crimes and 574 534

(41%) for non-priority crimes. Of priority crimes 22% were drug-related. Research has also found that between one in eight and one in thirteen adult men aged between 18 to 65 years are arrested annually in South Africa, assuming that no one is arrested more than once in a year. The data therefore indicate that large numbers of adult males are annually arrested for crimes that do not pose a serious threat to public safety.[417]

In addition, poor Black suspects cannot always access the legal services that may prevent harsher sentences or shorter detention periods. What we have, then, is a system in which poor Black people struggle to access the law on equal terms, and are punished disproportionately for it.

And yet democratic South Africa is drenched in mythologies of over-coming incarceration – from Nelson Mandela's triumph over Robben Island, to the Constitutional Court's foundation on the ruins of a former pass law jail. This mythology also assumes gendered dimensions, as the struggle over incarceration is often painted as men's struggle. Democratic South Africa's promise is bound up in breaking bondage. But, perhaps, a different allegory is more apt: the allegory of the Black prison warder. Perhaps Nongoloza, the inmate-turned-warder, and not Mandela, the inmate-turned-president, represents what has happened since the end of apartheid.

In the transition to democracy, jails once controlled by apartheid apparatchiks were transferred to the democratic government; from White management to Black management. In the correctional system, unlike the corporate boardroom, this transferral to Black management was relatively swift. But the chalice was poisoned. Black warders and correctional officials inherited a chronically unstable, grossly over-crowded and chaotically violent system which claimed their lives, limbs and psychological states. Black warders replaced White ones as the canvas upon which the Number sharpened its knives and elaborated its violent rituals. This chronic instability has lasted for the duration of the post-apartheid period. To be a South African correctional official today is still to dance with death. This is why the South African Correctional Services Workers' Union was forced to plead, in 2019:

> Enough is enough, this has to stop. It is high time that the department [of Correctional Services] be litigated for these negligent incidents from its side. The department gave offenders more rights than our own officials. The trend will show that offenders target the weekend knowing exactly that centres are short-staffed.[418]

This changeover of warders is allegorical of the democratic transition itself: the new Black government would assume responsibility for the larger prison of South Africa – still a place of townships, informal settlements and invisibly demarcated Bantustans. Black politicians would become accountable for resolving an infinity of 'wicked' socio-economic ills – as the warders of a new society still teeming with all the horrors of Pandora's box. They would become the new front line in a potentially unwinnable war. Meanwhile, the agents of apartheid would recede from view, no longer liable for the chaotic currents they had unleashed.

One crucial ingredient is still missing from the story of violent crime and growing incarceration: that of South Africa's harmful masculinities. For, if violent crime is caused by a history of social oppression, then Black women ought to be its main perpetrators. Instead, they are its major victims. Violence perpetrated by men against women is a defining feature of the new apartheid. In this realm, as in others, violence ranges from the incomprehensible to the macabre.

In February 2021, Mpho Thobane was sentenced to twenty years' imprisonment for dousing his girlfriend, Viwe Dalingozi, in petrol and setting her alight. Dalingozi died in hospital two days later after last-ditch attempts at resuscitation. It was just one drop in an ocean of violent crime directed at women by men. And, by 2021, it was a story that failed to capture the public imagination for more than a few hours.

The term 'femicide' denotes the killing of women by men and the inherent power relations involved in such killing. Femicide takes different forms: the killing of women by strangers, the killing of women by people known to them (and, within this category, by their intimate partners), and the killing of women after rape. This makes femicide a distinct form of violence.[419] In a study of South African femicide for the year 1999, Lisa Vetten found that 40 per cent of cases were intimate femicides (where the perpetrator was known to the woman) and 41 per cent were non-intimate (where the perpetrator was not known). That year, the femicide rate was a staggering 24.7 per 100 0000 women. Ten years later, the rate had dropped, in line with overall homicide, to 12.9 deaths per 100 000 women – still a staggering level. As Nechama Brodie observes:

> A 2016 Small Arms Survey report estimated that in Syria in 2015 this figure (for women) was 25.7 per 100,000, while that of intimate-partner femicide was 8.8/100,000 – at the time, the highest figure(s) reported in research anywhere in the world.[420]

Shanaaz Mathews, Rachel Jewkes and Naeemah Abrahams have investigated femicide through interviews with twenty incarcerated men who killed their partners.[421] They found that childhood adversity contributed to their subjects' actions but did not explain them fully. Rather, femicide was often seen by its perpetrators as an exaggerated display of masculinity. Theirs is a harrowing study of the words of murderers who continue to blame their victims for their own deaths; one which shows these men's deep-seated inability to reckon with their own sense of inadequacy. Their findings corroborate Jock Young's claim that violent crime often emanates from 'a solution to the deep-seated crisis of identity faced by young men . . . to delineate themselves more clearly by exaggerating or essentialising one attribute "the system" cannot easily take away: their masculinity'.[422]

Femicide is not new. Brodie shows, by investigating newspaper reports since the 1970s, that it has long plagued South Africa. The continued prevalence of femicide illuminates the resemblances between past and present South Africa. The mistaken assumption that democracy would automatically reduce social violence has proved deceptive. South African masculinity – forged in the multiple fires of colonialism, hyper-exploitation, crass consumerism and apartheid – is geared towards a toxic mix of violence and silence.[423] This destructive masculinity is key to appreciating the continued salience of violence – and violence against women – in the new apartheid.

The femicide epidemic reveals that apartheid was as much a project of gender engineering as one of racial engineering. Apartheid dictated through law that women's identities would be centred around the family. And, through this confinement to the domestic sphere, women became objects of gross oppression. One key example was the marital rape exemption, which granted immunity from prosecution to husbands who raped their wives; this lasted long into late apartheid.[424]

A Law Commission Report of 1985 recommended abolishing this exemption. But the virtually all-male apartheid Parliament rejected it: even as the NP was warming to negotiations with Black activists, it clung to a conception of women as care-givers and baby-making machines. Throughout apartheid, domestic violence was only addressed in laws dealing with neighbourly irritations like loud music. In its final throes, apartheid passed the Family Violence Act, which circumscribed the evil of violence against women in the context of the family home.[425]

This echoed beyond 1994, as the new government addressed an ever-expanding crisis of violence against women. The democratic government's response framed women in the context of vulnerability, often associating their plight with that of children. The 1995 Reconstruction and Development Programme promised to pay 'special attention to the problem of violence against women and children'. This framing obscured the political dimensions of violence against women and treated women as inherently fragile.

Indeed, men were – and are – more vulnerable to violence in South Africa than women, because the incidence of violence between women is far lower than violence between men. Women are only vulnerable because they are targeted for violence by men. The problem, then, is not the vulnerability of women but the vulnerability of men to violence.[426]

A second wave of governmental policy shifted focus to 'gender-based violence'.[427] This definition was, again, too vague to name the problem of men's violence against women. It suggested that violence against men by women was equally deserving of urgent attention. The ambiguity produced concrete problems: one of the measures envisaged in the policy was the creation of shelters for the victims of 'gender-based violence'. Soon, men began envisaging themselves as such victims, or pretending to be such victims to gain food and shelter. As a result, these shelters increasingly accommodated men.

Black women thus suffer a double oppression in the new republic: racism from White men and women, and patriarchy from White and Black men. The end of apartheid removed only legal barriers to the one, while leaving the other entrenched. Take, for instance, a study of sexual assault in Tshwane, which shows that

> Roughly 65% of recorded sexual crime occurs in Black African neighbourhoods compared with 25% in Mixed neighbourhoods and 10% in White neighbourhoods. Rape accounts for the majority of sexual crimes occurring in neighbourhoods across all racial groups and is almost seven times higher in Black African neighbourhoods than White neighbourhoods and more than two times higher than in Mixed neighbourhoods.[428]

The new apartheid has failed to generate alternative masculinities. Rather, the masculinities of old have adapted and evolved into the democratic era.[429] Violence against women remains entrenched even as democratic rights have expanded. The scale and extent of this violence call for a reappraisal of the gains made in the democratic transition itself. For violence against women, like other forms of violent crime, threatens to undermine the very social fabric of the new republic.

The persistence of violent crime also creates political vacuums into which opportunistic actors jump with abandon. The 'White genocide' myth is a case in point. This myth suggests that White people are being widely murdered by Black people *because* they are White. This, according to the myth, occurs especially on commercial farms. Here violent crime is converted into a pretext for racial seclusion and projects of White secession.

To be sure, White South Africans have suffered extreme violence since 1994. And, to be sure, extreme and unconscionable violence occurs on commercial farms – the vast majority of which are White-owned. But the deductive leap from this reality to a genocidal conspiracy strains the bounds of credulity – and, I might add, affronts real victims of genocide. White farmers are no different from the Black people who suffer violent crime, except that White farmers happen to own more agricultural land and property. The violence they face is real and senseless. So is the violence faced by the residents of informal settlements and suburbs.

As Brodie notes, claims of genocide 'exaggerated the level of killings of White South Africans while simultaneously ignoring the extremely high levels of fatal violence experienced by Black and Coloured South Africans'.[430] This claim is supported by Gregory Breetzke, who finds dramatic differences in people's experiences of crime, depending on their race. In Tshwane, about 58 per cent of violent crimes affect Black African neighbourhoods, as opposed to 29 per cent in '[racially] mixed' neighbourhoods and 13 per cent in White neighbourhoods.[431]

By contrast, household burglary disproportionately affects White neighbourhoods. Interestingly, crime was most pervasive in Tshwane's mixed neighbourhoods, but *violent* crimes were concentrated in Black neighbourhoods. Racialised patterns of farm murder are simply products of widespread violent crime, on the one hand, and racially unequal patterns of farm ownership, on the other. Separating these crimes from the crimes experienced by all other South Africans is only a ploy to build conservative solidarities.

In sum, violent crime has proven remarkably resilient in the new apartheid. It has also increasingly been privatised. In the political maelstrom of the early 1990s, over 14 000 people died in political violence.[432] After 1994, violent crime replaced political violence as a pre-eminent social fear; concern over private property and personal safety displaced anxiety over the political order. During apartheid, the question of violence had large public and political dimensions. Would the ANC renounce violence? Would the apartheid state cease its relentless violence? Would protests turn violent? And, while state violence remains a major concern in the new apartheid, private violence has come to dominate: private altercations which turn murderous; hidden acts of sexual violence known only to two people; robberies in bedrooms and kitchens. The anxiety of the new apartheid is an anxiety over private violence – a violence which, though it has diminished since the late 1990s, proceeds on a horrifying scale.

Violent crime thus continues to wrong-foot the ANC. Since 1995, its crime policy has dallied between appearing 'tough on crime' and embracing the new rights-based order. This tension is reflected in the Correctional Services Act of 1998, which on the one hand seeks 'the enhancement of human dignity', but, on the other, reinforces prison labour: 'all prisoners must . . . perform any labour which is related to any development programme or which generally is designed to foster habits of industry, unless the medical officer or psychologist certifies in writing that he or she is physically or mentally unfit to perform such labour'.[433] But, instead of stemming violent crime and curbing incarceration, the ANC has proved powerless against both. And this failure points to underlying problems with the democratic project itself. Beneath the glossy veneer of the 'rainbow nation' is a dark untold history, a history of gory crime and mass imprisonment. This history is no unfortunate by-product of an otherwise noble trajectory. Rather, it is a solemn warning about the fragility of the new republic itself.

POLICING AND JUSTICE

Apartheid has always needed violence to survive. Forced removals, political assassinations, massacres and mass imprisonments all maintained the apartheid state. Apartheid's notorious police force was a key institution in this violence. The conversion of violence from public to private institutions provides, therefore, an important window into the persistence of apartheid under democracy. The new apartheid uses a wide repressive apparatus of its own, designed to entrench power and property relations. But this apparatus exists parallel to state control, permeating malls, recreational areas, transport terminals and busy streets.

On any given weekday, Van Beek Street in Doornfontein, Johannesburg, is lined with hundreds of Black men. They vie for a qualification from the South African Security Academy – the key to a job in the sprawling private security industry. Now South Africa's fourth-largest employer, the private security industry spans around 10 000 companies and nearly half a million active private guards – a force bigger than the army and police service combined.[434] The industry has become central to the economy, accounting for nearly 4 per cent of employment and a similar size of GDP. South Africa's private guards protect and patrol the labyrinthine borders of the new apartheid.

Private security forces now control large parts of otherwise public space, increasingly usurping the role of the police. The privatisation of South Africa's most valuable commercial region, Sandton, illustrates the extreme end of this trend. City Improvement Districts (CIDs) style themselves as 'self-governed districts that are initiated and governed by property and business owners to operate within a designated urban and suburban area' on the basis of 'a reduced role for the local government and transferring the service provision responsibilities to private stakeholders'.[435] Or, in simple language, CIDs aim to replace the state.

According to the Sandton Central Management District, the umbrella body of three Sandton CIDs, 'these three improvement districts . . . manage the public space bound by Sandton Drive, Katherine Street into Wierda Road East and West, West Street, along Rivonia Road and including Grayston Drive'.[436] South Africa now has 50 CIDs, with 30 in Johannesburg alone. CIDs have also developed tax-collecting powers: Johannesburg CIDs currently collect approximately R100 million in taxes annually. Two-thirds of this expenditure goes to 'supplementary public space safety'.

However, this 'public safety' is inevitably equated with commercial safety rather than protecting people from violence. Security companies account not to the state but to the businesses which fund them, and they are prepared to use force against citizens, if necessary. Private security companies thus become the 'arbitrators of access to, and accepted conduct within', the areas under their control.[437] This loosens the state's grip on violence in important commercial centres – a central feature of legitimate state power.

Neighbourhood residents' associations play a similar role in formerly White suburbs. As this excerpt from the Saxonwold and Parkwood Residents' Association 2018/19 Annual Report shows, privatised security strategies are common occurrences:

> There have been a number of thefts of motor vehicles at the Woolworths parking lot in Wells Avenue. It is hoped that the recent erection of palisade fencing will reduce the number of incidents. Although there are security guards at the parking lot, they are unarmed and, understandably, unwilling to confront the thieves who are armed. A more effective security presence funded by the landlords and shop owners is needed.[438]

The extent of this private power cannot be underestimated. In a survey of security guards in the Sandton CID, 36 per cent of them said they would 'forcibly remove the homeless and vagrants from the space by physically manhandling them' while 61 per cent said they would arrest them if they did not cooperate. Guards also regularly confiscate goods from 'vagrants' and 'illegal' traders. They are also encouraged to crack down on 'dustbin hunting', rough sleeping, hawking and begging. Small traders who obtain licences to work inside the CID are, in turn, bound by by-laws which prevent them from 'creating nuisance'. But only 11 per cent of security guards had read these by-laws. CID security personnel admitted to targeting suspects by the clothes they wore, with an emphasis on 'torn clothes'.

The very lines between private and public policing have become intertwined. The private security industry is now so much a part of South African life that its legitimacy goes unquestioned. Criminals, too, are known to dress up as police before they hijack cars or steal watches. This creates a sense of insecurity within the new apartheid. One is never quite sure in South Africa whether a police vehicle is a vector of crime prevention, crime itself, or some collaboration of interests in-between.

The role of these new privatised police officers is ultimately to exclude certain categories of people from commercial centres. Although their task is not avowedly racist, the patterns of racial exclusion cannot be avoided. Sandton comes to represent all spaces of privilege in South Africa, from malls to universities. Black people moving through these spaces occupy an ambiguous role. They are either rightful residents deserving of protection, or they are threats who must be surveilled and policed. Hence, in order to avoid the attentions of these private police forces Black people must develop a sophisticated and unspoken language to project their legitimacy.

This language involves subtle hints in body language, acts of faux confidence and, most importantly, a set of economic signals through clothing and car ownership. But these signals cannot be too extreme, either, lest Black people be confused for drug dealers. This delicate balance cannot always be struck, and innocent Black people moving through these spaces of privilege inevitably conflict with private armies – also made up of Black guards – which are tasked with categorising Black bodies as dangerous or safe. The signals that Black people send as they move through these privately patrolled worlds are, in fact, similar to the pass books of old. They explain, in part, why even the most progressive Black people often revert to flashy symbols of opulence. These symbols offer protection from violence just as they confer social status.

But, tragically, they can also attract violence and moral condemnation. Black people cannot be too rich or too poor in the new apartheid. They must occupy a safe middle ground between the two. The regulations of the new apartheid are often unwritten and unspoken. But they are no less effective. The role of private police is ultimately to patrol these regulations by excluding suspicious persons. This exclusion is underwritten by private power.

Racial biases in policing have long been a feature of apartheid. Apartheid, like other forms of oppression, is about inequality of privilege *and* punishment: White people are easily excused, and Black people excessively penalised, for the same acts. White supremacy is founded on impunity for White people and unflinching harshness for everyone else. For example, between 1986 and 1989 Louis van Schoor – a White security guard – shot over 1 000 people, 39 of whom died. Yet police later testified that Van Schoor could not be held culpable for the killings and a coroner stated under oath that the killings were 'part of his job'. He was released after twelve years of his twenty-year sentence and was only ever convicted for seven murders. Another 1987 case, recounted by Parker and Mokhesi-Parker, underscores dramatic differentials in punishment under apartheid:

> Mr Eric Sambo drove a tractor over two of his employer's puppies. Two months later the employer, a Mr Jacobus Vorster, tied him to a tree, fired shots above his head and, over the next day, and punctuated by beer and a barbecue, he and a fellow farmer took turns kicking him, punching him, whipping him, until he died, whereupon Vorster drove the body to the police station. It was only publicity, however, that pushed the police into doing anything. The murder charges were soon converted into pleas of guilty to culpable homicide for Vorster and to assault for his friend. The judge fined the friend R500, Vorster R3 000, ordering him also to pay Mr Sambo's widow R130 a month for five years.[439]

By contrast, Black people were often sentenced extremely harshly for relatively minor crimes, like 'playing struggle songs', 'possessing subversive literature', or merely 'possessing a mug with ANC slogans on it'.[440] Even when Black and White people committed the same crime, as happened on the same day before the same judge in 1985 over parking infractions, the White person was fined R50 and the Black person R200. When members of the virulent White power organisation, the AWB, unlawfully stowed rifles and ammunition, Judge A. P. van Dyk,[441] who issued harsh sentences to ANC freedom fighters, averred that these extreme-right nationalists were 'civilised and decent people . . . the victims of an unfortunate combination of circumstances' and that 'the community would certainly not expect me to send them to jail for that'.[442]

This inequality of punishment is now administered by private police. But it is also executed by Black men. The racial hierarchy of the private security complex is a unique blend of old and new apartheid. Like the apartheid security apparatus, the industry is still controlled and managed by White men – some of them even drawn from the old apartheid security infrastructure.[443] However, unlike the apartheid police force, the industry's lower ranks are filled almost exclusively with Black men. This represents a great inversion. During apartheid, state repression relied on a large base of White policemen and military officers. In the private security industry, however, this is no longer the case. The logic of the market has produced an unlikely alliance: White financiers and business owners flock to the private security industry for profits; Black guards are drawn to private security to escape poverty. Together they police every corner of private privilege in the country.

Democracy has thus produced a pact between White security companies and Black security guards which subverts some racial hierarchies and preserves others. To be policed in South Africa now means to be policed by Black men. But to be Black is also to be the target of policing. White South Africans have managed to extricate themselves both from the suspicion of law enforcement and also from law enforcement's dirty work.

The role of private power extends beyond private policing. Today's major security companies have expanded their reach into investigation, financial services, surveillance and technology. These combined services are known in the industry as 'convergence' or the unification of once-unrelated security services. Through their superior convergence strategies, private security companies have even assumed responsibility for sensitive government buildings and institutions, like the South African Broadcasting Corporation, the South African Revenue Service, several airports and even the arms manufacturer Denel.

G4S, one of the main players in South Africa's private security and private prison sector, exemplifies this trend. First, G4S is a multinational conglomerate, operating in around a hundred countries and six different regions. It is listed on the London Stock Exchange. Founded as a merger between Danish security company Group 4 and British company Securicor, G4S has been at the centre of several human rights controversies over allegations of excessive force. In South Africa, G4S operates private prisons and has also faced allegations of inmate torture. Yet G4S also has South African ties: its current CEO, Ashley Almanza, is a South African who attended Durban High School. Almanza's origins are murky, but he is known to have served as a security guard in apartheid South Africa before emigrating in 1990.[444]

In the democratic era, G4S has extended its reach into an unprecedented array of sectors and functions. It secures mines and provides 'cash solutions' to retailers, ensuring that the cash that goes into registers is not stolen. G4S also transports cash for banks and makes ATM machines. In many ways, it plays the role of converting cash into wealth, by protecting vulnerable piles of cash flowing out of businesses until they can be deposited into bank accounts. It glues the spaces between points of purchase and wealth accumulation.

G4S is part of a larger set of 'converged' security companies. Local players include Bidvest (through its subsidiary Bidvest Protea Coin) and Mvelaserve, both companies with ties to senior ANC politicians. President Cyril Ramaphosa chaired the board of Bidvest from 2004 to 2013. Bidvest in turn benefited from several important government contracts in the period, in the aviation, security and logistics sectors. Mvelaserve was a subsidiary of Mvelaphanda Group, the holding company part-owned by the former Gauteng premier and prominent ANC member, Tokyo Sexwale. In 2013, the Competition Commission approved a merger between Bidvest and Mvelaserve. As these two entities reveal, the spoils of the private security complex have been shared with connected ANC figures.

The sprawl of private security would not be possible without the sprawl of crime. But both are tangled in the web of historical inequality. South Africa's crime problem, and its crime prevention strategies, reflect the new apartheid, which thrives on a 'bewildering array of security, investigative, and quasi-judicial services'[445] offered by a mix of 'private companies, civic and nongovernmental organisations, religious fraternities, traditional authorities, gangs, even taxi associations'. Or, as Claire Bénit-Gbaffou observes:

> The post-apartheid period is characterised by a twofold and somehow contradictory transformation of security governance. First, there is definitely an attempt to integrate the police system, through the redistribution of police personnel and resources towards deprived townships ... However, the parallel impact of security governance practices leads to fragmentation trends, *de facto* encouraging private security companies in the wealthier parts and community policing and patrolling in the poorer, while municipal policies, informed by the desire to build a globally competitive city, focus mainly on business areas, and *de facto* encourage segregationist practices, directly or indirectly. The regulation of these various local initiatives, which are recognised as fostering inequality, remains highly political.[446]

Privatisation has also spread to correctional facilities. 'We started with a batch of ten prisoners who moved in early in the morning.' These were the words of Correctional Services spokesperson Russel Mamabolo at the opening of South Africa's first private prison, Mangaung Maximum Security Prison, in 2001. Four companies, led by international security firm Group 4 (now G4S), with prison interests in the UK and Australia, founded the facility. The government would pay the company a fixed price per prisoner, then in the region of R90. Group 4 would take responsibility for building the prison and for 'medical treatment, nutrition, recreational and rehabilitation programmes'.

Unlike in the US, private prisons are still relatively rare in South Africa. Only three of South Africa's 240 correctional facilities are private. However, even if prisons themselves are not privatised, the correctional system has been increasingly outsourced since 1994 – from security and food supplies, to IT and logistical support. In this way, private interests have encroached on criminal punishment from within, even as prisons have remained state-controlled. As incarceration rates have increased, so the privatisation of punishment has expanded.

Scandals surrounding Bosasa (later renamed African Global Operations)[447] – a now-notorious corrupt prison contractor – illustrate the problem. Bosasa became a byword for graft in the Zuma era, as senior employees of the firm exposed a prodigious bribery racket between Bosasa and ANC politicians.

In testimony before the State Capture Commission in 2019, former Bosasa chief operating officer Angelo Agrizzi alleged that Bosasa paid gratuitous cash bribes for government contracts with the Department of Correctional Services. Bosasa was said to have kept around R5 million per month in a walk-in bribery vault, which was regularly raided by ANC politicians, who left with 'little grey security bags'.[448] Marked above the entrance to Bosasa's headquarters was an inscription from the book of Deuteronomy: 'You will be blessed when you come in and when you go out.'[449] Between 2013 and 2018, Bosasa scored over R7 billion in tenders from the Department of Correctional Services.[450] Bosasa also 'blessed' the ANC and its leaders, notably contributing R500 000 to President Cyril Ramaphosa's personal campaign for the ANC presidency in 2017.

Recently, privatisation has even encompassed the realm of public prosecution. In 2017, the controversial Afrikaner neo-nationalist group AfriForum announced that it would establish South Africa's first dedicated private prosecution unit. Headed by the renowned prosecutor Gerrie Nel – the advocate who successfully sunk Oscar Pistorius – the unit vowed to address crime and corruption. Upon its launch, Nel said:

I believe in the supreme authority of the law. AfriForum's newly founded private prosecuting unit gives me the opportunity within civilian society to help ensure that everyone, irrespective of position, is equal before the law. AfriForum and I are now in a position to prosecute ourselves corrupt persons who are not prosecuted by the NPA.[451]

The privatisation of justice has gained favour in governmental circles. In 2017, senior government officials began mooting proposals for allowing the NPA – the body tasked with public prosecution in South Africa – to accept private donations:

The potential risk relating to the impact of donor funding on the government, in general, to ensure the protection of objectivity and independence has been thoroughly considered throughout the years by our government . . . This risk has been properly managed through ensuring a proper framework under the auspices of the National Treasury, which regulates the acceptance and allocation of donor funding both internationally and locally.[452]

The National Director of Public Prosecutions, Shamila Batohi, supported this move. In an appearance before the National Assembly's Portfolio Committee on Justice, Batohi suggested:

We have to find a way in which we could access support quickly within the prescripts – with the Public Finance Management Act, the regulatory framework and whatever Treasury guidelines there are, but at the moment we are finding it challenging to quickly access external support that has come from various different entities . . . For example, business wants to support, there are individuals, there are other entities that want to assist the directorate. We really have to look at how we can find a quick mechanism to be able to deal with this.[453]

Batohi and Justice Minister Ronald Lamola do not seem to have learned the lessons of South Africa's history of state capture. It is difficult to see how these private donations could avoid perceptions of bias and escape subversion by wily corporations. How would donations be made transparent? What would happen if donors found themselves in the crosshairs of the NPA? What if wealthy politicians decided to donate to the institution to avoid prosecution? How would the NPA convince the public that they were able to ignore these donations? How would the motives of wicked actors be stopped? If the NPA fell into the hands of an unwise leader, it could potentially gift the entire institution to criminal syndicates. The idea that the NPA could neatly insulate its private donations from perceptions of bias and capture is an exercise in magical thinking. Such an outcome would represent the high point of criminal justice's privatisation. More worryingly, it reveals the extent to which state incapacity continues in effect to cede power to private actors.

CONCLUSION

In this chapter, I have investigated the privatisation of South Africa's criminal punishment system. Criminal punishment provides a unique window into South African society by unveiling power relations from an unfamiliar angle. By analysing how people are policed and incarcerated, we gain new insights into private power's inner logic, beyond grand constitutional proclamations.

How does this chapter advance the larger argument made in this book? Punishment links to all of the other cases already discussed. It links to technology, since the technologies of surveillance and categorisation interface with criminal punishment. It links to law, since privatised justice connects to private law. It links to space, because segregated spaces are often policed by private security corporations. And it links to wealth, since the security corporations instantiate the evolution of corporate wealth since 1994.

The analysis in this chapter leaves me with one abiding impression: to be South African is to be paradoxically surrounded by both punishment and impunity. Indeed, impunity is the evil and unspoken twin of 'reconciliation': if reconciliation underpins the 'new South Africa', then impunity undergirds the new apartheid. South Africa rests on amnesty for the powerful and extreme punishment for the powerless. This amnesty is increasingly extended to powerful ANC leaders. Poor Black people have become the sacrificial lambs from which the democratic order draws its legitimacy. This has produced nihilism, apathy and seething anger. The trauma of apartheid has been replaced with a secondary trauma: that of being sold a faulty product at a hefty price.

The impunity on which the new apartheid rests offends justice. If a negligent driver bumps into an innocent bystander, everyone accepts that the driver owes a duty to compensate the bystander for any damages caused by the driver's negligence. If the damage caused is serious, then the driver may also face punishment in addition to the need for compensation. How much more reparation, then, is due for centuries of oppression caused to all Black people by colonialism and apartheid? And, yet, restitution has proved elusive after democracy. Black people have been persuaded to trade justice for a hollow voting ritual. The new apartheid is a condition in which minor infractions are punished harshly while the gaping wound at the centre of society is ignored. It is a society in where petty violations are meticulously penalised, but gross injustices are perpetually indemnified.

Conclusion

There is thus reason to reopen the coffin and remind ourselves of what apartheid looks like in the flesh.

– J. M. Coetzee[454]

How did the concept of the 'post-apartheid' dissipate in the moment of the post-apartheid?

– Premesh Lalu[455]

Apartheid did not die; it was privatised. This is the single, simple thesis that I have explored in this book. This intuition is not new. Apartheid's persistence is commonly lamented in public discourse. But this lament is rarely pursued in its full depth. This book is thus a detailed reckoning with a common intuition. Its central claim is that apartheid continues in new and unsuspecting guises, despite democracy's inception. Indeed, the resemblances between South Africa's old and new order are stark and distressing. Since 1994, apartheid has adapted, resuscitated and even resurged. This is paradoxical because democracy is commonly seen as apartheid's cure. But democracy is not the antithesis of apartheid. Indeed, democracy can even enable apartheid.

Provocative residual questions flow from these contentions. In this conclusion, I tackle the implications, ambiguities and limitations of my argument. I begin by suggesting that South Africa must radically reform its political order. I then reflect on global debates about racial justice, inequality and democracy. I conclude by considering the shortcomings of my analysis while defending the theoretical potential of the new apartheid.

A NEW REPUBLIC

If what I have said in this book is true, then the country we now know as South Africa must consider far-reaching, even revolutionary political changes. And, so, I begin this conclusion with a provocation: perhaps the time has come to consider a new republic altogether.

What do I mean by a new republic? I mean a radical reformation of South Africa's very constitutional foundations. Grand policy shifts are not enough. Nor can new political parties turn the new apartheid's tides. Protest is insufficient, even if it spans the length and breadth of the country. The new apartheid will also be impervious to constitutional tinkering. Before South Africa can eradicate the new apartheid, it must reconstitute itself.

Sweeping and simultaneous constitutional reforms are, therefore, necessary. I shall venture here to sketch the outlines of such an agenda, though this endeavour requires deeper and wider collective deliberation. First, the arguments I have advanced in the chapter on law suggest that South Africa's Constitution commences from too meek, too mild and too moderate a philosophical departure point. As Tshepo Madlingozi observes, the Constitution omits even the word 'apartheid'.[456] How then can the current Constitution be the antithesis of injustices it is too tame to name? Therefore, reforming South Africa's political order starts with the very ideals on which the nation is founded. And justice as an ideal – not merely a legal mechanism – must take centre stage in a new republic.

Rights and South Africa's approach to them should also be reformulated. The Constitution's ambiguous declarations in section 25 on property rights must be clarified. There should be no room for ambiguity about racial, gender-based and other forms of reparation. These should be framed around the ideal of justice rather than equality. And they should not be called 'positive discrimination' as if to suggest that they are evils to be tolerated. Hence, Chapter 2 of the Constitution must also be closely scrutinised.

The nuts and bolts of political order also need examination. This requires reflection on at least four aspects of South Africa's current political make-up: the electoral system, the separation of powers, the devolution of power, and the extent of power vested in various arms and offices of government. This would require reforming Chapters 3, 4, 5, 6, 7 and 10 and Schedules 3, 4 and 4b of the Constitution.

First, the electoral system needs an overhaul. This includes changing how public representatives are selected to stand for election, and reconsidering the system of closed-list proportional representation, which in effect grants parties the power to choose their candidates without voter input. South Africa should consider the direct election of its president, and an executive which is able to draw from outside Parliament. This would allow for the president to draw members of cabinet from outside the legislature, thus further breaking the political party monopoly on power. This would also require a close inspection of the Electoral Act and various Independent Electoral Commission regulations.

Similarly, the powers of the president, and the president's relation to the executive and the legislature, must also be examined.[457] The president's sweeping powers of appointment rival those of twentieth-century dictators. And this near-imperial power is insufficiently constrained. Parliament must be re-fanged for presidential accountability. It is currently impotent to compel presidential accountability in the absence of the drastic steps of impeachment and a no-confidence vote.

Indeed, the legislature itself must be rethought. The ineffectual National Council of Provinces should be abolished and replaced with a directly elected upper chamber. The rules of Parliament, which stifle debate and protect the executive unduly, must be reformulated. Plenary time must move from prepared set pieces to deliberative debates. And the president must be more tightly constrained to appear before Parliament to explain his or her actions.

Some of these concerns could also be applied to the structure of the judiciary, especially the cumbersome system of appeal balanced between the Supreme Court of Appeal and the Constitutional Court. Proposals for the merger of those two courts ought also to be closely considered.

The devolution of power should also be on the table. The clumsy nine-province, three-tiered system of government is a relic of an outdated compromise. It hamstrings the executive and fails citizens. A more effective system should be sought which breaks the hold of ethnic provincial assumptions and maximises the central government's ability to deliver its policies. This would also reduce the complexity of South Africa's electoral process, by simplifying the number of provinces – or abolishing them altogether – and thereby reducing the number of ballots and elections required to confer executive authority. This would need a careful re-examination of Chapter 6 of the Constitution, as well as Schedules 4 and 4b.[458]

Even Chapter 9 of the Constitution requires further thought. Does the Human Rights Commission really grapple with South Africa's unique injustices and inequalities? Why should a new constitution not found an institution tasked with explicitly resolving the legacy of apartheid? Should constitutional institutions focused on gender equality not be re-imagined to curb the scourges of femicide, rape and domestic violence?

Is South Africa's corruption-fighting infrastructure fit for purpose? Does the Public Protector really work as an institution? Perhaps the tortuous litigation and ambiguous jurisprudence that have emerged around that office stem from a fundamental constitutional confusion. Could a new constitution not design more effective anti-graft institutions altogether, rather than spending decades waiting for the executive to muddle through?

These are all matters for debate, sketched in broad strokes. But they show plentiful possibilities for constitutional renewal. Such a broad reform agenda also answers the question often posed by constitutional triumphalists: what is the alternative to the Constitution? It places the burden on those who defend the Constitution in its current form to explain why at least some of the proposals I have mentioned would leave South Africa in a worse position.

I am also wide-eyed about the dangers of my call for a new republic. The first of these should be avoiding a slide towards authoritarianism. A new constitutional convention could attract a new and opportunistic majority. One virtue of the current Constitution, then, is its refusal to bow to majoritarian demands such as restoring the death penalty or eroding LGBTQI+ rights. The Constitution also extends important protections to migrant communities and religious minorities rendered hyper-vulnerable by the new apartheid. Such protections should be defended and even enhanced.[459]

Moreover, through the Constitution, many of the callous features of apartheid criminal law have been destroyed. The Constitution has abolished the death penalty, reversed judicial corporal punishment, and expanded the right to a fair trial. All these achievements are real and significant.

All the dangers of constitution-making existed in the 1990s when South Africa adopted its current constitution. And these dangers were indeed more present than they are now. Why, then, can South Africa not find the wisdom to remake itself now when it has found the wisdom to remake itself before?

My argument, then, is not that the Constitution should be entirely abolished but that it should be substantially transformed. I admit, and indeed celebrate, the Constitution's achievements and advances. I believe in constitutional democracy. And I do not take for granted the Constitution's role in extending the franchise and inaugurating the rule of law. Nor do I dismiss the virtue of South Africa's independent judiciary – one which has passed many tests in the democratic era. South Africa needs a constitutional and democratic order. I am simply not convinced that South Africa needs *this* and *only this* constitutional order forever. We must distinguish between the Constitution and constitutionalism itself.

I should not be lumped, then, with those mounting a vague attack on the Constitution for self-serving political ends. I simply disagree with those who believe that *this* constitution cannot be transcended. Rather, I see South Africa's first truly democratic constitution as a bridge between apartheid and its antithesis. Some pieces of that bridge should be preserved into that new future, and some should be discarded.

Constitutional reformation is further advantaged by the last three decades of experimentation. South Africa is in an infinitely better place today to assess the Constitution's wisdom than it was in 1996. Indeed, I concede that it would have been hard to predict how ineffectual the Constitution would prove to be prior to its inception. Today, however, South Africa's considerable pool of constitutional minds can turn their collective genius to a fresh constitutional project – one that would avert the mistakes of the first constitution and the first republic. What I am calling for, then, goes beyond reform and lies in the realm of reformation.

Constitutional reformation is common when one takes a long view of history. Diverse nations have reappraised their founding assumptions, and benefited from such reappraisal. Indeed, South Africa has been notably conservative in amending its Constitution since 1994, enacting fewer than twenty amendments at the time of writing. And, even then, many of these amendments have only toyed with the constitutional margins.

A comparative glance at constitutional history is instructive. The United Kingdom has overhauled electoral procedures, most notably in the Great Reform Acts of the nineteenth century, and in the extension of women's voting rights in the twentieth. Like many other European nations, it has reformed towards – and even now away from – European integration. And it has grappled over the extent of power accorded to Ireland (before home rule), Northern Ireland, Scotland and Wales.[460]

France's transition from the fourth to the fifth republic in 1958 brought widespread political change. And, since the fifth republic's inception, France has abolished the death penalty, devolved executive power, and changed the term limits of presidents.[461]

The United States has made far-reaching amendments to its political order since 1789. These involved revising election procedures for the vice president just four years after constitutional inception. This is to say nothing of the abolition of slavery and the conferral of voting rights on African Americans and women.

The Indian constitution has been amended 104 times since 1948. Brazil had four constitutions in the twentieth century alone. And its fourth constitution has been amended 108 times.[462] Tunisia remade its constitution after widespread popular uprisings in 2010, setting it on a more democratic course.[463]

To be sure, constitutional changes are not always progressive. African examples testify to their danger. The continent is replete with broken constitutions extending presidential power and restricting civic freedoms. Unlike Tunisia, Egypt squandered the chance to forge a democratic constitution after Mubarak's fall. In 2020, Guinea's president, Alpha Condé, joined a long line of African leaders who extended their presidential terms while in office.[464] Nevertheless, constitutional stagnancy presents a danger, too. History is littered as much with the sins of inaction as with those of action. South Africa should avoid both.

Whatever the wisdom of my briefly-sketched proposals, I suspect that the future historian will see South Africa's current period as an interregnum – a transitory passage between one order and another. This interregnum contains the seeds of a new order as it reaps the harvest of the old order. The shape of that future is unpredictable from the current vantage point. And there is no guarantee that it is desirable. But a failure to consciously imagine that future could end in the chaos of spontaneous social combustion. What seems certain is that the first democratic republic will be remembered as a purgatorial dance.

I reiterate: even radical constitutional reformation is not sufficient to reverse the new apartheid. The country's social and economic foundations must also be reassessed, as should South Africa's international relations. A vision of this magnitude will take multiple generations to execute. And only very few human communities have ever marshalled the foresight, wherewithal and wisdom to remake their nations. But failure to realise a new national vision will eventually wreak catastrophe or, worse, irreversible stagnation. South Africa will otherwise be doomed to remake apartheid in ever-changing guises. Complacency is South Africa's biggest danger. For, if South Africans fiddle in the midst of impending ruination, then we shall all perish like so many frogs in slow-boiling water. It is time for South Africans to realise that the noble experiment of the first republic has failed.

GLOBAL QUESTIONS

This book challenges the idea that democracy combats injustice and inequality. The vote cannot fix what denying the vote has broken. Voting, even with bold constitutional guarantees, is no guard against the rapacious appetite of entrenched power. Nominal rights and formal protections shrivel under the weight of unspoken conventions and undeclared alliances. Democracy is not the antithesis of apartheid. It is not the antithesis of injustice. It is not the antithesis of inequality. All these evils can survive under democracy's shroud.

And yet it is tempting to believe that political equality automatically leads to social and economic equality. The logic is seductive: giving votes to previously disenfranchised people means that they can shift policy by articulating their interests. Over time, these interests manifest in substantive equality in the economic and social spheres, as elites are toppled.

Like many myths, this story is plausible but untrue. For one thing, it assumes that political participation leads to political equality. But, as various political scientists stress, no such relationship obtains. Equality of participation does not mean equality of influence. And, indeed, as scholars like Thomas Ferguson and Larry Bartels have shown, the less power an individual voter holds, the less they can shape political outcomes.[465] By contrast, the more wealth a citizen enjoys, the more democratic influence she or he enjoys. Hence, economic inequality cannot be neatly severed from political inequality. Democracy and inequality are not only compatible, but often mutually reinforcing.

Examples old and new support this frustrating conclusion. Before the democratic waves of the twentieth century, democracy often coincided with great inequality and injustice. In nineteenth-century England, democracy emerged in a context of heightened social disparity, typified in tales of Dickensian deprivation. And, despite major reforms in the century leading to World War I, income inequality was not fundamentally altered by wider political participation.[466] In the comparatively equal realm of modern-day China, democracy failed to take root in the same period.

Even the French Revolution failed to guarantee lasting equality. As recent economic analyses of taxation data from the eighteenth and nineteenth centuries show, the revolutionary period only momentarily halted income inequality, which, by the mid-nineteenth century, had resurged to its previous levels.[467] Even great political realignments based on equality cannot guarantee it.

Indeed, a long-established philosophical tradition places democracy against equality – let alone justice. This conservative tradition views democracy as a technology of intra-elite compromise rather than a pathway to mass representation. To John Locke, democracy shielded propertied men from the excesses of the state. To Adam Smith, Thomas Malthus and David Ricardo, democracy guarded the propertied class against the tyranny of arbitrary taxation.[468] And, indeed, the racial democracies of Europe, the Americas, Australia and southern Africa protected White men (and subsequently all White people) from the claims of indigenous populations. Exclusionary democracy made colonies the *property* of their voters. At its most extreme, conservative democracy came to legitimise violent annexation and even genocide.[469]

A wide variety of contemporary examples reinforce democracy's tolerance for inequality. In Brazil, inequality continues to thrive alongside democracy. And, when inequality began to fall in the 2000s, this did not necessarily improve democracy.[470] In Europe and the US, inequality has soared since the 1980s, under democracy's cover.[471] In India and Indonesia the same pattern obtains.[472] And, of course, in Africa and especially in southern Africa, inequality has proved impervious to unprecedented democratic transformations in the same period.

From the perspective of the African continent, then, concerns about the lack of 'democratic consolidation' are misguided. Perhaps, rather, democracy is simply consolidating in a particularly rapacious form: one which makes democracy compatible with extreme political and economic injustice and inequality; one which ironically uses the mythology of democracy to legitimise this rapacity.[473] The problem, then, is not that Africa is not truly democratic. Rather, it is that democracy is not 'democratic' – where democracy is a byword for equality. African experiences of democracy tell us something about democracy rather than something about African aberrance.

African democracy has produced ephemeral victories and become, in the words of Claude Ake, 'a strategy for power, not a vehicle for empowerment'.[474] The South African experience – which continues to confound optimists – is no different. The hard question to be faced, then, is whether the ANC's commitment is to democracy or to power. For if its commitment is to power, then democracy is merely a convenient mask by which that power gains deceptive legitimacy. This question will produce an answer in the decades to come.

Democracy also tolerates state violence. When economic inequality and injustice peak, elites have more to lose in redistribution:[475] the price of repression becomes cheaper than the cost of losing wealth. This finding is supported by the economists Carrera and Policardo, who examine data on state violence from 51 countries between 1960 and 2008, concluding that 'a rich, powerful elite usually prefers repression when inequality and the cost of redistribution is high'.[476] Similarly, Magaloni and Rodriguez lament 'a grim picture of surviving authoritarian policies in democracy'[477] in various Latin American contexts.

Southern African experiences confirm this perspective, as liberation movements have opted for repression over redistribution. And Western democracies, too, have often chosen the baton over the ballot, through policies of mass incarceration and police brutality. South Africa shifts between these two currents – of southern African state repression and Western racial policing. It is little wonder, then, that South African democracy has become compatible with Black expendability – and, I dare add, the special dispensability of Black women.

Gross state repression and monstrous inequality should not mystify South Africans. They are fibres in the very fabric of the new apartheid, not unintended outcomes of constitutional wisdom. They are the shadows of a deformed economic order. Even without obvious state violence – as seen in the Marikana massacre or in the killing of innocent bystander Mthokozisi Ntumba during student protests in 2021 – South African democracy will continue to reproduce horrifying inequality. As Ansell and Samuels note: 'under democracy, elites do not necessarily need to threaten violence to preserve their standing, as they could simply bribe politicians or otherwise make their wealth indispensable to those who manage government affairs.'[478]

Ansell and Samuels make another provocative argument that bears on South Africa's democratic experiment. Specifically, they challenge the idea that a growing middle class signals inequality's decline. Instead, they claim that middle-class growth may produce – rather than threaten – inequality: 'in developing autocracies [income equality] does not indicate a large middle class, but rather that nearly everyone is equally poor. [Income inequality], by contrast, suggests the growth of the middle classes, which have strong interests in reining in the expropriative authority of the state.'[479] So, even sizeable middle classes can collude with elites rather than renouncing wealth and power.

And this explains a key paradox of the new apartheid. Many observers argue that South Africa's so-called Black middle class endangers inequality. Yet, since 1994, inequality has persisted and deepened despite the growth of this class. It follows, then, that South Africa's persistent economic inequality under democracy is not 'puzzling'. The Black middle class is incentivised to side with wealth and power against the impoverished majority. And this is precisely why the apartheid government itself was intent on creating a Black middle class in its final throes: not to reduce inequality but to preserve it.

The idea of 'inequality' itself requires reflection, because it has become so central to discourse in South Africa. In some ways, inequality is a dangerous term, because it decontextualises injustice. It also numericises inequity, suggesting a quantitative quandary distinct from everyday life. It breaks links between the past and present. Hence, equality without justice is futile; justice without equality is fruitless.

A second and related problem is that inequality is understood in narrow economic terms. Inequality has become synonymous with inequality of income or wealth. It is clearer, then, to speak of 'inequalities' than 'inequality',[480] because South Africa – like the rest of the world – suffers from deeper inequalities than those of income and wealth. It suffers from inequalities of power, inequalities of racial justice, inequalities of gender justice, inequalities of land, inequalities of property, inequalities of force, inequalities of speech, and inequalities of care. The combination of these inequalities gives the new apartheid its inhumane face, not merely the inequalities of income and wealth that undergird them. When I contend that democracy tolerates inequality, I refer to all these complex and intersecting inequalities.

South Africa has always been a unique place from which to understand deeper global forces. The new apartheid thus refracts global questions of private power and racial injustice. Apartheid inspired – and was inspired by – other systems of racial oppression, from Germany to Britain, and from the US to Australia and Brazil.[481] Likewise, the new apartheid draws from – and influences – twenty-first-century racial oppression and neo-colonialism. Therefore, if South Africa defeats the new apartheid, it will inspire other nations to contend with White supremacy; if it fails, this will demonstrate White supremacy's resilience.

In some respects, South Africa remains a unique experiment in racial injustice. In other ways, it has become more like the rest of the world since 1994. South Africa must now reckon with its mundanity and everydayness.[482] It must abandon pretensions to exceptionalism. Far from being a 'miracle', apartheid's demise has inaugurated the ordinary and the average. South Africa has taken its place among the world's disappointing democracies, where social victories are fleeting and the tactics of oppression have become subterranean. Indeed, global racism has become privatised. South Africa's present failure to transcend apartheid is, therefore, illuminating both in its uniqueness and in its familiarity.

PAST, PRESENT AND FUTURE

This book is about South Africa's pasts, presents and futures. It brings these different times into conversation, from a new historical vantage point. In doing so, it implies a radical departure from the 'end of history narrative' that surrounds South Africa's democratic transition.

It conceives anew South Africa's history, contemporary life, and future trajectories. The implications of this theoretical move require further reflection.

One of this work's underlying themes is the changing face of power. Power resides in unexpected places in South Africa, and it has adapted with remarkable rapidity and ingenuity around democratic constraints. Yes, power resides in the state. And, yes, power resides in the corporate sphere. But it also lives in unlikely corners: behind the walls of private enclaves, within the borders of mobile screens, in the abstract world of algorithms, in shopping malls, and in the seemingly quotidian domain of private contracts. All this points to a fundamental shift in the ratio of public to private authority. To appreciate apartheid's stubborn persistence in democratic South Africa, we must reappraise our understanding of power itself. For, as Foucault famously suggests, 'power is not a thing, but a relation'.[483]

Thus, just as South Africa transitioned to democracy, so power itself transitioned. The liberation movement proceeded from outdated assumptions of the state's centrality in South African life. When the ANC gained state power, state power itself was radically diluted by global and local actors. Whereas achieving state power meant one thing in the 1950s, it meant quite another in the 1990s. The compromises of the transition improved the South African state's legitimacy without necessarily improving its effectiveness. Thus, in addition to the ANC's plentiful failures, the disappointments of the democratic era can also be traced to the relative weakness of the South African state, when compared to private power.

I insist that apartheid history is yet to be fully written; that apartheid remains a live question in democratic South Africa; that apartheid has evolved from a tool of religious segregation, through to a state ideology, and then into an autonomous, self-regulating species of neoliberal domination.

Treating apartheid as a live question means rethinking its boundaries and breaking dominant paradigms. It means contesting assumed historiographies and even rethinking the nature of apartheid itself. For instance, this book has shown that apartheid was far more than just an ideology of separation. Rather, it was a paradox of separation and entanglement, or what I call 'entangled separation': a set of binary identities at once forcibly divided *and* interwoven. The pressure of apartheid's internal borders pushed races apart, but the pressure of South Africa's external borders, apartheid's goals of economic exploitation, and the sheer numerical dominance of the indigenous majority squeezed people together. Apartheid was founded on pronounced partition but also on inevitable intertwinement.

This paradox, of distant intimacy and exploitative interrelation, created an enigmatic political community, at once worlds apart and inescapably connected. As J. M. Coetzee observes: 'In its greed [apartheid] demanded Black bodies . . . in order to burn up their energy as labour. In its anxiety about Black bodies, it made iron laws to banish them from sight. Its essence was therefore from the beginning confusion, a confusion which it displaced wildly all around itself.'[484]

Rethinking apartheid also recasts the transformations of the 1990s as a period of multiple intersecting compromises. These were compromises between the different strands of the liberation movement; between different strands of the apartheid establishment; between the NP and ANC; between capital and labour; between Bantustan leaders and freedom fighters; and between the apartheid state and global capital. As such, the Constitution, and the republic that followed, often resemble an incoherent patchwork of pragmatic trade-offs.

This condition of constant compromise creates a climate of perpetual amnesty. This partly explains why the commission of inquiry has become such a dominant institution in democratic South Africa. Rather than questioning the ever-growing web of compromises on which democratic South Africa is founded, these commissions bury existential contradictions under the weight of deflective reports.

Apartheid was a set of laws, and an elaborate technology, but it was also more than these things. Apartheid lived in buildings and edicts, but it also lived in people's minds, in their emotions and their sadnesses. Indeed, to Mark Sanders, apartheid was the very denial of mourning itself.[485] It was the denial of collective bereavement that is so central to human emotional survival.

The new apartheid, like its predecessor, creates novel emotional dissonances: states of simultaneous hope and optimism alongside feelings of disillusionment, terror, anxiety and melancholy; a feeling of simultaneous remembrance and denial. These are the cumulative results of a society consumed with punishment and devoid of therapy, always on the precipice of some faint new optimism.

To live in South Africa today is to be surrounded by the remainders and reminders of apartheid. It is to be enveloped by apartheid's fallen facades and buried bones. And, so, in some ways this book has archaeological intentions. It seeks to excavate the foundations of apartheid so that South Africa might see their continued significance. Beyond the glossy promises of the 'new South Africa', beneath the myths of providential exceptionalism, are buried ancient structures of division. Democratic South Africa built on top of these foundations, sometimes even against them, but it never uprooted them. To live in South Africa is to be walking among living ruins.

This unique conjuncture of emotions is often reflected in song and literature. South African hip-hop culture – a genre forged in the new apartheid – reflects the competing tendencies of Black South African life: on one hand, a desires for opulence and radical financial liberty; on the other, a longing for political liberation.

In South Africa, as elsewhere, rappers aren't always exemplars of moral rectitude or prophets of social progress. Sometimes, the fantasies they conjure – and the personae they produce – unveil horror-filled presents or dystopian futures: from hyper-patriarchy to nauseating narcissism and virulent violence. Even in these moments, rap reflects society back at itself, by lifting the lid on the social id.

But rappers also paint utopian lyrical visions and sculpt affective scapes that expand the frontiers of freedom. Rappers like Dope Saint Jude, for instance, confound gender norms and subvert sexual stereotypes, restoring rap to the avant-garde of social criticism. Take Saint Jude's music video, 'Go High Go Low', which reflects on Coloured identity, flips gender roles, and explores life on the Cape Flats through vivid neon shop signs and the jarring notion of headlessness.

At its best, and its worst, rap captures the uneasy feeling of the 'post-apartheid', and the contradictory desires for spectacular wealth and revolutionary equality that mark it. Fists up, Bentleys out.

In the pages of South African speculative fiction, we find horrifying visions of tomorrow, where werewolves roam Soweto street corners and pandemics claim multitudes in Khayelitsha. Two years before coronavirus, Mohale Mashigo imagined a South African outbreak which turned people into phantoms, in her short story 'Ghost Strain N': 'By the time national newspapers, radio stations and TV stations were covering the "outbreak" it was too late for many. It happened so fast; in less than two weeks whole neighbourhoods were emptied.' Urban fantasy author Lauren Beukes's *Afterland* imagines a killer affliction that wipes out 99 per cent of men.[486]

The new apartheid's social fears are thus often translated through the fantastical. This is why themes of death defiance and resurrection resonate so powerfully in South Africa today. Zombies and ghosts conjure fear not only by their mythical status, but also by revealing the deeper fear of White supremacy's resurrection. As Beukes notes, fantasy eerily reminds us of 'the monsters in our past that come up from the depths to eat us alive when we least expect them'. The vampires and ghouls of apartheid that once seemed vanquished are omnipresent in fantasy and reality.

The living dead also pervade poetry. In the poem 'South Africa, you do not have a name', Lebo Mashile weaves themes of dying and death around the painful paradoxes of the new apartheid:

[South Africa,] Can you hear the Song of the Dead?
The rush of blood spilling daily in your breast?
We kill each other for your nameless name's sake,
To appease the hungry ghosts.
who keep asking, where do we look?
Where do we go?

The dead know more of living.
Than we, the living dead.[487]

While the poet Don Mattera laments:

I see them everyday,
Everywhere,
Non-people in non-transition,
Moving, shifting going nowhere,
Trapped in twilight zones of vacuous expectation,
Waiting between nothing and nothing.[488]

LIMITATIONS

A book of this theoretical ambition is inevitably constrained by certain limits and shortcomings. One key limitation of this work is its scope. My ideas still need to be extended, tested and critiqued against other areas of South African life, beyond the five I have examined here. Had I the luxury of infinite time and energy, I would have considered the new apartheid against at least three other examples: education, health care, and media. These three realms seem particularly ripe for the critique I have offered here.

For instance, the new apartheid may shed light on the crisis of the South African universities. The privatisation of university funding through students fees has dogged the university sector since 1994, leading to the conflagrations of Fees Must Fall and its echoes in subsequent years. The state's response to this problem, of patching together grants for low-income students, has proved fragile. South Africa's larger economic crisis, which has led to cuts in higher education, will further imperil this strategy.

This will open the door to an even more dangerous solution: handing over the entire system of student funding to the big banks – as suggested by former Wits vice chancellor Adam Habib and the Hefer

Commission of Inquiry into higher education. In one swoop, this would crush the South African university in the jaws of private power. It would also spark a debt crisis decades down the line, as a generation of students default on their payments.

The university sector also exemplifies my arguments about repression. The confluence of anti-Black police brutality and private policing, which is now commonly deployed against student protest, typifies apartheid's persistence in democracy. These and other prospects are ripe for detailed examination in the light of the concepts developed in this book.

The new apartheid also reframes massive inequalities in the schooling sector. Three decades of massive state expenditure in education have produced desperately disappointing results. The new apartheid helps to explain the stubbornness of this trend. The system of unequal schooling first perfected by the apartheid state has now become privatised and partially deracialised. Even within the public sector, those schools once designated for White students still enjoy massive advantages over those once served by Bantu Education. For this reason, various scholars continue to lament South Africa's 'two systems of education'.[489] As Nicholas Spaull argues: 'the strong legacy of apartheid and the consequent correlation between education and wealth have meant that, generally speaking, poorer South African students perform worse academically'.[490] The insights of the new apartheid could extend this line of inquiry.

Health care is another potentially useful example of the new apartheid. Inequalities of access and inequalities in outcomes are equally deserving of exploration. Recent scholarship continues to complain that 'race still significantly affects demand for public healthcare in South Africa'[491] and shows the 'significance of place in shaping access and health experiences'.[492] Hence, the arguments advanced in this book about the persistence of racial segregation and the increasing financialisation of wealth bear, too, on health care. Indeed, the two intersect, since access to health insurance often occurs along apartheid lines. Health care, then, is an omission from this book worthy of further detailed consideration.

The South African media constitute another sector calling for radical critique. The increased corporatisation and digitisation of South African media present new challenges for South African democracy. My arguments on technology and wealth should, therefore, be considered against these trends. The narrative of self-congratulation that pervades the South African journalistic world resembles the self-satisfaction of the 1994 moment. But beyond vague appeals to 'freedom of the press' and naive notions of journalistic sanctity, the South African media have corporatised, privatised and balkanised since democracy. They have also proved dangerously easy to co-opt. Like any system, the new apartheid has its propagandists. In this area, as with many others, the new apartheid provides fertile theory, ready for further development and extension.

Unlike scientific theories, social theories cannot be proved conclusively through neat experiments isolating specific variables. Rather, social theories are good in so far as they give explanatory insight. To be sure, the new apartheid cannot explain everything that happens in South Africa. This is not the ambition of my theory. Instead, my ambition is to explain more than existing theories of South Africa's democratic experience. Specifically, the new apartheid explains more than the optimistic and triumphant theory contained in the 'new South Africa' hypothesis that emerged after the democratic transition.

That theory suggests that apartheid was vanquished and that, in time, South Africa is on an ineluctable path to dignity, equality and freedom. Each of these theories elides detail. Yet each goes some way to explaining South Africa's present. The broader question is: which one explains more than the other? My argument is that the new apartheid explains more than the triumphalist account can.

My hope is that the shortcomings of this book are addressed by a new generation of scholars and public intellectuals under the frame of the new apartheid. My further challenge to South African social thinkers is to meet this novel social moment with a correspondingly ambitious social theory.[493]

PERORATION

This has been a difficult book to write. I have been constantly haunted by the feeling of rediscovering, and then inspecting and dissecting, some long-suppressed horror. Apartheid is hard to think about. It is even harder to reckon with. It is a form of mass constriction, mass confinement, mass punishment, mass suffering, mass grief, mass trauma, mass terror. Even those who fought apartheid seem to have buried their experiences in deep and inaccessible corners of their minds.

The evil of apartheid lies not in the number of people it killed – though it did kill many. Rather, its evil lies in the number of people it tyrannised. Apartheid was ultimately an ideology of colossal social control. The atrocity of this panoramic subjugation is yet to be fully comprehended. And the mass devastation it wrought is yet to be fully understood. Nor has the complexity of apartheid as a philosophical, social, legal, economic and governmental system yet been fully mined. The grimmest feature of this monstrous system is its capacity for self-reinvention. And, since 1994, apartheid has metastasised – free from the structures of human agency and central control. Apartheid is now dictated by markets rather than minds. Like a virus, it is neither dead nor alive, but survives through the people it afflicts.

Defining a central social problem takes generations. In hindsight, the struggle against formal apartheid appears coherent and premeditated. But identifying apartheid as *the* problem took eternities of debate, struggle and reflection. Similarly, democratic South Africa is confronted with a multitude of scourges. Since 1994, observers have struggled to identify *the* problem: now focusing on education, and now on unemployment; now on poverty, and now on inequality; now on racism and now gender oppression; now on queerphobia and now on xenophobia. None of these scourges are South Africa's final enemy. Neither is the enemy just governmental ineptitude or grand corruption. Nor is it simple corporate greed. The enemy is not state violence or crime. These are all symptoms of the virus. What is South Africa's enemy? The new apartheid.

South Africa needs a way to define its crises that captures their historical roots, their present complexity, and their future trajectories in a single frame. Only once we identify the problem can we define liberation. By defining the new apartheid, I have tackled this task and, in so doing, sought to define a generational mission.

This book is thus not about 'solving' South Africa's problems; it is about defining its central problem. Before we can dream of defeating the new apartheid, we must first behold its monumental scale and omnidirectional reach. Overcoming the new apartheid will require breathtaking imagination and unmatched wisdom over several generations. It demands the painful reassessment of long-held creeds. The defeat of new apartheid requires all the fortitude of a new liberation movement, fixed on the ideal of a second, true independence. For, in the words of Shireen Hassim, 'the central question of our time is: what was it that people were struggling for over centuries, and what have we got?'[494]

Acknowledgements

To my mother, who is always my first reader, editor and sounding board. Everything I have ever achieved is down to her sacrifice, love and unfailing kindness. She has sharpened my arguments and spurred my resolve. Our regular walks during the long, lonely days of lockdown clarified my thoughts and kept me determined. I owe endless gratitude to her maternal pen.

To my father, whose love and support are fundamental. For our long chats on the nature of law, property and the Constitution. The idea for the book was planted in my mind when he spoke one day of 'neo-apartheid'.

To my wife, Sumaya. For our conversations over the dining table, many of which found their way into these pages. For her insights on 'trickle-down constitutionalism', and her understanding of government's inner workings. And, for her unfailing support and affirming love. I hereby confirm, for all the world to know, that I owe her various dinners, holidays and desserts.

To Sarah Nuttall. For giving me an academic home at the Wits Institute for Social and Economic Research (WiSER) and showing untold patience as this book was postponed, time and again, because of the treacherous process of competing my DPhil and the Covid pandemic. I am grateful for her faith, encouragement and quiet reassurance.

To Achille Mbembe. Researching this book has repeatedly led me to his work and thought. Not only has his thought been an inspiration, but I have been lucky enough to gain his personal insights, in seminars at WiSER and in a long conversation in my office at the beginning of this project. This book, then, is a product of the considerable collective genius of the Mbembe–Nuttall household.

To my godfather Edwin Cameron. For conversations that greatly strengthened the sections on law and punishment. And for his insights on minimum sentences, drawn from deep wells of experience throughout the justice system.

To my colleagues at WiSER: Isabel Hofmeyr, Charne Lavery, Melanie Boehi, Bronwyn Kotzen, Mpho Matsipa, Souad Zeineddine, Richard Rottenburg, Keith Breckenridge, Hlonipha Mokoena, and Pamila Gupta. They all provided valuable feedback whether in person, in seminars or through their cited work.

To my siblings. Luc (for taking strange calls about fractals and cloning during Ramadan), Mnce, Letsema and Zwekazi. And to my other family, specially Fuad and Mimona Hendricks, and my siblings Fatima, Qutb, Towfiq, and their respective partners and children. To my nieces, Iman and Ayah, and nephew, Zinedine. And, to my siblings-in-law, Fiona, Jasmine, Fatima and Tayo.

To my friends in academia, Dr Warren Chalklen (for helpful early comments), Dr Vuyane Mhlomi, and Professor Simukai Chigudu. Thank you for your guidance and your friendship at various stages of this journey. You each contributed in foundational ways to the completion of this book. Thanks, also, to Professor Kalypso Nicolaïdis for her continued support and guidance.

To Nhlanhla Makenna, Ntokozo Mazibuko and Kaeden Arnold, for friendship and sanity, and various calls and chats as this book unfolded. And to Eusebius McKaiser for additional encouragement.

To the Academic and Non-Fiction Authors' Association of South Africa in collaboration with the Norwegian Embassy for proving a grant for this work.

To Tshepo Mosoeu for his unmatchable designer's eye. I owe him a great debt for the fascinating work he has done in bringing the book's cover to life and inspiring the visual feel for this overall project.

To my editor, Russell Martin, for rigorous and professional guidance and encouragement. His keen eye has greatly polished this work. I also thank Charl Blignaut for his helpful comments on the introduction and Sekoetlane Phamodi for useful advice on editing. Thanks also to Karyn Maughan for assistance in finding various documents, and to my typesetter Nazli Jacobs and proofreader Angela Voges.

To Makhosi Tshabalala. For her probing and productive questions in the early days of this work, which set it on a new trajectory. She is also responsible for the work's focus on gender. I thank her most profoundly for challenging me to talk about gender despite my compromised position as a man. And for her challenges to me about the title of this work, which gave me productive pause.

Finally, to my publisher, Tafelberg. First, to Kristin Paramoer, who was patient and kind in extracting this work over two years, and indeed extracted my first work. To Erika Oosthuysen, for believing in me before I had ever published, and guiding this work to completion. Thank you for making this the work that I hoped it would be. And, in advance, to Helené Prinsloo, for the work that will go into promoting and marketing this work. Thanks also to Sadé Walter for her work towards this book's completion.

To Advocate Tembeka Ngcukaitobi and Qaanitah Hunter, for generously providing 'shouts' for this book's cover. Their considerable credibility has lent this work credibility in turn.

Endnotes

INTRODUCTION

1   As alluded to in the front matter, this phrase comes from Chief Justice Mogoeng Mogoeng's 2019 address to the Pan African Bar Association of South Africa.

2   To borrow Katherine McKittrick's vivid phrase. See Katherine McKittrick and Alexander G. Weheliye, '808s and Heartbreak', *Propter Nos* 2, no. 1 (2017): 13–42.

3   Lebo Mashile and Majola, 'Thina Sizwe', track 1 on *Moya*, 2017, CD.

4   This phrase comes from a forthcoming volume edited by Louise Bethlehem, titled *Restless Itineraries: Anti-apartheid Expressive Culture and Global Imaginings of Freedom*. I heard the phrase in an internal seminar of the Wits Institute for Social and Economic Research where the work was presented.

5   These vivid phrases come from Eric Worby and Shireen Ally, 'The disappointment of nostalgia: Conceptualising cultures of memory in contemporary South Africa', *Social Dynamics* 39, no. 3 (2013): 457.

6   Explicating apartheid fully is a work on its own. Condensing apartheid into a single definition is inevitably telegraphic. My purpose here, however, is to give a sense of the way that I invoke the term throughout the rest of this work. The reader can only comprehend the full meaning of the way I define apartheid by reaching the end of the work.

7   For a fascinating meditation on the influence of American race laws on early Nazi German legal ideology, see James Q. Whitman, *Hitler's American Model: The United States and the Making of Nazi Race Law*, Princeton: Princeton University Press, 2017. This work rather puts paid to Giliomee's suggestion that Nazi ideology was not important to apartheid ideology. Giliomee suggests that American race laws were the true inspiration. He seems unaware, however, that Nazi legal ideology drew considerable inspiration from American race laws in any case. Hence, the triangular relationship between Nazi laws, American race laws and South African race laws cannot be ignored. For Giliomee's position, see Hermann Giliomee, 'The making of the apartheid plan, 1929–1948', *Journal of Southern African Studies* 29, no. 2 (2003): 373–92.

8   Verwoerd defined the system of apartheid laws as 'organic', for instance.

9   I thank Makhosazana Xaba for this piercing phrase, used in a conversation with me after I presented an early draft of this work to WiSER Internal Seminar in September 2019.

10   I expand on this definition in subsequent sections. Various qualifications are, of course, necessary for a full definition. The most succinct definition comes from Mbembe who defined privatisation as the processionals by which 'functions supposed to be public, and obligations that flow from sovereignty, are increasingly performed by private operators for private ends'. See Achille Mbembe, *On the Postcolony*, Berkeley, CA: University of California Press, 2001, 80.

11   Not all apartheid laws were, in fact, repealed, as I show in the chapter on law.

12   That part of law developed by precedent and custom rather than statutory enactments.

13   See, for instance, Anna Orthofer, 'Wealth inequality in South Africa: Evidence from survey and tax data', *Research Project on Employment, Income Distribution and Inclusive Growth* 15 (2016).

14   There were ten Bantustans. Four eventually gained 'independence'. The Bantustans emerged out of the 'native reserves', which themselves were the products of colonial segregation and eventually the Tomlinson Commission, which was established 'to devise "a comprehensive scheme for the rehabilitation of the Native Areas with a view to developing within them a social structure in keeping with the culture of the Native and based upon effective socio-economic planning"'. See Jack D. Krige and E. Krige, 'The Tomlinson report and the Lovedu', *Race Relations Journal* 23, no. 4 (1956): 12–25; Frederik Rothman Tomlinson, *Summary of the Report of the Commission for the Socio-economic Development of the Bantu Areas within the Union of South Africa*, UG 61-1955, Government Printer, South Africa, 1955.

15   By 1970, several new Acts further devolved administrative power to 'homelands' such as the Bantu Homelands Constitution Act (1970), the Black Affairs Administration Act (1971) and the Black Local Authorities Act (1983). See John Dugard, *Human Rights and the South African Legal Order*, Princeton, NJ: Princeton University Press, 2015 [1978].

16   Steve Biko, *I Write What I Like: Selected Writings*, Chicago, IL: University of Chicago Press, 2015, 62.

17   Daniel J. Kapust, *Republicanism, Rhetoric, and Roman Political Thought: Sallust, Livy, and Tacitus*, Cambridge: Cambridge University Press, 2011, 14.

18   Adam Tooze, 'Neoliberalism's world order', *Dissent* 65, no. 3 (2018): 132.

19   The same is, of course, true of White women, though their stake in White supremacy is greater.

20   See Nechama Brodie, *Femicide*, Cape Town: Kwela Books, 2020.

21   See Achille Mbembe, 'Apartheid futures and the limits of racial reconciliation',

Public Positions on History and Politics: Racism, Recognition and Justice (2015). The exact quote is taken from a speech similar to this text, which can be accessed at https://www.youtube.com/watch?v=NqWzsiT-U7E.

22 See Jean Comaroff and John L. Comaroff, *The Truth about Crime: Sovereignty, Knowledge, Social Order*, Chicago: University of Chicago Press, 2016, 2.

23 Peter Hudson, 'The reproduction of racial inequality in South Africa: The colonial unconscious and democracy', in Vishwas Satgar (ed.), *Racism after Apartheid: Challenges for Marxism and Anti-racism*, Johannesburg: Wits University Press, 2019, 158.

24 See Sampie Terreblanche, *Lost in Transformation: South Africa's Search for a New Future*, Johannesburg: KMM Publishing, 2012; Sampie Terreblanche, *A History of Inequality in South Africa, 1652–2002*, Pietermaritzburg: University of Natal Press, 2002. These negotiations are typically understood as the official conversations between the ANC and the NP – and, later, multiple political formations –between 1990 and 1994, followed by the parliamentary process which led to the final constitution in 1996. In truth, the negotiations were more fragmented and decentralised.

25 The major exception was the vast welfare state created under the ANC. However, welfarism is compatible with neoliberalism, as is clear from various European examples.

26 For instance, Cheryl Carolus was the only woman elected into the ANC's 'top six' in 1994. None of the NP's senior leaders were women in the transition period. The ANC has still never had a woman president, deputy president or secretary general. Men also dominated the economic talks.

27 Mbembe, 'Apartheid futures and the limits of racial reconciliation', 1.

28 See, for instance, Keith Beavon, 'Northern Johannesburg: Part of the "rainbow" or neo-apartheid city in the making', *Mots Pluriels* 13 (2000): 1–15; Tshepo Madlingozi, 'Social justice in a time of neo-apartheid constitutionalism: Critiquing the anti-black economy of recognition, incorporation and distribution', *Stellenbosch Law Review* 28, no. 1 (2017): 123–47; M. C. Jozana, 'Proposed South African Bill of Rights: A prescription for equality or neo-apartheid', *American University Journal of International Law and Policy* 7 (1991): 45; Charlotte Lemanski, 'A new apartheid? The spatial implications of fear of crime in Cape Town, South Africa', *Environment and Urbanization* 16, no. 2 (2004): 101–12; Charlotte Spinks, 'A new apartheid?: Urban spatiality,(fear of) crime, and segregation in Cape Town, South Africa', London School of Economics and Political Science, Development Studies Institute, 2001; Scott Warren, 'A new apartheid: South Africa's struggle with immigration', *Huffpost*, 6 December 2017.

29 Simukai Chigudu, *The Political Life of an Epidemic: Cholera, Crisis and Citizenship in Zimbabwe*, Cambridge: Cambridge University Press, 2020, 4.

30 Mbembe, *On the Postcolony*, 66–8. On p. 67, Mbembe avers, 'Because these new

technologies of domination are still being elaborated, they have not yet, generally, totally replaced those already present. Sometimes they draw inspiration from the old forms, retain traces of them, or even operate behind their facade.' Mbembe has himself elaborated on this process in the twenty years since in various works, especially *Necropolitics*, Durham, NC: Duke University Press, 2019; *Brutalisme*, Paris: La Découverte, 2020.

31   Béatrice Hibou, *Privatizing the State*, New York: Columbia University Press, 2004; Jean-François Bayart, Stephen Ellis and Béatrice Hibou, *The Criminalization of the State in Africa*, Leiden: African Studies Centre, 1999, especially their chapter 'From kleptocracy to the felonious state', 1-31; Béatrice Hibou, 'From privatising the economy to privatising the state: An analysis of the continual formation of the state', in Béatrice Hibou (ed.), *Privatizing the State*, New York: Columbia University Press, 2004: 1–47.

32   See, for instance, Safiya Umoja Noble, *Algorithms of Oppression: How Search Engines Reinforce Racism*, New York: NYU Press, 2018; Shoshana Zuboff, *The Age of Surveillance Capitalism: The Fight for a Human Future at the New Frontier of Power*, London: Profile Books, 2019; Jaron Lanier, *You Are Not a Gadget: A Manifesto*, New York: Vintage, 2010; Jaron Lanier, *Who Owns the Future?*, New York: Simon and Schuster, 2014. I survey this literature more carefully in the chapter on technology.

33   Any notion, therefore, that I am repeating arguments about African 'extraversion' or 'the privatisation of the state' from the late 1990s and early 2000s is mistaken, though I owe a scholarly debt to Bayart and Hibou.

34   This is inspired again by Mbembe, who insists that failing to regard multiple temporalities at once comes 'at the at the cost of an extraordinary impoverishment of reality', in *On the Postcolony*.

35   Sarah Nuttall, 'Afterword: the shock of the new old', *Social Dynamics* 45, no. 2 (2019): 280–5.

SPACE

36   Barry Ronge, 'Enemy at the Gates', *Sunday Times Magazine*, April 2003, 6.

37   See, for instance, Nico Kotze, Ruan Schoeman, Sanet Carow and Peter Schmitz, 'Orania – 24 years after apartheid: The sociopolitical reanimation of a small rural town in South Africa', *Smart Geography*, 2020: 217–30.

38   Humphrey Tyler, 'Apartheid switch: South African call for "whites only" homeland', *Christian Science Monitor*, 14 July 1980, https://www.csmonitor. com/1980/0714/071443.html.

39   The precursor of today's Vryheidsfront Plus party (Freedom Front Plus).

40   Nelson Mandela, *Dare Not Linger*, Johannesburg: Pan Macmillan, 2017.

41   Mandela, *Dare Not Linger*, 27.

42   Mandela, *Dare Not Linger*, 28.

43 Edward Cavanagh, 'The history of dispossession at Orania and the politics of land restitution in South Africa', *Journal of Southern African Studies* 39, no. 2 (2013): 396.

44 Right-Wing Directory, Independent Board of Inquiry, Wits Historical Papers, 1996, http://www.historicalpapers.wits.ac.za/inventories/inv_pdfo/AG2543/AG2543-2-3-7-01-jpeg.pdf.

45 Cavanagh, 'The history of dispossession at Orania', 400.

46 Interestingly, those pushing for a *volkstaat* had split by this time. The Afrikaner Freedom Foundation (AVSTIG) was initially in alliance with other right-wing organisations: the Conservative Party, the AWB and the HNP. However, the group split after the AVSTIG was prepared to seek a *volkstaat* in the country's west while the other organisations refused to abandon a *volkstaat* in the country's north.

47 Cavanagh, 'The history of dispossession at Orania', 402.

48 Cavanagh, 'The history of dispossession at Orania', 402.

49 Right-Wing Directory, Independent Board of Inquiry, Wits Historical Papers, 1996, http://www.historicalpapers.wits.ac.za/inventories/inv_pdfo/AG2543/AG2543-2-3-7-01-jpeg.pdf.

50 Right-Wing Directory, Independent Board of Inquiry, Wits Historical Papers, 1996, http://www.historicalpapers.wits.ac.za/inventories/inv_pdfo/AG2543/AG2543-2-3-7-01-jpeg.pdf.

51 'Mandela visits apartheid die-hards', *New York Times*, 16 August 1995, https://www.nytimes.com/1995/08/16/world/mandela-visits-apartheid-die-hards.html.

52 'Mandela visits apartheid die-hards', *New York Times*, 16 August 1995, https://www.nytimes.com/1995/08/16/world/mandela-visits-apartheid-die-hards.html.

53 President Zuma visits Orania, SABC News, 21 January 2020, https://www.youtube.com/watch?v=aJOXp29y0zI.

54 Rebecca Davis, 'Everyone in Orania is woke: A journey to SA's most notorious town', *Daily Maverick*, 21 January 2020, https://www.dailymaverick.co.za/article/2020-01-21-everyone-in-orania-is-woke-a-journey-to-sas-most-notorious-town/.

55 See, for instance, Brij Maharaj, 'The apartheid city', in Ruth Massey and Ashley Gunter (eds.), *Urban Geography in South Africa*, New York: Springer, 2020, 97–117.

56 Mpho Matsipa, 'The order of appearances: Urban renewal in Johannesburg', PhD thesis, UC Berkeley, 2014, 10.

57 These maps were created in 2016 but draw on data from 2011. A new census set for 2021 will reveal any change. Still, even if we consider the picture seventeen years after apartheid, the point stands. Note, also, that 'Indian' and 'Coloured' areas still bridge White urban centres and Black urban peripheries: the new apartheid city preserves racial boundaries *and* the hierarchies between these boundaries.

58 Aubrey Matshiqi, 'South Africa needs a new revolution', YouTube video, 21 January 2020, https://www.youtube.com/watch?v=ApsL29r7JR4&t=5s.

59 Tlou Ramoroka, 'Gated communities in South Africa's urban areas 20 years into

democracy: Old wine in newly designed bottles?', *Mediterranean Journal of Social Sciences* 5, no. 15 (2014): 58.

60   Karina Landman, 'Gated communities in South Africa: The challenge for spatial planning and land use management', *Town Planning Review* 75 (2004): 151–73.

61   Karina Landman, 'The transformation of public space in South Africa and the role of urban design', *Urban Design International* 21, no. 1 (2016): 78–92.

62   Karina Landman, 'Gated communities in South Africa: An emerging paradox', in Ruth Massey and Ashley Gunter (eds.), *Urban Geography in South Africa*, New York: Springer, 2020, 55.

63   Landman, 'Gated communities in South Africa: An emerging paradox', 55–74.

64   Gauteng is the province with the most gated communities in South Africa

65   Residential fortification is becoming increasingly widespread, even in townships. Gated communities are no longer confined to metropolitan centres. The middle class now also prefer gated living. As Spocter shows, there is an increasing trend towards de-urbanisation, where gated communities occur at a distance from traditional urban centres. See Manfred Spocter, 'Privatisation of municipal golf courses in small towns in the Western Cape, South Africa', *South African Geographical Journal* 99, no. 2 (2017): 113–33; Manfred Spocter, 'A toponymic investigation of South African gated communities', *South African Geographical Journal* 100, no. 3 (2018): 326–48.

66   Lynsey Chutel, 'South Africa's gated communities are building higher walls in an already divided society', *Quartz*, 9 January 2018, https://qz.com/africa/1175370/johannesburgs-gated-communities-echo-apartheid-era-segregation-in-south-africa/.

67   Teresa Dirsuweit and Alex Wafer, 'Scale, governance and the maintenance of privileged control: The case of road closures in Johannesburg's northern suburbs', *Urban Forum* 17, no. 4 (2006): 396.

68   Anine Kriegler and Mark Shaw, *A Citizen's Guide to Crime Trends in South Africa*, Cape Town: Jonathan Ball Publishers, 2016.

69   Tunde Agbola. *The Architecture of Fear: Urban Design and Construction in Response to Urban Violence in Lagos*, Ibadan: African Book Builders, 1997.

70   Ha-Joon Chang, *23 Things They Don't Tell You about Capitalism*, London: Bloomsbury, 2012.

71   See, for instance, a fascinating auto-ethnographic study of walking on Rissik Street by Temba Middelmann, 'Rhythm and connection on Rissik Street: Reflecting on public space research in inner-city Johannesburg', *Anthropology Southern Africa* 42, no. 1 (2019): 99–113.

72   Charlotte Lemanski, 'A new apartheid? The spatial implications of fear of crime in Cape Town, South Africa', *Environment and Urbanization* 16, no. 2 (2004): 107.

73   Roger Southall, 'Botha reformism, the Bantustan strategy and the marginalization of the South African periphery', *Labour, Capital and Society/Travail/Capital et Société* 15, no. 2 (1982): 6–39.

74 Meaning 'white person-stan'.

75 Keith Bevon and Pauline Larsen, 'Sandton Central, 1969–2013: From open veld to new CBD?', in Philip Harrison, Graeme Gotz, Alison Todes and Chris Wray (eds.), *Changing Space, Changing City: Johannesburg after Apartheid*, Johannesburg: Wits University Press, 2014.

76 Dirsuweit and Wafer, 'Scale, governance and the maintenance of privileged control', 396.

77 Grace Blakeley, *Stolen: How to Save the World from Financialisation*, London: Watkins Media Limited, 2019, Kindle edition.

78 The protest also echoed previous demonstrations in Cape Town over the city's use of the bucket toilet system in townships. Revolted by this demeaning attempt at solving the city's sanitation crisis, the Ses'khona People's Rights Movement had established faeces as a symbol for economic inequality in the politics of Cape Town. See Colin McFarlane and Jonathan Silver, 'The poolitical city: "Seeing sanitation" and making the urban political in Cape Town', *Antipode* 49, no. 1 (2017): 125–48; Tawanda Nyawasha, 'The nation and its politics: Discussing political modernity in the "other" South Africa', *Journal of Southern African Studies* 42, no. 2 (2016): 229–42.

79 Maxwele himself had lived in Khayelitsha.

80 Although protests continued for three years, the main moment of protest happened in 2015.

81 I cover the extent of fees increases in Sizwe Mpofu-Walsh, 'Myth Two: Free education is unachievable', in *Democracy and Delusion: 10 Myths in South African Politics*, Cape Town: Tafelberg, 2017, 14–24.

82 Lwandile Fikeni, 'Protest, art and the aesthetics of rage: Social solidarity and the shaping a post-rainbow South Africa', Ruth First Lecture, University of the Witwatersrand, 17 August 2017, http://witsvuvuzela.com/wp-content/uploads/2016/08/Final-1-Lwandile-2016.pdf.

83 See, for instance, Mamdani's argument on the importance of student movements. Mahmood Mamdani, 'University crisis and reform: A reflection on the African experience', *Review of African Political Economy* 20, no. 58 (1993): 7–19.

84 The word 'Bantustan' was created by the anti-apartheid movement to satirise carving South Africa into ethnic states. It is a portmanteau of 'Bantu' (denoting the Bantu people) and '-stan', a term often used to describe fractured Central Asian states.

85 There were four of these in the 1980s: Transkei, Ciskei, Venda, and Bophuthatswana. There were also six 'self-governing' territories: Lebowa, Gazankulu, KwaNdebele, Qwaqwa, KaNgwane, and KwaZulu.

86 Laura Phillips, 'History of South Africa's Bantustans', in *Oxford Research Encyclopedia of African History*, 2017.

87 Black people were legally confined to only 13% of the South African landmass.

88 Bertil Egerö, 'South Africa's Bantustans: From dumping grounds to battlefronts', Nordic

Africa Institute, 1991; Laura Evans, 'South Africa's Bantustans and the dynamics of "decolonization": Reflections on writing histories of the homelands', *South African Historical Journal* 64, no. 1 (2012): 117–37.

89   Phillips, 'History of South Africa's Bantustans'.

90   Phillips, 'History of South Africa's Bantustans'.

91   Despite the upheaval of 'betterment planning', the democratic government chose not to restitute to its victims, since they were already deemed to have lived inside the Bantustans.

92   Arianna Lissoni and Shireen Ally, 'Bantustan states', *African Historical Review* 50 no. 1 (2018): 1–3.

93   Phillips, 'History of South Africa's Bantustans'.

94   Ivor Chipkin and Sarah Meny-Gibert, 'Why the past matters: Studying public administration in South Africa', *Journal of Public Administration* 47, no. 1 (2012): 107. Some of these civil servants also went into national government.

95   Holomisa was initially an ANC Deputy Minister. He was ironically expelled from the party for alleging before the TRC that then Minister of Public Enterprises, Stella Sigcau, was guilty of soliciting a bribe while she was a Bantustan official. See Eric Naki, *Bantu Holomisa: The Game Changer*, Johannesburg: Picador Africa, 2017.

96   The isiXhosa word for 'chief'.

97   In some ways, this was a return to an earlier form of ANC politics in the early twentieth century, when leaders like Seme viewed the ANC as a 'parliament of traditional leaders'. See, for instance, Bongani Ngqulunga, *The Man Who Founded the ANC: A Biography of Pixley ka Isaka Seme*, Johannesburg: Penguin Random House, 2017.

98   Supra Mahumapelo, Ace Magashule and David Mabuza, respectively.

99   Mahmood Mamdani, 'Democracy, dictatorships, and ethical leadership in post-colonial Africa', YouTube video, Tambo Foundation, 21 October 2020, https://www.youtube.com/watch?v=K7DKfAyuz64&t=6128s.

100   Elsewhere, I have explored newer proposals for land reform which also reinforce the problem. See, for example, the third chapter in Mpofu-Walsh, *Democracy and Delusion*. Among the pieces of legislation which have reified these land relations are the Governance Framework Act of 2003, the Communal Land Rights Act of 2004 and the Traditional Courts Bill of 2012.

101   Andisiwe Makinana, 'Pensioners head for high court', News24, 14 June 2014, https://www.news24.com/citypress/news/pensioners-head-for-high-court-20160611.

102   Anton van Zyl, 'Another chapter finishes in the Venda pension fund saga', *Zoutnet*, 18 September 2020, https://www.zoutnet.co.za/articles/news/53124/2020-09-18/another-chapter-finishes-in-venda-pension-fund-saga.

103   Roger Southall, 'The ANC for sale? Money, morality and business in South Africa', *Review of African Political Economy* 35, no. 116 (2008): 281–99; Ray Hartley, *Cyril*

Ramaphosa: The Path to Power in South Africa, Cape Town: Oxford University Press, 2018. Millennium Consolidated Investments would later morph into the Shanduka Group.

104 Walter Sisulu, We Shall Overcome: Reflections in Prison, Cape Town: Zebra Press, 2001, 85.

105 See, for instance, Nigel Worden, Slavery in Dutch South Africa, Cambridge: Cambridge University Press, 1985; Wayne Dooling. Slavery, Emancipation and Colonial Rule in South Africa, Athens, OH: Ohio University Press, 2008.

106 This quote comes from a judgment of the Constitutional Court authored by Deputy Chief Justice Dikgang Moseneke. See Department of Land Affairs and Others v Goedgelegen Tropical Fruits (Pty) Ltd (CCT69/06) [2007] ZACC 12; 2007 (10) BCLR 1027 (CC); 2007 (6) SA 199 (CC) (6 June 2007).

107 Michael Cowling, Donna Hornby and Laurel Oettlé, Research Report on the Tenure Security of Labour Tenants and Former Labour Tenants in South Africa', Pietermaritzburg: AFRA, 2017.

108 The Restitution of Land Rights Act of 1994, The Land Reform (Labour Tenants) Act of 1996, The Extension of Security of Tenure Act of 1997, and the Prevention of Illegal Evictions from and Unlawful Occupation of Land Act of 1998.

109 This comes from section 25(9) of the Constitution.

110 Mwelase and Others v Director-General for the Department of Rural Development and Land Reform and Another (CCT 232/18) [2019] ZACC 30; 2019 (11) BCLR 1358 (CC); 2019 (6) SA 597 (CC) (20 August 2019). See, also, Elmien du Plessis, 'The Msiza-case: The perpetuation of injustices by the miscalculation of "just and equitable" compensation', European Property Law Journal 8, no. 2 (2019): 211–26.

111 See J. M. Pienaar, 'Approaching systemic failure? A brief overview of recent land reform case law: Aantekeninge', Journal of South African Law/Tydskrif vir die Suid-Afrikaanse Reg 2020, no. 3 (2020): 536–46.

112 Mwelase and Others v Director-General for the Department of Rural Development and Land Reform and Another, 16. This is put in the way that only Justice Cameron could put it.

113 Mwelase and Others v Director-General for the Department of Rural Development and Land Reform and Another, 13.

114 The section reads: '23(1) The owner of affected land or any other person whose rights are affected shall be entitled to just and equitable compensation as prescribed by the Constitution for the acquisition by the applicant of land or a right in land.'

115 Msiza v Director-General for the Department of Rural Development and Land Reform and Others (LCC133/2012) [2016] ZALCC 12; 2016 (5) SA 513 (LCC) (5 July 2016).

116 Msiza v Director-General for the Department of Rural Development and Land Reform and Others, 11.

117 *Uys N.O. and Another v Msiza and Others* (1222/2016) [2017] ZASCA 130; 2018 (3) SA 440 (SCA) (29 September 2017), 12.

118 'Labour tenancy', Custom Contested, 2018, https://www.customcontested.co.za/laws-and-policies/labour-tenancy/.

119 To quote Teju Cole from 'Speech to the graduating class of the Harvard Graduate School of Design', YouTube video, 31 May 2019, https://www.youtube.com/watch?v=y-TIaxEgQ9kM.

LAW

120 Dikgang Moseneke, 'Transformative constitutionalism: Its implications for the law of contract', *Stellenbosch Law Review* 20, no. 1 (2009): 7.

121 The difference between statute and common law is that statutory law is law passed by legislation, whereas common law is law which develops organically from legal judgments. Public law and private law differ as to who is affected: public law applies to all of society, whereas private law applies to private parties, usually contracting between and among themselves. These distinctions are fundamental to my argument about the new apartheid, because I claim that the logic of apartheid has migrated to the private domain, so that common law, private law, and the law of contract become key venues for understanding the preservation of apartheid oppression.

122 Ndumiso Dladla, 'The liberation of history and the end of South Africa: Some notes towards an Azanian historiography in Africa, South', *South African Journal on Human Rights* 34, no. 3 (2018): 415.

123 To quote Fukuyama.

124 Karin van Marle, 'The spectacle of post-apartheid constitutionalism', *Griffith Law Review* 16, no. 2 (2007): 411.

125 See, for instance, Edwin Cameron, *What You Can Do with Rights*, Law Commission, 2012; Jonathan Michael Berger and Amy Kapczynski, 'The story of the TAC case: The potential and limits of socio-economic rights litigation in South Africa', in Deena R. Hurwitz and Margaret L. Satterthwaite (eds.), *Human Rights Advocacy Stories*, St Paul, MN: Foundation Press, 2009.

126 Cyril Ramaphosa, 'State of the nation address 2019', http://www. thepresidency. gov. za/state-of-the-nation-address/state-nation-address-president-republic-south-africa%2C-mr-cyril-ramaphosa.

127 Jacob Zuma, '20th anniversary of the Constitution of the Republic of South Africa', https://www.gov.za/speeches/constitution-12-dec-2016-0000.

128 Roelf Meyer, 'Celebrating South Africa's peaceful transition: A Conversation with the SA Reconciliation Barometer', http://reconciliationbarometer.org/?page_id=2890.

129 Helen Zille, 'Remarks at the FW de Klerk Foundation conference on the South African Constitution: Quo vadis the Constitution', https://gosouth.co.za/helen-zille-quo-vadis-the-constitution/.

130 This section states:

We, the people of South Africa,

Recognise the injustices of our past;

Honour those who suffered for justice and freedom in our land;

Respect those who have worked to build and develop our country; and

Believe that South Africa belongs to all who live in it, united in our diversity.

We therefore, through our freely elected representatives, adopt this Constitution as the supreme law of the Republic so as to

Heal the divisions of the past and establish a society based on democratic values, social justice and fundamental human rights;

Lay the foundations for a democratic and open society in which government is based on the will of the people and every citizen is equally protected by law;

Improve the quality of life of all citizens and free the potential of each person; and

Build a united and democratic South Africa able to take its rightful place as a sovereign state in the family of nations.

May God protect our people. Nkosi Sikelel' iAfrika. Morena boloka setjhaba sa heso. God seën Suid-Afrika. God bless South Africa. Mudzimu fhatutshedza Afurika. Hosi katekisa Afrika.

131 For the problems with this conception, see Sizwe Mpofu-Walsh, 'Myth Six: Racial justice is unjust', in *Democracy and Delusion: 10 Myths in South African Politics*, Cape Town: Tafelberg, 2017.

132 The Constitution of India, 26 January 1950, https://www.refworld.org/docid/3ae6b5e20. html. For a deeper analysis of the Indian Constitution, see the magisterial work of Indian Constitutional Court judge F. S. Nariman. For example, Nariman, 'Fifty years of human rights protection in India: The record of 50 years of constitutional practice', *National Law School of India Review* (2013): 13–26.

133 The Constitution of India.

134 Constitution of Brazil, 5 October 1988, https://www.refworld.org/docid/4c4820bf2. html.

135 Constitution of Brazil.

136 Dikgang Moseneke, *My Own Liberator: A Memoir*, Johannesburg: Picador Africa, 2016, Kindle edition.

137 Moseneke, *My Own Liberator*, Kindle edition.

138 This section states:

The amount of the compensation and the time and manner of payment must be just and equitable, reflecting an equitable balance between the public interest and the interests of those affected, having regard to all relevant circumstances, including—

(a) the current use of the property;

(b) the history of the acquisition and use of the property;

(c) the market value of the property;

(d) the extent of direct state investment and subsidy in the acquisition and beneficial capital improvement of the property; and

(e) the purpose of the expropriation.

139 This section states:

No provision of this section may impede the state from taking legislative and other measures to achieve land, water and related reform, in order to redress the results of past racial discrimination, provided that any departure from the provisions of this section is in accordance with the provisions of section 36(1).

Section 36(1), in turn, asserts:

The rights in the Bill of Rights may be limited only in terms of law of general application to the extent that the limitation is reasonable and justifiable in an open and democratic society based on human dignity, equality and freedom, taking into account all relevant factors, including—

(a) the nature of the right;

(b) the importance of the purpose of the limitation;

(c) the nature and extent of the limitation;

(d) the relation between the limitation and its purpose; and

(e) less restrictive means to achieve the purpose.

140 Rights guaranteed are housing, health care, food, water, and social security.

141 The limitations of rights have been recounted at length elsewhere. Here, I am not interested in recounting that record at length.

142 Jessica Whyte, *The Morals of the Market: Human Rights and the Rise of Neoliberalism*, London: Verso Books, 2019, Apple Books edition.

143 Whyte, *The Morals of the Market*, Apple Books edition.

144 Peter Mwipikeni, 'Ubuntu, rights, and neoliberalism in South Africa', *International Journal of African Renaissance Studies: Multi-, Inter- and Transdisciplinarity* 14, no. 2 (2019): 82.

145 Adam Tooze, 'Neoliberalism's world order', *Dissent* 65, no. 3 (2018): 133.

146 Edwin Cameron, 'Judges, justice, and public power: The constitution and the rule of law in South Africa', *Oxford University Commonwealth Law Journal* 18, no. 1 (2018): 73–97.

147 See, for instance, Xia Jisheng, 'Evolution of South Africa's racist constitutions and the 1983 constitution', *Issue: A Journal of Opinion* 16, no. 1 (1987): 18-23, doi:10.2307/1166413.

148 Jisheng, 'Evolution of South Africa's racist constitutions and the 1983 constitution', 18.

149 Johan van der Walt, 'Vertical sovereignty, horizontal constitutionalism, subterranean capitalism: A case of competing retroactivities', *South African Journal on Human Rights* 26, no. 1 (2010): 105.

150 See, for instance, M. B. Ramose, 'Towards a post-conquest South Africa: Beyond the constitution of 1996', *South African Journal on Human Rights* 34, no. 3 (2018): 326–41.

151 Here I paraphrase Audre Lorde's now-famous statement that 'the master's tools will never dismantle the master's house'.

152 Tembeka Ngcukaitobi, *The Land Is Ours: South Africa's First Black Lawyers and the Birth of Constitutionalism*, Cape Town: Penguin Books, 2018.

153 Richard R.W Brooks, 'The banality of racial inequality', *Yale Law Journal* 124 (2014): 2626.

154 Tshepo Madlingozi, 'Social justice in a time of neo-apartheid constitutionalism: Critiquing the anti-black economy of recognition, incorporation and distribution', *Stellenbosch Law Review* 28, no. 1 (2017): 125. See, also, Tshepo Madlingozi, 'South Africa's first black lawyers, amaRespectables and the birth of evolutionary constitution: A review of Tembeka Ngcukaitobi's *The Land is Ours: South Africa's First Black Lawyers and the Birth of Constitutionalism*', *South African Journal on Human Rights* 34, no. 3 (2018): 517–29.

155 Madlingozi, 'Social justice in a time of neo-apartheid constitutionalism', 125.

156 Madlingozi, 'Social justice in a time of neo-apartheid constitutionalism', 146.

157 Madlingozi, 'Social justice in a time of neo-apartheid constitutionalism', 125.

158 Moseneke, 'Transformative constitutionalism', 3.

159 Deeksha Bhana, 'The horizontal application of the Bill of Rights: A reconciliation of sections 8 and 39 of the Constitution', *South African Journal on Human Rights* 29, no. 2 (2013): 357. See, also, Deeksha Bhana and Marius Pieterse, 'Towards a reconciliation of contract law and constitutional values: Brisley and Afrox revisited', *South African Law Journal* 122 (2005): 865; Deeksha Bhana, 'The law of contract and the Constitution: Napier v. Barkhuizen (SCA)', *South African Law Journal* 124 (2007): 269; D. Bhana and C. J. Visser, 'The concurrence of breach of contract and delict in a constitutional context', *South African Journal on Human Rights* 35, no. 1 (2019): 94–120. For an alternative view, see Stu Woolman, 'Category mistakes and the waiver of constitutional rights: A response to Deeksha Bhana on Barkhuizen', *South African Law Journal* 125 (2008): 10.

160 J. C. van der Walt and Johan Willem Gous van der Walt, *Law and Sacrifice: Towards a Post-apartheid Theory of Law*, Abingdon: Psychology Press, 2005.

161 Moseneke, 'Transformative constitutionalism', 8.

162 Incidentally, some apartheid statutes survive. The Riotous Assemblies Act is a key example. Sections 16, 17 and 18 are all that remain of the substance of the 1956 Act. But, curiously, these sections are fundamental to the original spirit. Section 18, in particular, deals with the crime of 'incitement'. It was expressly intended to stultify political opposition to apartheid, and imposed harsh criminal sanctions on 'inciteful' speech.

Apartheid's Parliament intentionally defined this crime broadly so that incitement could be punished in even the most tenuous of cases. No link between the incitement and any eventual act of violence was necessary to secure guilt. This was a powerful tool in the apartheid state's repressive armoury. Yet it survives in democratic South Africa. The crime of incitement is not, in itself, unconstitutional. The problem with the Act is the draconian definition of incitement—as was the original intention. Not only has this law been preserved, but it has also been defended by the democratic government in the context of its use against opposition parties on the grounds of law and order.

The National Key Points Act is a second example. This Act, which was only repealed in 2019, was intended to defend privately owned sites considered 'strategic' to the apartheid state. According to Pierre de Vos, 'it enabled the apartheid government to compel private owners, as well as state-owned corporations, to safeguard such sites owned by them at their own cost'. The Act was famously invoked by the ANC government to justify the extravagant expense incurred at President Zuma's private residence in Nkandla. Other statutes like the Native Administration Act of 1927, the Coloured Persons Education Act of 1963, the Indians Education Amendment Act 60 of 1967, and the Tear Gas Act of 1964 have all caused controversy late into democracy, and some still survive. The quotes in this note come from Pierre de Vos, 'Why are the Riotous Assembly Act and other apartheid-era laws still in place?', *Daily Maverick*, 21 February 2020, https://www.dailymaverick.co.za/opinionista/2020-02-21-why-are-the-riotous-assembly-act-and-other-apartheid-era-laws-still-in-place/. For further background, see Dirk Lambrechts and Alice Maree, 'The law in South Africa regarding state security', *Acta Criminologica: Southern African Journal of Criminology* 11, no. 1 (1998): 50–8. On state security, see also Dale T. McKinley, 'State security and civil-political rights in South Africa', *Strategic Review for Southern Africa* 35, no. 1 (2013): 118. The National Key Points Act was replaced by the Critical Infrastructure Protection Act, which was signed into law on 20 November 2020.

163 See David Keyt, *Aristotle: Politics, Books V and VI*, Oxford University Press, 1999; Robert Nozick, *Anarchy, State, and Utopia*, New York: Basic Books, 1974; Christian Lund, 'Property and citizenship: Conceptually connecting land rights and belonging in Africa', *Africa Spectrum* 46, no. 3 (2011): 71–5.

164 Karl Marx, *Capital, volume I*, Harmondsworth: Penguin, 2004; Karl Marx and Friedrich Engels, *The Communist Manifesto*, Harmondsworth: Penguin, 2002. For a useful brief meditation on Marx's position, see George G. Brenkert, 'Freedom and private property in Marx', *Philosophy and Public Affairs* (1979): 122–47.

165 Matthew D. Fails and Jonathan Krieckhaus, 'Colonialism, property rights and the modern world income distribution', *British Journal of Political Science* (2010): 487–508.

166 Emile Zitzke, 'A decolonial critique of private law and human rights', *South African Journal on Human Rights* 34, no. 3 (2018): 500.

167 Zitzke, 'A decolonial critique of private law and human rights', 492.

168 A key case dealing with this question is the Constitutional Court's *Jaftha* case, where eviction was precluded on the basis of the right to housing guaranteed in the Constitution.

169 *Beadica 231 CC and Others v Trustees for the Time Being of Oregon Trust and Others* (CCT 109/19), 40.

170 See, for instance, John Rawls, *Lectures on the History of Political Philosophy*, Cambridge, MA: Harvard University Press, 2008; John Locke, *The Second Treatise of Civil Government*, 1690; Jean-Jacques Rousseau, *Rousseau: The Social Contract and Other Later Political Writings*, Cambridge: Cambridge University Press, 2018.

171 See, for instance, Charles W. Mills, *The Racial Contract*, Ithaca, NY: Cornell University Press, 2014; Charles W. Mills, 'Racial liberalism', *PMLA* 123, no. 5 (2008): 1380-1397.

172 See, for instance, John Rawls, *A Theory of Justice*, Cambridge, MA: Harvard University Press, 2009.

173 Moseneke, 'Transformative constitutionalism', 9.

174 Here I paraphrase David P. Weber, 'Restricting the freedom of contract: A fundamental prohibition', *Yale Human Rights and Development Law Journal* 16 (2013): 51.

175 I stress race here but there was also class, gender and sexual orientation discrimination.

176 *Truth and Reconciliation Commission of South Africa Report*, vol. 1, 1998, 495. These Acts also criminalised 'desertion, insolence, drunkenness, negligence and strikes'.

177 *Weinerlein v Goch Buildings Ltd* 1925 AD 282, 292.

178 This case was heard before the Supreme Court of the Transvaal, where Innes served as Chief Justice from 1902 to 1910.

179 *Burger v Central African Railways* 1903 TS 571.

180 *Moller v Keimoes School Committee* 1911 AD 635. For context, see Peter Parker and Joyce Mokhesi-Parker, *In the Shadow of Sharpeville: Apartheid and Criminal Justice*, London: Palgrave Macmillan, 1998, 38.

181 Parker and Mokhesi-Parker, *In the Shadow of Sharpeville*, 38.

182 *Minister of Posts and Telegraphs v Rasool* 1934 AD 167; *R. v Herman* 1937 AD 168.

183 The highest court in the Union of South Africa.

184 Parker and Mokhesi-Parker, *In the Shadow of Sharpeville*, 38. See *Mokhatle v Union Government (Minister of Native Affairs)* 1926 AD 71.

185 *Sibanyoni v University of Fort Hare* 1985 (1) SA 19 (Ck) 301.

186 *Lucas' Trustee v Ismail and Amad* 1905 TS 239, 247; *Minister of the Interior v Lockhat*

1961 (2) SA 587 (A); *S v Adams, S v Werner* 1981 (1) SA 187 (A); *R. v Pitje* 1960 (4) SA 709 (A). In 1962, an appeal court upheld a conviction for contempt of court when a Black lawyer refused to speak from a desk reserved for Blacks in court.

187 For example, former Chief Justice Pius Langa instituted a commission into racism in the judiciary soon after the new Constitution was adopted, highlighting this problem. Interestingly, both Chief Justice Mogoeng and Deputy Chief Justice Zondo contributed to this commission.

188 Section 35(3) only invoked a 'duty' on behalf of the judiciary to regard the Bill of Rights, which caused judicial confusion in the years before 1996.

189 Moseneke, 'Transformative constitutionalism', 9. See *Du Plessis and Others v De Klerk and Another* (CCT8/95) [1996] ZACC 10; 1996 (3) SA 850; 1996 (5) BCLR 658 (15 May 1996).

190 *Du Plessis and Others v De Klerk and Another* (CCT8/95) [1996] ZACC 10; 1996 (3) SA 850; 1996 (5) BCLR 658 (15 May 1996)

191 *Du Plessis and Others v De Klerk and Another.*

192 See, for instance, Leo Boonzaier, 'Rereading Botha v Rich', *South African Law Journal* 137, no. 1 (2020): 1–12; Dale Hutchison, 'From bona fides to ubuntu: The quest for fairness in the South African law of contract', *Acta Juridica*, no. 1 (2019): 99–126. In its *Beadica* decision, the Constitutional Court went as far as remarking: 'The Supreme Court of Appeal's failure to either apply or distinguish *Botha* in this matter is most unfortunate. The fundamental doctrine of precedent is a core component of the rule of law. This doctrine has been endorsed by both this Court and the Supreme Court of Appeal. To deviate from it is to invite legal chaos and undermine a founding value of our Constitution. The Supreme Court of Appeal failed to properly engage with this Court's reasoning in *Botha*. It went further, chastising the High Court for not following its decisions, whilst at the same time departing from the decisions of this Court.'

193 See, for instance, *Brisley v Drotsky* 2002 (4) SA 1 (SCA); *Afrox Healthcare Bpk v Strydom* 2002 (6) SA 21 (SCA); *Barkhuizen v Napier* 2007 (5) SA 323 (CC); *Everfresh Market Virginia (Pty) Ltd v Shoprite Checkers (Pty) Ltd* 2012 (1) SA 256 (CC). See, also, F. D. J. Brand, 'The role of good faith, equity and fairness in the South African law of contract', *South African Law Journal* 126 (2009): 71; Carole Lewis, 'The uneven journey to uncertainty in contract', *Journal for Contemporary Roman Dutch Law* 76 (2013): 80; L. T. C. Harms, 'The puisne judge, the chaos theory and the common law', *South African Law Journal* 131 (2014): 3; Malcolm Wallis, 'Commercial certainty and constitutionalism: Are they compatible?', *South African Law Journal* 133 (2016): 545; F. D. J. Brand, 'The role of good faith, equity and fairness in the South African law of contract: A further instalment', *Stellenbosch Law Review* 27 (2016): 238.

194 See Drucilla Cornell and Nyoko Muvangua (eds.), *Ubuntu and the Law: African Ideals and Postapartheid Jurisprudence*, New York, NY: Fordham University Press, 2012.

195 Moseneke, 'Transformative constitutionalism', 10.

196 Lewis, 'The uneven journey to uncertainty in contract', 80–94.

197 The Constitutional Court had already said in *Botha* and *Barkhuizen* that notions of fairness and reasonableness could be considered beyond strict definitions of contractual freedom.

198 The actual respondent was Trustees for the Time Being of the Oregon Trust. Incidentally, the owner of Sale's Hire was also a trustee in the Oregon Trust, hence benefiting both from the franchises and from the property leases.

199 The initial term was five years, with the option to renew for a further five years.

200 Davis had relied on *Botha v Rich*, in which the Constitutional Court had weighed the importance of contractual adherence against the potential impact of non-adherence.

201 Deeksha Bhana, 'The implications of the right to equality in terms of the Constitution for the common law of contract', *South African Law Journal* 134 (2017): 158.

202 Bhana, 'The implications of the right to equality in terms of the Constitution for the common law of contract', 158.

203 See Johan Beckmann, 'Exclusion and education in South Africa: An education law perspective of emerging alternative understandings of exclusion', *Bulgarian Comparative Education Society* (June 2016).

204 At the time of writing, an inquiry into racial discrimination in medical aid schemes in the context of section 59 of the Medical Schemes Act.

205 Some cases of racism have made it to the Constitutional Court, such as *South African Revenue Service v Commission for Conciliation, Mediation and Arbitration and Others* (CCT19/16) [2016] ZACC 38; *Duncanmec (Pty) Limited v Gaylard NO and Others* (CCT284/17) [2018] ZACC 29. The SARS case was particularly egregious given that SARS is a state organ, and the epithet 'kaffir' was used. See, also, Bongani Khumalo, 'Racism in the workplace: A view from the jurisprudence of courts in the past decade', *SA Mercantile Law Journal* 30, no. 3 (2018): 377–94.

206 See, for instance, Lisa R. Pruitt, 'No Black names on the letterhead: Efficient discrimination and the South African legal profession', *Michigan Journal of International Law* 23 (2001): 545.

207 For a meditation on this battle, see Timothy Gibbs, 'Apartheid South Africa's segregated legal field: Black lawyers and the Bantustans', *Africa: The Journal of the International African Institute* 90, no. 2 (2020): 293–317; J. Klaaren, 'African corporate lawyering and globalisation', *International Journal of the Legal Profession* 22, no. 2 (2016): 226–42; J. Klaaren, 'The contemporary South African legal profession and its transformations', in R. Abel, O. Hammerslev, U. Schultz and H. Sommerlad (eds.), *Lawyers in 21st-Century Societies*, London: Hart Publishing, 2020.

208 Parker and Mokhesi-Parker, *In the Shadow of Sharpeville*, 36.

209 Bhana, 'The horizontal application of the Bill of Rights', 351.

210 Bhana, 'The horizontal application of the Bill of Rights', 353.

211 National Party of South Africa, *Constitutional Rule in a Participatory Democracy*, https://omalley.nelsonmandela.org/omalley/index.php/site/q/03lv01538/04lv01584/05lv01594.htm (1991).

212 Moseneke, *My Own Liberator*, Kindle Edition.

213 National Party of South Africa, *Constitutional Rule*, 1.

WEALTH

214 Paul Williams and Ian Taylor, 'Neoliberalism and the political economy of the "new" South Africa', *New Political Economy* 5, no. 1 (2000): 21.

215 The commission later moved to a public building, partly due to funding constraints.

216 J. A. Lombard, 'The evolution of the theory of economic policy', *South African Journal of Economics* 53, no. 4 (1985): 204–14.

217 Lombard, 'The evolution of the theory of economic policy', 205.

218 Lombard, 'The evolution of the theory of economic policy', 210.

219 Lombard, 'The evolution of the theory of economic policy', 210.

220 Lombard, 'The evolution of the theory of economic policy'.

221 Lombard, 'The evolution of the theory of economic policy', 211.

222 Lombard, 'The evolution of the theory of economic policy', 331.

223 David Yudelman, *The Emergence of Modern South Africa: State, Capital, and the Incorporation of Organized Labor on the South African Gold Fields, 1902–1939*, Cape Town: David Philip, 1984.

224 Stuart Jones and Jon Inggs, 'An overview of the South African economy in the 1980s', *South African Journal of Economic History* 9, no. 2 (1994): 1–18.

225 Jones and Inngs, 'An overview of the South African economy in the 1980s', 3.

226 Seeraj Mohamed, 'Financialization of the South African economy', *Development* 59, no. 1-2 (2016): 137–42.

227 Anton Rupert, *Priorities for Coexistence*, Cape Town: Tafelberg, 1981, 81.

228 Wasserman published a book in the 1970s entitled *The Assault on Free Enterprise: Freeway to Communism*, which crystallised the argument.

229 See Marco Lorusso and Luca Pieroni, 'Causes and consequences of oil price shocks on the UK economy', *Economic Modelling* 72 (2018): 223–36; Marc Gronwald, 'Large oil shocks and the US economy: Infrequent incidents with large effects', *Energy Journal* 29, no. 1 (2008).

230 See Desmond King and Stewart Wood, 'The political economy of neoliberalism: Britain and the United States in the 1980', in *Continuity and Change in Contemporary Capitalism* , Cambridge: Cambridge University Press, 1999, 371–97; David Harvey, *A Brief History of Neoliberalism*, New York: Oxford University Press, 2007.

231 Andrew Bowman, 'Parastatals and economic transformation in South Africa: The political economy of the Eskom crisis', *African Affairs* 119, no. 476 (2020): 395–431.

232 Bowman, 'Parastatals and economic transformation in South Africa'.

233 Seeraj Mohamed, 'The political economy of accumulation in South Africa: Resource extraction, financialization, and capital flight as barriers to investment and employment growth', PhD dissertation, University of Massachusetts, 2019, iv, https://scholarworks.umass.edu/dissertations_2/1533.

234 See David Parker, *The Official History of Privatisation*, vol. I: *The Formative Years 1970–1987*, London: Routledge, 2009.

235 Friedrich A. Hayek, 'Economics and knowledge', *Economica* 4, no. 13 (1937): 33–54; see also F. A. Hayek, *The Road to Serfdom*, London: Routledge, 2014.

236 By maximising their own utility.

237 John Maynard Keynes, *The End of Laissez-Faire: The Economic Consequences of the Peace*, Buffalo, NY: Prometheus Books, 2009.

238 F. J. van Biljon, *State Interference in South Africa*, London: King and Son, 1939.

239 Privatisation also refers to the transition of a company from being publicly traded to becoming privately held in 'corporate privatisation'.

240 Parker, *The Official History of Privatisation*, vol. I, 22.

241 Dexter Whitfield, 'A typology of privatisation and marketisation', European Services Strategy Unit, 2006.

242 Arundhati Roy, *Capitalism: A Ghost Story*, London: Verso Books, 2014; Franco Berardi, *After the Future*, Chico, CA: AK Press, 2011; Franco Berardi, *Futurability: The Age of Impotence and the Horizon of Possibility*, London: Verso Books, 2017.

243 Béatrice Hibou, *Privatizing the State*, New York: Columbia University Press, 2004.

244 Hibou, *Privatizing the State*. Elsewhere, I discuss how the Gupta empire was essentially a privatised version of the South African state. See Sizwe Mpofu-Walsh, 'Myth 6: State participation in the economy is dangerous', in *Democracy and Delusion: 10 Myths in South African Politics*, Cape Town: Tafelberg, 2017.

245 Hibou, *Privatizing the State*.

246 Another goal of this period was creating a Black middle class. This would remove economic power from the state and displace it to the corporate world, while also enmeshing a 'black buffer' class into the economy. This enmeshment would conflict Black people between material and political aspirations. And it would come to characterise most of the new apartheid, as this class was quickly expanded in the new democracy. See Roger Southall, 'Political change and the black middle class in democratic South Africa', *Canadian Journal of African Studies/La Revue Canadienne des Etudes Africaines* 38, no. 3 (2004): 521–42.

247 RSA, White Paper on Privatisation and Deregulation in the Republic of South Africa 1987, Government Printer, South Africa, 1987.

248 Rex Mckenzie, 'Privatisation in South Africa', in Seeraj Mohamed (ed.), *The South African Financial System*, FESSD, 2016, 136–54, http://www.fessud.eu.

249 White Paper on Privatisation, 2.

250 White Paper on Privatisation, 2.

251 White Paper on Privatisation, 7.

252 F. W. de Klerk, 'Speech to the Opening of Parliament', Parliament of the Republic of South Africa, Cape Town, 1990.

253 Grietjie Verhoef, '"Not to Bet the Farm": Sanlam and internationalisation, 1995–2010', *Business History* 58, no. 6 (2016): 947–73. Sanlam stands for Suid-Afrikaanse Nasionale Lewens Assuransie Maatskappij Beperk (South African National Life Assurance Company Limited).

254 Grietjie Verhoef, *The Power of Your Life: The Sanlam Century of Insurance Empowerment, 1918–2018*, Oxford: Oxford University Press, 2019, 157.

255 Open Secrets, 'Declassified: Apartheid profits – Who funded the National Party?', *Daily Maverick*, 1 August 2017, https://www.dailymaverick.co.za/article/2017-08-01-declassified-apartheid-profits-who-funded-the-national-party/.

256 Hennie van Vuuren, *Apartheid, Guns and Money: A Tale of Profit*, Johannesburg: Jacana Media, 2017.

257 Open Secrets, 'Declassified: Apartheid profits – Who funded the National Party?'

258 Open Secrets, 'Declassified: Apartheid profits – Who funded the National Party?'

259 F. W. de Klerk, 'Speech to the Joint Sitting of Parliament', Parliament of the Republic of South Africa, Cape Town, 1993.

260 Belarus and Ukraine transferred their nuclear arsenals to Russia rather than renouncing nuclear weapons outright. See John W. de Villiers, Roger Jardine and Mitchell Reiss, 'Why South Africa Gave Up the Bomb', *Foreign Affairs* 72 (1992): 98; William C. Potter, 'The politics of nuclear renunciation: The cases of Belarus, Kazakhstan, and Ukraine', Henry L. Stimson Center, Occasional paper no. 22, 1995.

261 F. W. de Klerk, 'Letter form South African President de Klerk to President Bush', Office of the South African State President, 31 August 1990, https://digitalarchive. wilsoncenter.org/document/114187.pdf?v=e672caaf11d42a890e106474d085cd9c.

262 James Jude Hentz, 'The two faces of privatisation: Political and economic logics in transitional South Africa', *Journal of Modern African Studies* 38, no. 2 (2000), 203.

263 See Mohamed, 'The political economy of accumulation in South Africa'.

264 Apart from Sanlam and SA Mutual (later, Old Mutual), these companies can be traced to four main families: the Oppenheimer family controlled AAC, the Gordon family controlled Stanbic, the Rupert family controlled Rembrandt, and the Menell and Hersov families controlled Anglovaal. To complicate matters further, the unbundled parts of these companies sometimes merged with the subsidiaries of other conglomerates, creating cross-ownership.

265 Gilad Lee Isaacs, 'Financialisation in post-apartheid South Africa', PhD dissertation, SOAS, University of London, 2018, 243. See also Jason Bell, Sumayya Goga, Pamela Mondliwa and Simon Roberts, 'Structural transformation in South Africa: Moving towards a smart, open economy for all', CCRED working paper, 2018.

266 Isaacs, 'Financialisation in post-apartheid South Africa'.

267 I should note that the private sphere is not just the domain of big capital, however. In South Africa, as freedom to trade has bloomed, so a private informal sector exists in the shadows of the formal economy. This sector has boomed, increasing the bifurcated landscape of production and consumption. This informal sector—of minibus taxis, hair salons, fruit and vegetable sellers, etc.—is largely divorced from economic policy.

268 Isaacs, 'Financialisation in post-apartheid South Africa', 244.

269 Mohamed, 'The political economy of accumulation in South Africa', 2.

270 Anglo American plc., *Annual Report*, Johannesburg, 1999.

271 Anglo American plc., *Annual Report*, 1999.

272 National Treasury of South Africa, *A Safer Financial Sector to Serve South Africa Better*, Pretoria, 2011, http://www.treasury.gov.za/twinpeaks/20131211%20-%20Item%202%20A%20safer%20financial%20sector%20to%20serve%20South%20Africa%20better.pdf.

273 National Treasury of South Africa. *A Safer Financial Sector to Serve South Africa Better*.

274 For further context, see L. Ndikumana and J. K. Boyce, 'Capital flight from Africa: Updated methodology and new estimates', PERI research report, 1 June 2018: 'capital flight is defined as unrecorded capital flows and measured as discrepancies between recorded inflows and outflows of foreign exchange as reported in the country's official Balance of Payments. Net foreign exchange inflows consist mainly of additions to the stock of external debt and capital inflows in the form of foreign direct investment, portfolio investment and other investment.'

275 This amount exceeds R1tn in today's prices. See also Ben W. Smit and B. A. Mocke, 'Capital flight from South Africa: Magnitude and causes', *South African Journal of Economics* 59, no. 2 (1991): 101–17.

276 National Treasury of South Africa, *Research Report of the National Treasury: Ownership of JSE-Listed Companies*, Pretoria, September 2017, http://www.treasury.gov.za/comm_media/press/2017/2017100301%20Ownership%20monitor%20-%20Sept%202017.pdf. Specifically, see Table 7 on p. 20 of this report.

277 National Treasury of South Africa, *Research Report of the National Treasury: Ownership of JSE-Listed Companies*.

278 Keys only resigned from the board of BHP Billiton in 2002.

279 Tim Cohen, 'Derek Keys: A fearsome intellectual who led our fiscal discipline

model', *Business Day*, 2 May 2018, https://www.pressreader.com/south-africa/busine ss-day/20180502/282016147947097.

280 Nelson Mandela, 'Mandela on Derek Keys' resignation', Associated Press Archives, 21 July 2015, https://www.youtube.com/watch?v=ne86K8Dn_UY.

281 Kate Burgess and Scheherazade Daneshkhu, 'SAB: Last of London's international-ists', *Financial Times*, 13 November 2015.

282 T. Dunbar Moodie, 'Becoming a social movement union: Cyril Ramaphosa and the National Union of Mineworkers', *Transformation: Critical Perspectives on Southern Africa* 72, no. 1 (2010): 152–80.

283 Anthony Butler, *Cyril Ramaphosa*, Johannesburg: Jacana Media, 2011; Ray Hartley, *Cyril Ramaphosa: The Path to Power in South Africa*, Cape Town: Oxford University Press, 2018.

284 Bill Freund, 'South Africa: The end of apartheid and the emergence of the "BEE Elite"', *Review of African Political Economy* 34, no. 114 (2007): 661–78.

285 NAIL was founded by Dr Nthato Motlana. Other major executives were former Deputy Chief Justice Dikgang Moseneke and Jonty Sandler.

286 At inception, the Ramaphosa family owned 30% of Shanduka. Standard Bank and Investec also owned 30% while 25% was owned by management and 15% by associates and community trusts. Later, the China Investment Corporation became a significant shareholder.

287 Thanti Mthanti and Stephanie Townsend, 'Shanduka black umbrellas: Giving impetus to Black enterprises', Wits Business School, 2016.

288 Patrick Bond and Christopher Malikane, 'Inequality caused by macro-economic policies during overaccumulation crisis', *Development Southern Africa* 36, no. 6 (2019): 803–20.

289 He was criticised by his former partner in NAIL, Dr Motlana, for doing so.

290 See Ronit Frenkel and Pamila Gupta, 'Yo-yo culture: Thinking South Africa after Marikana', *Social Dynamics* 45, no. 2 (2019): 175–82; Bill Dixon, 'Power, politics and the police: Lessons from Marikana', *Journal of Modern African Studies* 57, no. 2 (2019): 203–21.

291 The margin was 179, meaning 90 people could have swung the election.

292 See, for instance, Cebelihle Bhengu, 'Maimane still wants answers from Ramaphosa, despite Mkhwebane court ruling', *Sunday Times*, 11 March 2020, https://www. timeslive.co.za/news/south-africa/2020-03-11-maimane-still-wants-answers-from-ramaphosa-despite-mkhwebane-court-ruling/; Karyn Maughan, 'Ramaphosa's bank statements won't be made public but other CR17 campaign info might', *Sunday Times*, 15 August 2019, https://www.timeslive.co.za/politics/2019-08-15-ramapho-sas-bank-statements-wont-be-made-public-but-other-cr17-campaign-info-still-might/.

293 Ferial Haffajee, 'How Ramaphosa's campaign spent R400 million and why it matters', *Daily Maverick*, 26 August 2019, https://www.dailymaverick.co.za/article/2019-08-26-how-ramaphosas-campaign-spent-r400-million-and-why-it-matters/26 August 2019.

294 Meanwhile, the Public Protector's report which impugned Ramaphosa was set aside by the Pretoria High Court. This ruling was appealed at the Constitutional Court and is reserved for judgment at the time of writing. The specific issue of campaign disclosure grew into a second court case also yet to be determined at the time of writing. This case may itself reach the Constitutional Court for a final decision. See *President of the Republic of South Africa v Office of the Public Protector and Others* (91139/2016) [2017] ZAGPPHC 747; 2018 (2) SA 100 (GP). See, also, Oxford Analytica, 'South Africa's Ramaphosa campaign scrutiny will linger', *Emerald Expert Briefings*, https://doi.org/10.1108/OXAN-ES246002; Oxford Analytica, 'South Africa's Protector will divert Ramaphosa focus', *Emerald Expert Briefings*, https://doi.org/10.1108/OXAN-DB245328.

295 Truth and Reconciliation Commission of South Africa. Business Sector Hearing, Day 3, Johannesburg, 13 November 1997, https://www.justice.gov.za/trc/special/business/busin3.htm.

296 Hermann Giliomee, 'Six aspects of the rise of Afrikaner capital and Afrikaner nationalism in the Western Cape, 1870–1915', in Wilmot James and Mary Simons (eds.), *Class, Caste and Colour: A Social and Economic History of the South African Western Cape*, Cape Town: David Philip, 1989, 63.

297 Michael J. Meyer, 'Privatising South Africa by dictum: A review', *New Contree* 42 (1997): 52.

298 Cited in Meyer, 'Privatising South Africa by dictum'. The original quote comes from the *Sunday Times*, 26 May 1995.

299 See Vishnu Padayachee and Robbie van Niekerk, '"Shadows of liberation": ANC economic and social policy from African Claims to GEAR', *New Agenda: South African Journal of Social and Economic Policy* 2017, no. 67 (2017): 12–18.

300 Michael J. Meyer, 'Globalisation: An issue of contestation and struggle in South Africa', *Mots Pluriels* 13 (2000).

301 R. Rumney, 'Restructuring of state assets versus privatisation in South Africa: What's in a name', *Policy Brief* 45 (2005).

302 Rumney, 'Restructuring of state assets versus privatisation in South Africa'.

303 Peter A. Hall, *The Political Power of Economic Ideas: Keynesianism across Nations*, Princeton: Princeton University Press, 2020. One of the best short explanations of Keynesianism is found in Chapter 11 of Barack Obama, *A Promised Land*, New York: Crown, 2020.

304 Michael Hiltzik, *The New Deal: A Modern History*, New York: Simon and Schuster, 2011.

305 See Justin Yifu Lin, Fang Cai, and Zhou Li, *The China Miracle: Development Strategy and Economic Reform*, Hong Kong: Chinese University of Hong Kong Press, 2003.

306 Social grants account for about 15% of governmental expenditure.

307 See Genius Murwirapachena and Forget Mingiri Kapingura, 'Determinants of external debt in South Africa: A VAR-based approach', *International Journal* 8, no. 2 (2015): 138–52.

308 The Department of Rural Development and Land Reform's total expenditure estimate for 2021 was just over R11bn. The amount dedicated to land reform was R2bn and the amount dedicated to land restitution was R3.5bn. South Africa's total budget at the time of writing is about R2tn.

309 Philip Hirschsohn, 'From grassroots democracy to national mobilization: Cosatu as a model of social movement unionism', *Economic and Industrial Democracy* 19, no. 4 (1998): 633–66.

TECHNOLOGY

310 Population Registration Act 29 of 1950, https://www.sahistory.org.za/sites/default/files/DC/leg19500707.028.020.030/leg19500707.028.020.030.pdf.

311 Deborah Posel, 'Race as common sense: Racial classification in twentieth-century South Africa', *African Studies Review* (2001): 87–113.

312 And, of course, people with white ancestors who were not deemed racially 'pure' were categorised as non-white.

313 Here, 'Coloured' referred to Black, Coloured, and Asian people.

314 Immorality Act 5 of 1927.

315 See, for instance, Carol E. Kaufman, 'Reproductive control in apartheid South Africa.' *Population Studies* 54, no. 1 (2000): 105–14; Jeremy Sarkin, 'Patriarchy and discrimination in apartheid South Africa's abortion law', *Buffalo Human Rights Law Review* 4 (1998): 141.

316 Quoted in John M. Coetzee, 'The mind of apartheid: Geoffrey Cronjé (1907–)', *Social Dynamics* 17, no. 1 (1991): 27. The work quoted is Geoffrey Cronje, *Regverdige rasse-apartheid*, Stellenbosch: Christen-Studentevereniging maatskappy, 1947.

317 Prohibition of Mixed Marriages Act 55 of 1949.

318 Keith Breckenridge, *Biometric State*, Cambridge: Cambridge University Press, 2014; Keith Breckenridge, 'The biometric state: The promise and peril of digital government in the new South Africa', *Journal of Southern African Studies* 31, no. 2 (2005): 267–82. Breckenridge also has an interesting chapter on the concept of the state itself in Chapter One. A detailed analysis of this is outside the scope of this book. Another interesting part about his book is the section on Gandhi, which recasts his activism in South Africa around the question of biometric governance in the form of fingerprinting. Other fascinating insights include the visits of the founder of

eugenics, Francis Galton, to South Africa, and his influence on the implementation of fingerprinting in South Africa.

319 Kathleen Kuehn, 'Surveillance and South Africa', *The Political Economy of Communication* 6, no. 2 (2019); Sheperd Moyo, 'Evaluating the use of CCTV surveillance systems for crime control and prevention: Selected case studies from Johannesburg and Tshwane, Gauteng', PhD dissertation, University of Maryland, 2019.

320 Perhaps because I was researching the topic I received one of the ads.

321 Abeba Birhane, 'The algorithmic colonization of Africa', *Real Life*, 18 July 2019, 391.

322 The gendered aspects of the app also merit concern. The racially ambiguous woman is the face of Snaplate, precisely because divining one's 'true' racial identity is a question linked to beauty. And female beauty becomes the key advertising venue on which this quest is premised. Users, who download the app, are presumably able to upload photos and determine their own racial identity.

323 Yilun Wang and Michal Kosinski, 'Deep neural networks are more accurate than humans at detecting sexual orientation from facial images', *Journal of Personality and Social Psychology* 114, no. 2 (2018): 246.

324 Wang and Kosinski, 'Deep neural networks'.

325 Michal Kosinski, David Stillwell and Thore Graepel, 'Private traits and attributes are predictable from digital records of human behavior', *Proceedings of the National Academy of Sciences* 110, no. 15 (2013), 5802–5.

326 Roberto J. González, 'Hacking the citizenry? Personality profiling, "big data" and the election of Donald Trump', *Anthropology Today* 33, no. 3 (2017): 9–12; Mark Goodman and John Goodman, 'Psychographics on steroids: The attacks on democratic governments', *Media Watch* 11, no. 1 (2020): 4–20.

327 Jim Isaak and Mina J. Hanna, 'User data privacy: Facebook, Cambridge Analytica, and privacy protection', *Computer* 51, no. 8 (2018): 56–9.

328 Jaron Lanier, *Who Owns the Future?*, New York: Simon and Schuster, 2014.

329 Jason Lanier, 'Fixing the digital economy', *New York Times*, 8 June 2013, https://www.nytimes.com/2013/06/09/opinion/sunday/fixing-the-digital-economy.html.

330 Lori Ioannou, 'Silicon Valley's Achilles' heel threatens to topple its supremacy in innovation', CNBC, 20 June 2018, https://www.cnbc.com/2018/06/20/silicon-valleys-diversity-problem-is-its-achilles-heel.html.

331 Birhane, 'The algorithmic colonization of Africa'.

332 Dale McKinley, 'New terrains of privacy in South Africa', Right2Know Campaign. 2016, https://www.r2k.org.za/wp-content/uploads/Monograph_New_Terrains_of_Privacy_in_South_Africa_2016.pdf.

333 The most relevant pieces of legislation are: The Protection of Personal Information Act 4 of 2013, The Financial Intelligence Centre Act 38 of 2001 (FICA), The Regulation of Interception of Communications and Provision of Communication-

Related Information Act 70 of 2002 (RICA), and Electronic Communications and Transactions Act 25 of 2002 (ECTA).

334 Jane Duncan, *Stopping the Spies: Constructing and Resisting the Surveillance State in South Africa*, New York: NYU Press, 2018, 13.

335 McKinley, 'New terrains in privacy'.

336 Paulo Vaz and Fernanda Bruno, 'Types of self-surveillance: From abnormality to individuals "at risk"', *Surveillance and Society* 1, no. 3 (2003): 274.

337 Lanier, 'Fixing the digital economy'.

338 Or some combination of humans and computers.

339 Lanier, *Who Owns the Future?*

340 Solon Barocas and Andrew D. Selbst, 'Big data's disparate impact', *California Law Review* 104 (2016): 674.

341 Barocas and Selbst, 'Big data's disparate impact', 671.

342 Maya Ganesh and Stina Lohmüller, 'Spectres of AI', *Spheres: Journal for Digital Cultures*, 5 (2019): 1–6.

343 Hüseyin Bilal Macït, Gamze Macït and Orhan Güngör, 'A research on social media addiction and dopamine driven feedback', *Mehmet Akif Ersoy Üniversitesi İktisadi ve İdari Bilimler Fakültesi Dergisi* 5, no. 3 (2018): 882–97.

344 Robert Bartlett, Adair Morse, Richard Stanton and Nancy Wallace, 'Consumer-lending discrimination in the FinTech era', National Bureau of Economic Research, no. 25943, 2019.

345 The same search results were presented when I tried this at the time of writing, two years later.

346 Ferial Haffajee, 'South Africa's white squatter camps: How Google's easily skewed results spread disinformation', *Huffington Post*, 19 June 2018, https://www.huffingtonpost.co.uk/ferial-haffajee/sas-white-squatter-camps-how-googles-easily-skewed-results-spread-misinformation_a_23461415/.

347 UN Women, 'UN Women ad series reveals widespread sexism', United Nations, 21 October 2013, https://www.unwomen.org/en/news/stories/2013/10/women-should-ads.

348 Maya Indira Ganesh and Stina Lohmüller, '# 5 spectres of AI', *Spheres: Journal for Digital Cultures* 5 (2019): 2.

349 Gina Neff and Peter Nagy, 'Automation, algorithms, and politics| talking to Bots: Symbiotic agency and the case of Tay', *International Journal of Communication* 10 (2016): 17.

350 Mark Molloy, 'Microsoft "deeply sorry" after AI becomes "Hitler-loving sex robot"', *The Telegraph*, 25 March 2016, https://www.telegraph.co.uk/technology/2016/03/26/microsoft-deeply-sorry-after-ai-becomes-hitler-loving-sex-robot/.

351 Molloy, 'Microsoft "deeply sorry" after AI becomes "Hitler-loving sex robot"'.

352 Even after returning to Twitter after the fiasco, Tay once again devolved into strange musings before being indefinitely retired.

353 Christian Katzenbach and Lena Ulbricht, 'Algorithmic governance', *Internet Policy Review* 8, no. 4 (2019): 5.

354 Katzenbach and Ulbricht, 'Algorithmic governance', 4.

355 Cathy O'Neil, *Weapons of Math Destruction: How Big Data Increases Inequality and Threatens Democracy*, New York: Broadway Books, 2016, 70.

356 Vincent Chenzi, 'Fake news, social media and xenophobia in South Africa', *African Identities* (2020): 1–20.

357 Herman Wasserman and Dani Madrid-Morales, 'An exploratory study of "fake news" and media trust in Kenya, Nigeria and South Africa', *African Journalism Studies* 40, no. 1 (2019): 107–23.

358 David Foster-Wallace, *The Pale King*, Harmondsworth: Penguin Books, Kindle Edition, 82.

359 Achille Mbembe, 'Capitalisms: A global history; A conversation between Achille Mbembe and Dilip Menon', WiSER Podcast, 2020, https://wiser.wits.ac.za/event/wiser-podcast-episode-5-achille-mbembe-and-dilip-menon.

360 At the time of writing, Facebook, for instance, is granted a non-exclusive licence to photos posted by its users. They do not own them in the strict sense but reserve the right to make copies of them on their servers and display them on the site. In reality, people often forget what they have posted to Facebook, and their only memory of such posts is the annual reminder they receive of such posts on Facebook.

361 Lincoln S. Robards and Harris Pinkard, 'Remembering through Facebook: Mediated memory and intimate digital traces', in A. Dobson, B. Robards and N. Carah (eds.), *Digital Intimate Publics and Social Media*, Palgrave Studies in Communication for Social Change, London: Palgrave Macmillan, 2018, https://doi.org/10.1007/978-3-319-97607-5_5.

362 Ana Lúcia Migowski and Willian Fernandes Araújo, '"Looking back" at personal memories on Facebook: Co-constitutive agencies in contemporary remembrance practices', *Journal of Aesthetics and Culture* 11 (2019).

363 Artie Konrad, 'Facebook memories: The research behind the products that connect you with your past', Facebook Research, 6 September 2017, https://research.fb.com/facebook-memories-the-research-behind-the-products-that-connect-you-with-your-past/.

364 Sophia Drakopoulou, '"We can remember it for you": Location, memory, and commodification in social networking sites', *SAGE Open* 7, no. 3 (2017).

365 Drakopoulou, '"We can remember it for you"', 1.

366 See, for instance, Sanjam Garg, Shafi Goldwasser and Prashant Nalini Vasudevan, 'Formalizing data deletion in the context of the right to be forgotten', in *Annual*

International Conference on the Theory and Applications of Cryptographic Techniques, New York: Springer, 2020, 373–402.

367 Avani Singh, 'Do South Africans have a right to be forgotten? European court says not yet', Alt Advisory, 15 October 2019, https://altadvisory.africa/2019/10/15/do-south-africans-have-a-right-to-be-forgotten-european-court-says-not-yet/.

368 Singh, 'Do South Africans have a right to be forgotten?'

369 Singh, 'Do South Africans have a right to be forgotten?'

370 Julia Wong, 'Former Facebook executive: Social media is ripping society apart', *The Guardian*, 12 December 2017.

371 Trevor Haynes, 'Dopamine, smartphones and you: A battle for your time', *Science in the News* 30 (2018); Rogers Brubaker, 'Digital hyperconnectivity and the self', *Theory and Society* (2020): 1–31.

372 This phrase comes from K. C. Berridge and M. L. Kringelbach, 'Affective neuroscience of pleasure: reward in humans and animals', *Psychopharmacology* 199, no. 3 (2008): 457–80. It is quoted, in this context, in Mark Tschaepe, 'Undermining dopamine democracy through education: Synthetic situations, social media, and incentive salience', *Pragmatism Today* 7, no. 1 (2016): 34.

373 Joshua D. Berke, 'What does dopamine mean?', *Nature Neuroscience* 21, no. 6 (2018): 787–93.

374 Business Fibre, 'Screen time: UK vs US vs the rest of the world compared', 15 July 2019, https://businessfibre.co.uk/screen-time/.

375 Macït, Macït and Güngör, 'A research on social media addiction and dopamine driven feedback'. This study combined data from Hootsuite and We Are Social digital reports on social media usage, and is valuable in translation from the Turkish.

376 Abou Farman and Richard Rottenburg, 'Measures of future health, from the nonhuman to the planetary', *Medicine Anthropology Theory* 6, no. 3 (2019): 2.

377 John Eybers and Peter Zamayirha, 'Racist ranter Catzavelos stays in Greece', *City Press*, 26 August 2018, https://www.news24.com/news24/southafrica/news/racist-ranter-adam-catzavelos-stays-in-greece-20180826.

378 Canny Maphanga, 'Catzavelos pleads guilty to *crimen injuria* for k-word slur video', News24, 15 December 2019, https://www.news24.com/news24/southafrica/news/just-in-catzavelos-pleads-guilty-to-crimen-injuria-for-k-word-slur-video-20191205.

379 The observant reader will note that the thought experiment in the chapter about law which relates to a fictional racist estate agent is not far-fetched.

380 Likewise, White estate agent Penny Sparrow spewed racial slurs on her Facebook page comparing black beachgoers to monkeys. Sparrow, too, was found guilty of hate speech in 2016 and ordered to pay R150 000 to the Adelaide and Oliver Tambo Foundation. See Kaveel Singh, 'Penny Sparrow, whose racist post sparked furs, has

died', News24, 15 July 2019, https://www.news24.com/news24/southafrica/news/breaking-penny-sparrow-has-died-20190725.

381 Stephen Eskilson, *The Age of Glass: A Cultural History of Glass in Modern and Contemporary Architecture*, London: Bloomsbury Publishing, 2018.

382 James Bridle, *New Dark Age: Technology and the End of the Future*, London: Verso Books, 2018.

383 Jean Comaroff and John L. Comaroff, 'Occult economies and the violence of abstraction: Notes from the South African postcolony', *American Ethnologist* 26, no. 2 (1999): 277.

384 Brubaker, 'Digital hyperconnectivity and the self', 3.

385 O'Neil, *Weapons of Math Destruction*.

386 Cornel West interviewed by John Ehrenberg, 'Left matters: An interview with Cornel West', *New Political Science* 33, no. 3 (2011): 357–69, doi: 10.1080/07393148.2011.592023.

PUNISHMENT

387 Jean Comaroff and John Comaroff, *The Truth about Crime: Sovereignty, Knowledge, Social Order*, Chicago: University of Chicago Press, 2016, 181.

388 Jonny Steinberg, *The Number: One Man's Search for Identity in the Cape Underworld and Prison Gangs*, Cape Town: Jonathan Ball Publishers, 2010.

389 This figure was arrived at by combining the UNODA report up to 2019 with the South African Crime Statistics for the two years thereafter.

390 Haroon Bhorat, Adaiah Lilenstein, Jabulile Monnakgotla, Amy Thornton and Kirsten van der Zee, 'Socio-economic determinants of crime in South Africa: An empirical assessment', Development Policy Research Unit, University of Cape Town, 2017, 13.

391 John Gramlich, 'What the data says (and doesn't say) about crime in the United States', Pew Research Center, November 2020, https://www.pewresearch.org/fact-tank/2020/11/20/facts-about-crime-in-the-u-s.

392 United Nations Office on Drugs and Crime, 'Global study on homicides', 2019, https://www.unodc.org/unodc/en/data-and-analysis/global-study-on-homicide.html.

393 This figure was arrived at by comparing statistics for murder in different regions of South Africa with the UNODC data.

394 Between 1994 and 2011, violent crime fell but it rebounded in the decade after then, though not to the levels of the 1990s.

395 Ngozi Adeleye and Abdul Jamal, 'Dynamic analysis of violent crime and income inequality in Africa', *International Journal of Economics, Commerce and Management* 8 no. 2 (2020): 1–25.

396   Bhorat, Lilenstein, Monnakgotla, Thornton and Van der Zee, 'Socio-economic determinants of crime in South Africa'.

397   Gabriel Demombynes and Berk Özler, 'Crime and local inequality in South Africa', *Journal of Development Economics* 76, no. 2 (2005): 265–92.

398   Jeanne-Marie Versluis and Jan de Lange, 'Rising crime, low prosecution rates: How law enforcement in SA has all but collapsed', News24, 21 October 2019, https:// www.news24.com/citypress/News/rising-crime-low-prosecution-rates-how-law-enforcement-in-sa-has-all-but-collapsed-2019102.

399   These statistics are slightly misleading. They are calculated by taking the total number of cases reported in a given year and the total number of convictions in the same year. Some crimes may take more than one year to reach conviction. These figures should be seen, then, as a ratio of crimes committed for a given year versus crimes convicted in the same year. See Versluis and De Lange, 'Rising crime, low prosecution rates'.

400   Pablo Fajnzylber, Daniel Lederman and Norman Loayza, 'What causes violent crime?', *European Economic Review* 46, no. 7 (2002): 1323–57; Marcus Noland, 'The distribution of income in North Korea', Peterson Institute for International Economics, 19 February 2013, https://www.piie.com/blogs/north-korea-witness-transformation/distribution-income-north-korea.

401   Don Pinnock and Dudu Douglas-Hamilton, *Gangs, Rituals and Rites of Passage*, Cape Town: African Sun Press with the Institute of Criminology, University of Cape Town, 1997; Don Pinnock, *Gang Town*, Cape Town: Tafelberg, 2016.

402   Peter Parker and Joyce Mokhesi-Parker. *In the Shadow of Sharpeville: Apartheid and Criminal Justice*, London: Palgrave Macmillan, 1998, 53.

403   Richard James Thompson, 'Cecil Rhodes, the Glen Grey Act, and the labour question in the politics of the Cape Colony', PhD dissertation, Rhodes University, 1991.

404   Parker and Mokhesi-Parker, *In the Shadow of Sharpeville*.

405   The definitive work on Nongoloza's history is Charles van Onselen, 'Crime and total institutions in the making of modern South Africa: The life of "Nongoloza" Mathebula, 1867–1948', *History Workshop Journal* 19 (1985): 62–81. This eventually become a book: Van Onselen, *The Small Matter of a Horse: The Life of 'Nongoloza' Mathebula, 1867–1948*, Johannesburg: Ravan, 1985. See also Jonny Steinberg, 'Writing South Africa's prisons into history', in Michelle Kelly and Claire Westall (eds.), *Prison Writing and the Literary World: Imprisonment, Institutionality and Questions of Literary Practice*, Abingdon: Routledge, 2020, 110.

406   Paul La Hausse, '"The cows of Nongoloza": Youth, crime and amalaita gangs in Durban, 1900–1936', *Journal of Southern African Studies* 16, no. 1 (1990): 79–111.

407   Sisonke Msimang, 'Nongoloza's ghosts: The legacy of violence in the struggle for

freedom in South Africa', *Lapham's Quarterly*, 21 December 2020, https://www. laphamsquarterly.org/democracy/nongolozas-ghost.

408   Jonny Steinberg, *Nongoloza's Children: Western Cape Prison Gangs during and after Apartheid*, Braamfontein: Centre for the Study of Violence and Reconciliation, 2004, 2.

409   Van Onselen, *The Small Matter of a Horse*, 20.

410   J. M. Lötter, 'Prison gangs in South Africa: A description', *South African Journal of Sociology* 19, no. 2 (1988): 67–75.

411   Chris Giffard and Lukas Muntingh, 'The effect of sentencing on the size of the South African prison population', Open Society Foundation for South Africa, 2006.

412   Africa Watch Prison Project, 'Prison conditions in South Africa', Human Rights Watch, 1994, https://www.hrw.org/reports/pdfs/s/safrica/safrica942.pdf.

413   Africa Watch Prison Project, 'Prison conditions in South Africa', 54.

414   Mandatory life sentences are imposed on premeditated murder, murder of a law enforcement official or potential state witness, murder connected to rape or robbery with aggravated circumstances, rape committed more than once, gang rape, rape of a minor. Mandatory fifteen-year sentences are placed on robbery, drug-related offences, weapons-related offences or 'any offence relating to exchange control, extortion, fraud, forgery, uttering, theft'. Sentences cannot be suspended and time awaiting trail cannot be added to mandatory minimum sentences.

415   Constitutional cases which have dealt with this question include *Centre for Child Law v Minister for Justice and Constitutional Development and Others* 2009 ZACC 18; *M T v The State; A S B v The State; Johannes September v The State* 2018 ZACC 27.

416   Edwin Cameron, 'Imprisoning the nation: Minimum sentences in South Africa', Dean's Distinguished Lecture, University of the Western Cape Faculty of Law, 2017. See also Edwin Cameron, 'The crisis of criminal justice in South Africa', *South African Law Journal* 137, no. 1 (2020): 32–71; Dirk van Zyl Smit, 'Mandatory sentences: A conundrum for the new South Africa?', *Punishment and Society* 2, no. 2 (2000): 197–212.

417   Civil Society Prison Reform Initiative, Just Detention International and Lawyers for Human Rights, 'A submission to the UN Human Rights Committee in response to the initial report by South Africa under the International Covenant on Civil and Political Rights at the 116th session of the Human Rights Committee', March 2016, 9, https://tbinternet.ohchr.org/Treaties/CCPR/Shared%20Documents/ZAF/INT_CCPR_CSS_ZAF_23064_E.pdf.

418   Penwell Dlamini, 'Union has had enough of attacks on warders', *Sowetan*, 23 April 2019, https://www.sowetanlive.co.za/news/south-africa/2019-04-23-union-has-had-enough-of-attacks-on-warders/.

419   See Nechama R. Brodie, 'Using mixed-method approaches to provide new insights

into media coverage of femicide', PhD dissertation, University of the Witwatersrand, 2019; Nechama Brodie, *Femicide in South Africa*, Cape Town: Kwela Books, 2020.

420   Brodie, 'Using mixed-method approaches to provide new insights into media coverage of femicide', 79.

421   Shanaaz Mathews, Rachel Jewkes and Naeemah Abrahams, '"So now I'm the man": Intimate partner femicide and its interconnections with expressions of masculinities in South Africa', *British Journal of Criminology* 55, no. 1 (2015): 107–24.

422   Jock Young, *The Exclusive Society: Social Exclusion, Crime and Difference in Late Modernity*, London: Sage, 1999, 94.

423   See, for instance, K. Breckenridge, 'The allure of violence: Men, race and masculinity on the South African gold mines, 1900–1950', *Journal of Southern African Studies*, 24 (1998): 669–83; R. Morrell, 'Of boys and men: Masculinity and gender in southern African studies', *Journal of Southern African Studies*, 24 (1998): 605–30; R. Morrell, R. Jewkes and G. Lindegger, 'Hegemonic masculinity/masculinities in South Africa: Culture, power, and gender politics', *Men and Masculinities* 15, no. 1 (2012): 11–30; Lahoucine Ouzgane and Robert Morrell, *African Masculinities: Men in Africa from the Late Nineteenth Century to the Present*, London: Palgrave Macmillan, 2005.

424   Lisa Vetten, 'The ghost of families past: Domestic violence legislation and policy in post-apartheid South Africa', *Agenda* 28, no. 2 (2014): 48–57. See also Amanda Gouws, 'Women's activism around gender-based violence in South Africa: Recognition, redistribution and representation', *Review of African Political Economy* 43, no. 149 (2016): 400–15.

425   Anna van der Hoven, 'Domestic violence in South Africa', *Acta Criminologica: Southern African Journal of Criminology* 14, no. 3 (2001): 13–25.

426   See Pumla Dineo Gqola, 'How the "cult of femininity" and violent masculinities support endemic gender-based violence in contemporary South Africa', *African Identities* 5, no. 1 (2007): 111–24.

427   See Thenjiwe Meyiwa, Charmaine Williamson, Thandokazi Maseti and Gladys-Magdeline Ntabanyane, 'A twenty-year review of policy landscape for gender-based violence in South Africa', *Gender and Behaviour* 15, no. 2 (2017): 8607–17.

428   Gregory Dennis Breetzke, 'Modeling violent crime rates: A test of social disorganization in the city of Tshwane, South Africa', *Journal of Criminal Justice* 38, no. 4 (2010): 17.

429   See, for example, Morrell, Jewkes and Lindegger, 'Hegemonic masculinity/masculinities in South Africa'; Tamara Shefer, Kopano Ratele and Anna Strebel (eds.), *From Boys to Men: Social Constructions of Masculinity in Contemporary Society*, Cape Town: Juta, 2007; Sakhumzi Mfecane, 'Towards African-centred theories of masculinity', *Social Dynamics* 44, no. 2 (2018): 291–305.

430 Brodie, 'Using mixed-method approaches to provide new insights into media coverage of femicide', 2.

431 Breetzke, 'Modeling violent crime rates: A test of social disorganization in the city of Tshwane, South Africa', 13.

432 David Bruce, 'Political killings in South Africa: The ultimate intimidation', Institute for Security Studies, October 2014, https://media.africaportal.org/documents/PolBrief64.pdf.

433 Correctional Services Act of 1998, http://www.dcs.gov.za/wp-content/uploads/2016/08/DCS-Act-111-of-2008.pdf.

434 There are actually closer to 2.5 million private guards if one counts those not on active duty.

435 K. Manuel and A. Gunter, 'Privatisation of public space: Security guards and policing by non-state authorities in city improvement districts', *South African Geographers* 1 (2018): 27.

436 Sandton Central Improvement District, 'About Sandton Central', https://sandton-central.co.za/about-sandton-central.

437 Manuel and Gunter, 'Privatisation of public space', 31.

438 Manuel and Gunter, 'Privatisation of public space', 34.

439 Parker and Mokhesi-Parker, *In the Shadow of Sharpeville*, 44. These authors go on to list umpteen cases where acts of White brutality went unpunished or were leniently punished, and acts of similar Black violence were excessively punished in apartheid South Africa. They conclude on the resounding note that 'when one asks, therefore, why judges found the roasting, beating, kicking and slicing of blacks by whites and their employees so readily understandable, the short answer is the racism of the attacker chimed with the racism of the judge, the one acting out the feelings of the other'.

440 Parker and Mokhesi-Parker, *In the Shadow of Sharpeville*, 46.

441 The same judge who convicted Barbara Hogan to ten years' imprisonment.

442 Parker and Mokhesi-Parker, *In the Shadow of Sharpeville*, 46.

443 The privatisation of the security industry cannot be separated from South Africa's history of racialised violence. Many of South Africa's private security firms trace their history to the apartheid security apparatus. Some founders, investors and managers were part of the SADF, the South African Police and even the notorious Bureau of State Security. At the end of apartheid, these security operatives, some of whom were even granted amnesty, established lucrative private security businesses. The ownership and management structure of these companies is often murky. They do not often transparently list their shareholders or directors. In the same way, the financial sector is heavily invested in the private security sector. For instance, one of South Africa's main financial services businesses, FirstRand, is an investor in one of the biggest security companies, Fidelity. Here the privatisation of violence meets the

financialisation of the economy, and vice versa.

444 Jamie Nimmo, 'Ashley Almanza: "G4S is not for sale—at least at this price"', *The Times*, 1 November 2020, https://www.thetimes.co.uk/article/ashley-almanza-g4s-is-not-for-sale-at-least-at-this-price-vsrrvw93r.

445 Comaroff and Comaroff, *The Truth about Crime*, 182.

446 Claire Bénit-Gbaffou, 'Unbundled security services and urban fragmentation in post-apartheid Johannesburg', *Geoforum* 39, no. 6 (2008): 1948.

447 Bosasa is now called African Global Operations.

448 Kyle Cowan, 'Agrizzi's little black book of bribes', Corruption Watch, 29 March 2019. Interestingly, Bosasa also paid bribes to union bosses, to put pressure on companies to grant Bosasa contracts.

449 Adriaan Basson, *Blessed by Bosasa: Inside Gavin Watson's State Capture Cult*, Cape Town: Jonathan Ball, 2019. See also James-Brent Styan and Paul Vecchiatto, *The Bosasa Billions: How the ANC Sold Its Soul for Braaipacks, Booze and Bags of Cash*, Pretoria: LAPA Uitgewers, 2019.

450 Basson, *Blessed by Bosasa*. See the infographic at the opening of the book for a useful breakdown of Bosasa's state contracts including with the departments of Home Affairs and Social Development.

451 AfriForum, 'Adv Gerrie Nel appointed as head of AfriForum's Private Prosecutions Unit', 31 January 2017, https://afriforum.co.za/en/adv-gerrie-nel-appointed-head-afriforums-private-prosecuting-unit/.

452 Ethan van Diemen, 'Private donor funding for NPA has been "thoroughly considered"—Lamola', News24, 27 August 2019, https://www.news24.com/news24/SouthAfrica/News/private-donor-funding-for-npa-has-been-thoroughly-considered-lamola-2019082.7

453 Andisiwe Makinana, 'SA prosecutors inundated by donors, but can't use funds to fight crime—yet', *Sunday Times*, 10 July 2019, https://www.timeslive.co.za/politics/2019-07-10-sa-prosecutors-inundated-by-donors-but-cant-use-funds-to-fight-crime-yet/.

CONCLUSION

454 John M. Coetzee, 'The mind of apartheid: Geoffrey Cronjé (1907–)', *Social Dynamics* 17, no. 1 (1991): 1–35.

455 This quote is paraphrased from Premesh Lalu, 'Between history and apocalypse: Stumbling', YouTube video, 6 May 2015, https://www.youtube.com/watch?v=KN-T8ALsvfi8.

456 Tshepo Madlingozi, 'The proposed amendment to the South African Constitution: Finishing the unfinished business of decolonisation', Critical Legal Thinking, 6 April 2018, https://criticallegalthinking.com/2018/04/06/the-proposed-amend-ment-to-the-south-african-constitution/.

457 This question has already been raised by former Deputy Chief Justice Moseneke.

See, for instance, Mtendeweka Mhango and Ntombizozuko Dyani-Mhango, 'Deputy Chief Justice Moseneke's approach to the separation of powers in South Africa: Justice Moseneke, judicial engagement and the separation of powers', *Acta Juridica 2017*, Cape Town: Juta, 2018, 75–98. See also Dikgang Moseneke, 'The President wields too much power', *Business Day*, 17 November 2014, https://www.businesslive.co.za/rdm/politics/2014-11-17-the-president-wields-too-much-power/.

458 On the question of provinces, see Thabo Rapoo and Tshepo Moloi, 'A future in dispute: Political perspectives on South Africa's provincial system', Centre for Policy Studies, 2008, https://media.africaportal.org/documents/RR109.pdf.

459 See, for example, Edwin Cameron and Leo Boonzaier, 'Venturing beyond formalism: The Constitutional Court of South Africa's equality jurisprudence', *Rabels Zeitschrift für ausländisches und internationales Privatrecht/The Rabel Journal of Comparative and International Private Law* 84, no. 4 (2020): 786–840.

460 See, for example, William Stubbs, *The Constitutional History of England, in Its Origin and Development*, vol. 1, Oxford: Clarendon Press, 1880; Michael Rush, 'Constitutional history of the United Kingdom', *Representation* 41, no. 2 (2005): 127–8; Vernon Bogdanor, *Beyond Brexit: Towards a British Constitution*, London: Bloomsbury Publishing, 2019.

461 See Sudhir Hazareesingh, *In the Shadow of the General: Modern France and the Myth of de Gaulle*, Oxford: Oxford University Press, 2012.

462 Valentina Rita Scotti, 'Constitutional amendments and constitutional core values: The Brazilian case in a comparative perspective', *Revista de Investigações Constitucionais* 5, no. 3 (2018): 59–76.

463 Tofigh Maboudi, 'Reconstituting Tunisia: Participation, deliberation, and the content of constitution', *Political Research Quarterly* 73, no. 4 (2020): 774–89.

464 See, for instance, Heinz Klug, 'Constituting the state in postcolonial Africa: Fifty years of constitution-making toward an African constitutionalism', in Rogers M. Smith and Richard R. Beeman (eds.), *Modern Constitutions*, Philadelphia: University of Pennsylvania Press, 2020, 261. See also Oxford Analytica, 'Guinea's Conde may exploit opposition poll divisions', *Emerald Expert Briefings*, https://doi.org/10.1108/OXAN-DB256622.

465 See, for example, Thomas Ferguson, Paul Jorgensen and Jie Chen, 'How much can the US Congress resist political money? A quantitative assessment', Institute for New Economic Thinking Working Paper Series 109 (2020); Thomas Ferguson, *Golden Rule: The Investment Theory of Party Competition and the Logic of Money-Driven Political Systems*, Chicago: University of Chicago Press, 1995; Larry M. Bartels, *Unequal Democracy*, Princeton: Princeton University Press, 2016.

466 See, for example, Guido Alfani, 'Economic inequality in preindustrial times: Europe and beyond', *Journal of Economic Literature* 59, no. 1 (2021): 3–44. For further nuance on the question of the UK's inequality in the nineteenth century, see Moshe

Justman and Mark Gradstein, 'The Industrial Revolution, political transition, and the subsequent decline in inequality in 19th-century Britain', *Explorations in Economic History* 36, no. 2 (1999): 109–27. See also Thomas Piketty and Emmanuel Saez, 'Inequality in the long run', *Science* 344, no. 6186 (2014): 838–43.

467 Christian Morrisson and Wayne Snyder, 'The income inequality of France in historical perspective', *European Review of Economic History* 4, no. 1 (2000): 59–83.

468 This point is made by Ben W. Ansell and David J. Samuels, *Inequality and Democratization*, Cambridge: Cambridge University Press, 2014.

469 See Roy N. Lokken, 'The concept of democracy in colonial political thought', *William and Mary Quarterly: A Magazine of Early American History* (1959): 568–80.

470 Marcos Mendes, *Inequality, Democracy, and Growth in Brazil: A Country at the Crossroads of Economic Development*, Cambridge, MA: Academic Press, 2014.

471 David Dollar, 'Globalization, poverty, and inequality since 1980', *World Bank Research Observer* 20, no. 2 (2005): 145–75.

472 Ishan Anand and Anjana Thampi, 'Recent trends in wealth inequality in India', *Economic and Political Weekly* 51, no. 50 (2016): 59; Michele Ford and Thomas B. Pepinsky, 'Beyond oligarchy?: Critical exchanges on political power and material inequality in Indonesia', *Indonesia* 96, no. 1 (2013): 1–9.

473 See, for example, Thorsten Benner, Ricardo Soares de Oliveira, M. Berdal and D. Zaum, 'Statebuilding and the political economy of the extractive industries in post-conflict states', in Mats Berdal and Dominik Zaum (eds.), *Political Economy of Statebuilding: Power after Peace*, Abingdon: Routledge, 2013, 122–36; Will Jones, Ricardo Soares de Oliveira and Harry Verhoeven, 'Africa's illiberal state-builders', University of Oxford, Refugee Studies Centre, 2013.

474 Claude Ake, 'The unique case of African democracy', *International Affairs* 69, no. 2 (1993): 239–44.

475 See, for instance, Daron Acemoglu, Suresh Naidu, Pascual Restrepo and James A. Robinson, 'Democracy, redistribution, and inequality', in Anthony B. Atkinson and François Bourguignon (eds.), *Handbook of Income Distribution*, vol. 2, Amsterdam: Elsevier, 2015, 1885–966. See also Daron Acemoglu and James A. Robinson, *Economic Origins of Dictatorship and Democracy*, Cambridge: Cambridge University Press, 2006.

476 Laura Policardo and Edgar J. Sánchez Carrera, 'Can income inequality promote democratization?', *Metroeconomica* 71, no. 3 (2020): 526.

477 Beatriz Magaloni and Luis Rodriguez, 'Institutionalized police brutality: Torture, the militarization of security, and the reform of inquisitorial criminal justice in Mexico', *American Political Science Review* 114, no. 4 (2020): 1014.

478 Ben Ansell and David Samuels, 'Inequality and democratization: A contractarian approach', *Comparative Political Studies* 43, no. 12 (2010): 1547.

479 Ben W. Ansell and David J. Samuels, *Inequality and Democratization*, Cambridge:

Cambridge University Press, 2014, especially Chapter 5.

480 Robert D. Drennan, Christian E. Peterson and Jake R. Fox, 'Degrees and kinds of inequality', in *Pathways to Power*, New York: Springer, 2010, 45–76.

481 The relations between different racial states is fascinatingly covered in James Q. Whitman, *Hitler's American Model: The United States and the Making of Nazi Race Law*, Princeton: Princeton University Press, 2017.

482 This is a point made by Achille Mbembe, 'Democracy and the ethics of common life', YouTube video, Place Culture Politics, https://www.youtube.com/watch?v=YYrzeq9gHkA&t=2649s.

483 Here, he is paraphrasing Marx. See Michel Foucault, *Discipline and Punish: The Birth of the Prison*, New York: Vintage, 2012.

484 Coetzee, 'The mind of apartheid: Geoffrey Cronjé (1907–)', 26.

485 Mark Sanders, 'Remembering apartheid', *Diacritics* 32, no. 3/4 (2002): 60–80.

486 See Joanna Woods, 'On contemporary speculative short fiction in southern Africa', *Scrutiny2* (2020): 1–13.

487 This poem can be accessed in a recording of a performance: Lebo Mashile, 'Going through race', https://www.youtube.com/watch?v=q_73IDC9G8c.

488 Don Matterra, 'Second Hugh Masekela Annual Lecture – Fishbowl Discussion', Online video, YouTube, 11 September 2015, https://www.youtube.com/watch?v=-bUHprpJ2tA&t=404s

489 Nicholas Spaull, 'Poverty and privilege: Primary school inequality in South Africa', *International Journal of Educational Development* 33, no. 5 (2013): 436.

490 Spaull, 'Poverty and privilege', 437.

491 Acheampong Yaw Amoateng, Elizabeth Biney and Olusegun Sunday Ewemooje, 'Social determinants of chronic ill-health in contemporary South Africa: A social disadvantage approach', *Social Science Journal* (2021): 1.

492 David Mhlanga and Rufaro Garidzirai, 'The influence of racial differences in the demand for healthcare in South Africa: A case of public healthcare', *International Journal of Environmental Research and Public Health* 17, no. 14 (2020): 5043.

493 I would also urge those reading this conclusion to consider my arguments from the introduction in which I outline what I am *not* arguing. This section gives further clarity on the limitations and shortcoming of this book, and pre-empts various possible objections.

494 Shireen Hassim, 'Winnie Madikizela Mandela: The politics of refusal', Wits Institute for Social and Economic Research, Podcast, 25 September 2020, https://wiser.wits.ac.za/wiser-podcast-season-2-episode-4-shireen-hassim-and-sisonke-msimang.

Index

About the author

Photo: Sumaya Hendricks

SIZWE MPOFU-WALSH is a Post doctoral Fellow at the Wits Institute for Social and Economic Research (WiSER). He holds a DPhil in International Relations from the University of Oxford. His first book, *Democracy and Delusion: 10 Myths in South African Politics*, was an instant topseller. It won the City Press-Tafelberg Nonfiction Award and was longlisted for the Sunday Times-Alan Paton Nonfiction Award. The book was accompanied by a rap album of the same name. Mpofu-Walsh's popular YouTube channel the Sizwe Mpofu-Walsh Xperience (SMWX) explores South African politics through interviews and analysis. He is based in Johannesburg. For more, visit: sizwempofuwalsh.com